THE

PUBLICATIONS

OF THE

Northamptonshire Record Society

FOUNDED IN DECEMBER, 1920

VOLUME XXV

FOR THE YEAR ENDED 31 DECEMBER 1972

THE NORTHAMPTONSHIRE MILITIA AT BRACKLEY, 1807
by Thomas Rowlandson

Northamptonshire Militia Lists 1777

1777

EDITED BY

Victor A. Hatley

Printed for
The Northamptonshire Record Society
by Dalkeith Press Limited
Kettering, Northamptonshire
1973

PRINTED IN GREAT BRITAIN

CONTENTS

TABLES

ILLUSTRATIONS

v

ACKNOWLEDGEMENTS

MY gratitude is willingly given to various people who, in one way or another, assisted me in the production of this edition of the 1777 militia lists for Northamptonshire.

Mr. P. I. King, Chief Archivist of the Northamptonshire Record Office, allowed me to make a photocopy of the lists, thus enabling the work of transcription to be done at home. He and his staff also helped on various occasions with advice and information.

Mr. Bruce A. Bailey, Librarian of the College of Further Education, Northampton, and Mr. Stephen Green, formerly on the staff at the Northamptonshire Record Office but now Curator of the M.C.C. (Lords), both read through my original transcription and saved me from many errors.

Dr. Edmund King, General Editor of the Northamptonshire Record Society, undertook the duties of his office with good humour, exemplary patience and exact scholarship. His wife, Mrs. Jenny King, made the index of names, a formidable task which she performed with distinction. Much of the manuscript was typed for me by Mrs. Dorothy Roberts.

Mr. Philip Cox of the Dalkeith Press, Kettering, co-operated fully with Dr. King and myself, and, so far as I was concerned, made the production of this book a pleasant experience. Any errors which it may contain are solely my responsibility.

The coloured frontispiece showing the Northamptonshire Militia Regiment parading at Brackley in 1807 is reproduced by kind permission of Sir Hereward Wake, Bart., M.C., of Courteenhall.

Books published by the Northamptonshire Record Society do not carry dedications, but if they did this one would commemorate the name of Mrs. Grace Pearse (1892-1971), for many years a member of the Society's Council, and to me a good and kind friend.

December 1972   Victor A. Hatley

NOTE ON EDITORIAL METHOD

THE militia lists are, on the whole, straightforward documents, some of them neatly and carefully written and laid out, others just the reverse. I have tried to edit them so that the character of the original is maintained so far as is possible. Spelling remains the same as on the lists, but capitalization has been adapted to modern usage. As far as possible the original punctuation on the lists has been retained—many have no punctuation at all, and some are punctuated in the wrong places—but certain additions and alterations have been made to assist the modern reader. Of these the most important is that where names are followed by an occupation, status or some information, the surname has been separated from the next word by a comma (e.g. George Leeson, servant; Samuel Thomson, infirm; Thomas Line, now a substitute). A name enclosed by ⟨ ⟩ indicates that it has been crossed off the list, the man concerned being exempted from service in the militia. The lists for the hundreds of Chipping Warden, Cleyley, Greens Norton, Kings Sutton and Towcester carry the signatures of two deputy lieutenants and one justice of the peace before whom, at the first subdivisional meeting, the constables made a statutory verification upon oath that their returns were accurate; these signatures, which are the same for each hundred, have been omitted from the transcription. Also omitted is a number which appears on many of the lists, and which represents the total of men liable for service from the parish concerned. Thus the signatures of two deputy lieutenants, Michael Wodhull and William H. Chauncy, and a justice of the peace, Charles Fox, and also the number of men liable for militia service, fourteen in this case, appear on the list for Adstone, illustrated opposite p. 53.

THE NORTHAMPTONSHIRE HUNDREDS

INTRODUCTION

SERIES of militia lists for Northamptonshire exist for 1762, 1771, 1774, 1777, 1781 and 1786. Those for 1777 are reproduced in this book; they cover all the county except, unfortunately, Nassaburgh Hundred (better known as the Soke of Peterborough), and are nearer to being complete than any of the other series.[1]

The English militia was a force raised for the defence of the realm against invasion or rebellion. It was not liable for service overseas. Under the Militia Act of 1662 all owners of property were charged with the provision of horses, arms and men, in accordance with the value of their property, but this liability was removed from the individual to the parish by the Militia Act of 1757, itself modified by a series of subsequent acts. Each county had now to contribute a quota of men for militia service, 640 in the case of Northamptonshire; elsewhere the quotas ranged from 1600 each for Devonshire and Middlesex, 1240 for the West Riding of Yorkshire and 1200 for Lincolnshire, down to 240 each from Monmouth and Westmorland, and only 120 for tiny Rutland. Responsibility for raising the militia and providing it with officers lay with the lord lieutenant of each county and his deputies.

Liability to serve in the militia rested on able-bodied men between the ages of 18 and 45 years. However, peers of the realm, clergymen (including dissenting ministers), articled clerks, apprentices, seamen and parish constables were exempt. So also were poor men who had three or more children born in wedlock, a number which was reduced to one in 1786. Service in the militia was for three years and determined by ballot, but any man whose name was drawn had the right to provide a substitute. In the opinion of Professor J. R. Western, the most thorough historian of the eighteenth century militia, few men whose names were drawn in the ballot actually served in person.[2] Those who could afford to pay for a substitute usually did so; moreover, statutory powers were available for parishes to provide volunteers in place of drawn men (who, if they served, might have dependents, the responsibility for whose subsistence would fall on the parish itself), and groups of individuals would sometimes raise by mutual subscription a sum of money sufficient to indemnify any of their number who were unfortunate in the ballot. At Crick, for example, it will

[1] The militia lists for Northamptonshire are all held at the Northamptonshire Record Office. Lists for the following hundreds are missing:—
1762; Cleyley, Fawsley, Guilsborough, Nobottle Grove, Spelhoe, Towcester, Wymersley.
1771; Cleyley, Nassaburgh, Towcester.
1774; Cleyley, Nassaburgh, Polebrook, Towcester.
1777; Nassaburgh.
1781; Fawsley, Guilsborough, Nassaburgh.
1786; Chipping Warden, Cleyley, Corby, Fawsley, Greens Norton, Guilsborough, Hamfordshoe, Higham Ferrers, Huxloe, Kings Sutton, Nassaburgh, Navisford, Orlingbury, Polebrook, Rothwell, Towcester, Willybrook.
[2] J. R. Western, *The English Militia in the Eighteenth Century* (1965), chapter x ('Raising the Men'), esp. pp. 255-64.

be noticed that, out of the fourteen men listed in 1777 who were granted exemption because they had previously been drawn for the militia, thirteen had served 'by substitute' and only one, a weaver, 'in person'. Nineteen men at Wellingborough were stated to be 'Serving in other county's militia', presumably as substitutes.

Militia men were trained and exercised for a period of 28 days annually, when they were billeted in public houses and paid according to a scale laid down by Act of Parliament. For the Northamptonshire militia regiment this usually took place at Northampton during May and June, although in 1771, because of an epidemic of smallpox in Northampton, the men were divided between two detachments, one stationed at Welling-borough and the other at Kettering.[3] It was customary for the regiment to celebrate the birthday of George III, which occurred on 4 June, by assembling in Northampton's spacious market square and firing three volleys of blanks.

The thirteen North American colonies proclaimed their independence in July 1776, material assistance being rendered to them by France. War was declared between Great Britain and France in March 1778. In the following month the Northamptonshire regiment of militia, together with the militia from several other counties, was for the first time embodied for prolonged service. On 11 and 12 June 1778 it set out for a camp which had been formed at Warley Common, near Brentwood in Essex, leaving Northampton, according to the enthusiastic account in the *Northampton Mercury*, 'with repeated huzzas, and (what is the glory of Britons!) with spirits animated to repulse the designs that may be formed by the enemies to their king and country'.[4] During the next five years it remained on duty at various places in the home counties and, for a few months during 1780-1, at Northampton itself. Newly-balloted men and substitutes who joined the colours in 1782 were marched from Northampton to Maidstone where their units were stationed. The regiment was discharged in March 1783, not to be called upon for other than routine training and exercises until 1793 when war was again declared between Great Britain and France.

* * * * * * * * *

The militia in each county was raised by the lord lieutenant and his deputies who, to quote Professor Western, 'used what was in effect the ordinary machinery of local government. The general and subdivision meetings which directed the work were simply military equivalents of quarter and petty or local sessions respectively; justices of the peace could attend and do most of the business provided at least one deputy lieutenant was present.'[5] The subdivisions consisted, in practice, of two or more of the hundreds, rapes, lathes or wapentakes into which the county was divided. At the first general meeting, held on the last Tuesday in May or October, a precept was issued to the chief constable of each hundred requiring him to produce 'fair and true lists, in writing, of the names of all the men usually and at that time dwelling within their respective parishes, tythings and places, between the ages of eighteen and forty-five

---

[3] C. A. Markham, *The History of the Northamptonshire & Rutland Militia* (1924), p. 13. This is the standard work on the Northamptonshire militia, and I have used it extensively in this introduction.

[4] *Northampton Mercury* (hereafter cited as *N.M.*), 15 June 1778.

[5] Western, p. 247.

years, distinguishing their respective ranks and occupations ... and which of the persons so returned labour under any infirmities, incapacitating them from serving as militia men ... '.[6] Before being delivered to the first subdivisional meetings, dates for which were fixed by the general meeting, each list had to be displayed on the door of the parish church for the space of a Sunday morning. Any person who considered that his name ought not to be included, or that the name of some other person had been wrongfully omitted, was entitled to an appeal at his subdivisional meeting. The lists, amended where necessary, were now passed to a second general meeting at which was determined the number of men to be raised from each hundred. At the same time copies were made of the lists, and these were sent to second subdivisional meetings which determined the number of men to be raised from each parish. The next step was third subdivisional meetings at which the balloting took place; these meetings had to be held within three weeks of the previous meetings. The men whose names were drawn in the ballot were informed of this by their parish constable, and they or their substitutes were required to attend fourth subdivisional meetings at which they took an oath of allegiance to the king, and their names were entered on a militia roll. This roll was returned to the county authorities, and at a third general meeting the militia was organized into regiments, battalions and companies, according to the number of men available. The minimum size of a militia regiment was eight companies of 60 to 80 men each, from which it may easily be calculated that Northamptonshire was able to provide one regiment for the defence of Great Britain in time of war. The colonel commanding the Northamptonshire militia in 1777 was Henry Yelverton, third Earl of Sussex, who lived at Easton Maudit, and who held the appointment from 1763 to 1784.

* * * * * * * * *

In 1777 the first general meeting for Northamptonshire was held on the last Tuesday in October, hence the date in November or December which appears on many of the lists (e.g. Great Brington and Higham Ferrers). The names of farmers and other substantial inhabitants are usually recorded first, sometimes with the distinction of rank in the form of 'Mr.'. An excellent example of village hierarchy may be seen on the list for Yardley Gobion which carries, in order, the names of four farmers and two farmers' sons, each dignified by 'Mr.', two bakers, two tailors, a butcher, a horse-dealer, a hog-dealer, five servants, two men who asserted that they had already been drawn for militia service (their names not being deleted, it would seem that they were unable to convince the subdivisional meeting that they were telling the truth), and nine labourers, followed by seven men who were physically defective and whose claim for non-service was allowed. However, this list, like many of the others, does not carry any indication where or when the subdivisional meeting was to be held; presumably, in a small community, those persons who wished to attend would have had no difficulty in discovering these details from the parish constable or some other rural worthy. Not all the constables obeyed the letter of the law by recording the names of men who claimed exemption because of physical infirmity. If Yardley Gobion was the dwelling place of

[6] 2 Geo. III, cap. 20, s. 42 ('An Act to explain, amend, and reduce into one Act of Parliament, the several Laws, now in being, relating to the Raising and Training the Militia, within that part of Great Britain called England'). The Militia Act of 1762.

seven such persons, it is hard to believe that certain other parishes with larger populations (e.g. Irchester and Ringstead) had none at all. Nor, it seems, did the constable always record impoverished fathers with three or more legitimate children, and he sometimes overlooked the apprentices. Clergymen seldom make their appearance on the lists. In a few cases the occupations of the men listed were omitted, either wholly or for most of the names (e.g. Desborough and West Haddon).

The standard of literacy displayed on the lists varies, as would be expected, from high to very low. Sometimes the writer was not the constable himself, although, with only one or two exceptions (e.g. Cosgrove), his signature appears at the end of the document. The list at Ashley, for example, is written in a mature hand which would do credit to any modern penman, but contrasts strangely with the scrawling signature of William Whiteman, the constable, which appears in the bottom left-hand corner. The village schoolmaster, where he existed, or some other well-disposed literate, was probably sought for by many an anxious constable whose skill with pen and ink was limited. Spelling on some of the lists approximates to twentieth century practice, but on others it certainly does not! No word was more frequently mis-spelt than 'militia' itself; variations include 'militsha', 'milita', 'milata', 'militi', 'militian', 'militta', 'melisha', 'malitia', 'melesher', 'millitia', 'millita', 'militry', 'militerry', 'malititicia', etc. Forenames and surnames are frequently mangled. Tubal Cain Mellows, mason and prominent nonconformist at Northampton (North Ward: his monument may be seen at College Street Baptist Chapel), was unkindly recorded as 'Too Ball Cane Mellows'; 'Canity Gautharn', also at Northampton (North Ward), appears in the printed pollbook for 1774 (a more reliable source) as 'Kennedy Gaudern'. Phonetic or semi-phonetic spellings abound throughout the lists; Thomas Numan (Newman) at Thenford, Richard Yomans (Yeomans) at Desborough, John Willeby (Willoughby) at Preston Capes, John Willabe (also Willoughby) at Eydon. The reader will easily be able to find other examples for himself.

Occasionally the surname of an eligible man was not recorded by the constable; either the man did not know it himself, or he would not reveal what it was. 'George at Mr. Johnsons as servant' (Oundle) is one example, and two more are 'James, Mr. Walton shay [chaise] man' (Evenley) and 'Samwell at Mr. Gudgins Lodge, note [not] tell his name' (Kingsthorpe). 'Yorkshire John, under hostler' makes his appearance at Northampton (Chequer Ward). In the case of 'Mrs. Johnsons futtman' (West Ward, Northampton) it seems that the constable did not know, or had been unable to discover, even the man's forename.

Alongside the name of Henry Gordon, a servant at Warkworth, appears the mysterious word 'black'. 'Gordon' was an unusual surname in the rural Northamptonshire of 1777 (but not unique, e.g. Steven Gorden and John Gordeain, both at Apethorpe), so Henry may have been a negro employed as a house-servant by the local squire or parson. Perhaps he had been born in the West Indies, and brought to England by an officer who had served overseas or by a merchant who traded with the Americas.

No renowned man was recorded in the Northamptonshire militia lists for 1777, but one was missed by just two years. William Carey, the pioneer missionary to India, had been born in 1761; already working as an apprentice shoemaker at Hackleton, he was too young to be liable for militia service. The Hackleton constable did list him in 1781. Clarke Nichols, his first master at Hackleton, and Thomas Old, his second, both appear on the list for that hamlet. Joshua Ringrose and John Trestler (or Tresler),

Table 1: Men recorded in each hundred.

Chipping Warden	376	Navisford	247
Cleyley	458	Nobottle Grove	884
Corby	1078	Orlingbury	522
Fawsley	1269	Polebrook	357
Greens Norton	360	Rothwell	842
Guilsborough	1254	Spelhoe	1244
Hamfordshoe	784	Towcester	407
Higham Ferrers	607	Willybrook	467
Huxloe	1069	Wymersley	602
Kings Sutton	914		

whom their historically minded vicar, the Rev. John Mastin, considered to be 'two very able and ingeneous mechanics', were both recorded by the constable at Naseby.[7] At least three very minor poets put in an appearance on the lists: Benjamin West (Weedon Bec) and Thomas Trinder (Chequer Ward, Northampton) were schoolmasters, and William Chown (Moulton) was a shoemaker who later also turned over to teaching.[8] Descending the moral scale, William Smith, Richard Law and William Terrill, all listed at Culworth, were members of the notorious 'Culworth Gang' which terrorized south-west Northamptonshire for several years.[9] Law, a carpenter, was hanged in 1787 for his part in the gang's activities. William Abbot, listed as a labourer at nearby Sulgrave, may also have been a member of the gang; a shoemaker with the same name who was parish clerk there in 1787 is said to have hidden some of the stolen goods in Sulgrave church. This man received sentence of transportation for life. William Parker, a weaver at Kettering, was found guilty by a coroner's jury in 1780 of murdering his apprentice, but absconded before he could be arrested.[10] John Saul, a cooper at Byfield, hurriedly left that village in 1783; he was suspected of murdering a young woman, but could not be traced and thus escaped arrest and trial.[11]

* * * * * * * * *

The names of 13,741 men appear on the Northamptonshire militia lists for 1777. Table 1 shows the number of men recorded in each hundred.

Seventeen places each recorded more than 100 names on their list or lists. Obviously, the number of names appearing on any list depended on the size of the place concerned; however, by including apprentices and men in exempted occupations, men with physical defects, men who had

[7] John Mastin, *The History & Antiquities of Naseby* (1792), pp. 52-4. Ringrose, who was a carpenter as well as a joiner, also had 'works' at Cransley and Kelmarsh, *N.M.*, 27 May 1776.

[8] Benjamin West, *Miscellaneous Poems, Translations, & Imitations*, Northampton (1780); William Chown, *Original Miscellaneous Poems*, Northampton (1818); T. Trinder, *Geographical & Astronomatical Definitions . . .* , Newport Pagnell (1833). Trinder's volume was published posthumously.

[9] An account of the Culworth Gang, written in 1837-8 by Alfred Beesley, the Banbury historian, is reprinted in *Cake & Cockhorse* (Banbury Historical Society), Vol. 3, 1965-8, pp. 3-6. Terrill=Turrill on the Culworth list.

[10] *N.M.*, 28 Feb. 1780.

[11] *N.M.*, 24 Mar. 1783.

Table 2: Places recording more than 100 men. The second column gives the total population in 1801.

1.	Northampton (5 lists)	805	7020
2.	Wellingborough	456	3325
3.	Daventry	408	2582
4.	Kettering	387	3011
5.	Crick	188	961
6.	Towcester	187	2030
7.	Long Buckby	183	1600
8.	Welford	158	931
9.	Rothwell	156	1409
10.	Oundle	153	1956
11.	West Haddon	138	806
12.	Brackley (3 lists)	134	1495
13.	Raunds	120	890
14.	Rushden	109	818
15.	Kingsthorpe	107	909
16.	Middleton Cheney	104	1153
17.	Brington	101	772

already been drawn for militia service, and penurious fathers with three or more legitimate children, a conscientious constable (such as Thomas Harris at Crick) might produce an unexpectedly long list of male inhabitants aged between 18 and 45 years.

* * * * * * * * *

Out of the 13,741 men recorded on the lists for 1777, the occupations or status of 11,955 (87.0%), perhaps two-thirds of the males aged 18 to 45 years living in the county at that date, were recorded by the parish constables. These lists, together with the other series of surviving lists, are the nearest approach to an occupational census which is available for Northamptonshire prior to the table of occupations included in the printed abstract of the 1831 census of Great Britain, and the enumerators' books (Public Record Office) from the 1841 census.

The constables, of course, did not work to an agreed schedule of occupations. Thus there is much variation of terminology on the lists, e.g. 'apothecary' and 'druggist', 'barber' and 'hairdresser', 'wheelwright' and 'wheeler'. In Table 6 (the complete list of occupations), and to a lesser extent the occupational tables which precede the lists for each hundred, like has been grouped with like in order to promote clarity and to cut down in length. For certain occupations—the making of shoes is an example—only a consolidated figure appears in Table 6, the categories of men employed in these occupations appearing elsewhere in this introduction.

Also in Table 6, but with the exception of men who were listed as 'farmer's son', sons have been placed under the same occupational headings as their fathers (e.g. the figure for blacksmiths also includes all the sons of blacksmiths when they were listed as such by the constables). Apprentices have also been placed in their occupation when the constable recorded what it was. Apprentices whose occupation was not recorded have been placed under the heading 'no occupation or status given', and

Table 3: Numerical order of occupations (100 men and over); the second column gives this as a percentage of the grand total of occupations (Table 6: 11,955 men).

1.	'Servant'	2481	20.8
2.	Labourer	2291	19.2
3.	'Farmer'	1332	11.1
4.	Weaving & framework knitting	1164	9.7
5.	Shoemaking	705	5.9
6.	Carpenter/joiner	398	3.3
7.	'Wool'	317	2.7
8.	Tailor	281	2.4
9.	'Farmer's son'	224	1.9
10.	Blacksmith/smith	220	1.8
11.	'Inn-keeping'	214	1.8
12.	Butcher	213	1.8
13.	Baker	198	1.7
14.	Mason	189	1.6
15.	Shepherd	160	1.3
16.	Miller	127	1.1

so have the eighteen 'clerks and apprentices' from Daventry. On the other hand, servants, with or without qualification, have all been placed under the heading of 'servant'. Most of the rural 'servants' would have been 'servants in husbandry',[12] many of them young unmarried men who boarded at the farm where they were employed.

The militia lists contain many erratic spellings and contractions, and a glossary of some words which may cause difficulty for a modern reader will be found at the end of this introduction. A certain number of ambiguities or obscurities have also been included in this list, examples being the 'cotther' and the 'jaroser' at Polebrook, the 'cakeman' at Bozeat, the 'culer' at Irthlingborough, and the 'grit maker' at Broughton.

*　*　*　*　*　*　*　*　*

The complete list of occupations will be found in Table 6. A whole volume could obviously be written on the economy of Northamptonshire at the time of the militia lists, but limitations of space make it impossible here to do more than elaborate the groupings which appear in Tables 3, 5 and 6, and to indicate some of the principal features revealed by the analysis of the 11,955 men whose occupations or status were recorded by the constables in 1777.

Of the 1332 men appearing under the heading 'farmer', 1060 were listed as such by the constables, 109 as graziers, 81 as husbandmen, 79 as yeomen, and 3 as landholders. 'Farmer's son' includes 199 men who were the sons of farmers, 15 the sons of graziers, 6 the sons of husbandmen, 2 the sons of yeomen, and 2 the sons of landholders.

---

[12] This term is used by the constable at Great Oakley. 'Farmer's servant' appears on a number of lists (e.g. Blisworth).

Table 4: Weaving and Framework-knitting.

Weaving		Framework-knitting	
Cloth-joiner	1	Framework-knitter	84
Clothier	2	Framework-knitter (silk)	2
Harrateen-maker	2	Hosier	1
Manufacturer	5	Stockinger	4
Serge-maker	12		—
Weaver	1036		
Weaver (plush)	5		91
Weaver (sack)	1		
Weaver (shag)	6	Weaving	1073
Weaver (silk)	1	Framework-knitting	91
Weaver (stocking)	2		—
	—		1164
	1073		

'Innkeeping' (214 men) includes all persons who were described by the constables as the landlords of licensed premises (e.g. 'innkeeper', 'victualler', 'public house', 'ale-draper', etc.); they number 145, and range from Clark Hillyard, landlord of the mighty George Inn at Northampton (Chequer Ward), down to humble keepers of obscure village ale-houses. In addition there are four men who were the sons of landlords. Men who were employed at inns, or who would have been based on them, also appear under the heading of 'innkeeping'; they comprise 7 drawers, 26 ostlers, 29 post-boys, post-chaise drivers or postilions, and 3 waiters.

'Weaving & framework-knitting' accounts for 1164 men, 1073 of whom were weavers and 91 were framework-knitters. Table 4 indicates how these figures are made up.

701 weavers, two-thirds of the total number, lived in one or other of four contiguous hundreds, Corby, Huxloe, Rothwell and Guilsborough (see Table 5). The town of Kettering, where the worsted industry had been established since the second half of the seventeenth century,[13] contained easily the largest concentration of weavers in Northamptonshire (149 plus 5 manufacturers), followed by Rothwell (65), Northampton (56), Crick (52), and Welford (38). The constables at Desborough and West Haddon, each of which was a centre of weaving, did not provide a record of occupations in their respective lists for 1777. 31 weavers were recorded out of a total of 64 men at Braybrooke (48%), 23 out of 49 at Cottingham (47%), 17 out of 41 at Great Oxendon (41%), 28 out of 73 at Corby (38%), 18 out of 52 at Ashley (35%), and 8 out of 24 at Cransley (33⅓%). Only Navisford Hundred listed no weavers among its men liable for militia service, although Polebrook Hundred listed only one and Higham Ferrers three.

Framework-knitters made stockings, and the machines on which they worked were known as frames. In the Northamptonshire militia lists for 1777 two villages accounted between them for almost half the total of knitters, Middleton Cheney (24) and Abthorpe (20). ('The Stocking Frame' public house in Abthorpe closed only in 1957.) Other places which recorded framework-knitters were Daventry, Flore and Lilbourne (8 each),

[13] John Morton, *The Natural History of Northamptonshire* (1712), p. 26. See also Adrian Randall, 'The Kettering Worsted Industry of the Eighteenth Century', *Northamptonshire Past & Present*, Vol. 1V, Nos. 5 & 6 (1970-1, 1971-2), pp. 312-20, 349-56.

Chacombe and Towcester (6 each), Pattishall (4), Maidford (3), Blakesley (2, both working in silk), Alderton and Dallington (1 each). The militia list for Lilbourne, a tiny village at the point where Northamptonshire meets Warwickshire and Leicestershire, also includes the names of 8 weavers; out of a total of 27 men listed, no fewer than 16 (59%) were concerned with the production of textiles, a proportion unsurpassed by any other town or village in the county.

Eighteenth century Northamptonshire was an important wool-growing county, much of the wool being exported to other parts of England where the weaving or hosiery industries flourished.[14] Some of it was retained at home for use by Northamptonshire's own weavers and knitters; but before it could be spun into yarn—women's work, although 3 male spinners are recorded on the lists, 1 each at Kettering, Thorpe Malsor and Ravensthorpe—it had to pass through the hands of combers who were responsible for causing the fibres to lie parallel to each other. They did this by sprinkling the wool with oil and then drawing it through the teeth of two heated wool-combs, heavy rake-like implements one of which had previously been attached at head-height to a post. The names of 289 combers appear on the lists, 122 (42%) of them in the hundreds of Guilsborough and Nobottle Grove (see Table 5). Long Buckby recorded more combers than anywhere else in the county, 40 in all.[15] Kettering recorded 31 combers, Ravensthorpe 12, Kilsby and Welford 11 each, Whilton and Kislingbury 9 each, and Spratton 7. None of the hundreds represented in the lists for 1777 failed to record at least one wool-comber among their men liable for militia service. A solitary wool-winder is listed at Kettering.

The purchasing and marketing of wool was undertaken by wool-staplers, 12 of whom appear on the lists, 6 at Northampton, 3 at Kingsthorpe, and 1 each at Hardingstone, Little Harrowden and Stoke Albany. Richard Baker, a stapler at Northampton (North Ward), was the father of George Baker (1781-1851), the premier historian of Northamptonshire. 12 wool-sorters are also recorded, 7 at Northampton, 3 at Kettering, and 1 each at Hardingstone and Moulton. The total of 317 men classified under the heading 'wool' in Tables 3 and 6, is made up by 289 combers, 12 staplers, 12 sorters, 3 spinners and 1 winder.

705 men identified with shoemaking were listed by the constables in 1777: 697 shoemakers, 1 shoemaker and currier, 4 heel-makers, 2 flat-makers, and 1 clog-maker. In pre-industrial England the village shoemaker serving his own community was a familiar figure, hence it is not surprising that most of the larger Northamptonshire villages and many of the smaller ones could produce at least one shoemaker among their inhabitants liable for militia service. However, wholesale shoemaking for markets outside the county, and sometimes outside the country, had for more than a century been a speciality at Northampton, and by the second half of the eighteenth century Wellingborough and several villages within a few miles of that town had also developed a bias towards the shoe industry. 142 men were recorded on the five Northampton lists (20% of all the shoemakers listed in the county), and 113 on the Wellingborough list (16%). Irthlingborough recorded 17 shoemakers, Raunds 16, Earls Barton 11, Rushden

---

[14] Morton, p. 16; James Donaldson, *General View of the Agriculture of the County of Northampton* . . . , Edinburgh (1794), pp. 11-12; William Pitt, *General View of the Agriculture of the County of Northampton* . . (1809), pp. 241-2 (quotes Donaldson, but with additions of his own).

[15] For wool-combing at Long Buckby, see Victor A. Hatley, 'Blaize at Buckby', *Northamptonshire Past & Present*, Vol. IV, No. 2 (1967-8), pp. 91-6.

Table 5: Numbers of men employed in weaving and framework-knitting, wool-combing and shoemaking, giving in parenthesis each figure as a percentage of all men in that hundred whose occupations were stated.

Hundred	All occupations	Weaving & framework-knitting	Woolcombing	Shoemaking
Chipping Warden	360	14 (3.9)	8 (2.2)	19 (5.3)
Cleyley	443	9 (2.0)	2 (0.5)	15 (3.4)
Corby	787	145 (18.4)	17 (2.2)	24 (3.0)
Fawsley	1036	78 (7.5)	25 (2.4)	32 (3.1)
Greens Norton	285	8 (2.8)	3 (1.1)	9 (3.2)
Guilsborough	981	198 (20.1)	71 (7.2)	32 (3.3)
Hamfordshoe	751	35 (4.7)	6 (0.8)	136 (18.1)
Higham Ferrers	528	3 (0.6)	1 (0.2)	45 (8.5)
Huxloe	1007	185 (18.4)	35 (3.5)	55 (5.5)
Kings Sutton	733	59 (8.0)	11 (1.5)	20 (2.7)
Navisford	234		3 (1.3)	13 (5.6)
Nobottle Grove	796	62 (7.8)	51 (6.4)	36 (4.5)
Orlingbury	471	34 (7.2)	9 (1.9)	13 (2.8)
Polebrook	349	1 (0.3)	2 (0.6)	14 (4.0)
Rothwell	643	181 (28.1)	9 (1.4)	22 (3.4)
Spelhoe	1225	91 (7.4)	32 (2.6)	158 (12.9)
Towcester	387	34 (8.8)	2 (0.5)	24 (6.2)
Willybrook	424	17 (4.0)	1 (0.2)	15 (3.5)
Wymersley	515	10 (1.9)	1 (0.2)	23 (4.5)
	11,955	1164 (9.7)	289 (2.4)	705 (5.9)

10, and Wollaston 7; all these villages subsequently became important centres of shoe manufacturing in Northamptonshire. Daventry is revealed by its list not yet to have developed the considerable shoe industry which had become apparent there by 1810; in 1777, out of 408 men listed by the constables and thirdboroughs of Daventry and Drayton (a hamlet within the parish of Daventry), only 15 were shoemakers, 5 of whom were stated to be masters and the rest journeymen.[16]

Weaving and framework-knitting, wool-combing and shoemaking: these were the principal industries in Northamptonshire when the militia lists for 1777 were compiled. The number and proportion of weavers and knitters, wool-combers and shoemakers to all listed men in each of the hundreds is set out in Table 5.

* * * * * * * * *

'Leather' accounts for a total of 86 men on the lists. 20 tanners were recorded, a low figure which, however, does not conflict with the statement made by James Donaldson in 1794 that the leather used by Northamptonshire shoemakers was 'purchased partly in this and neighbouring

---

[16] Victor A. Hatley and Joseph Rajczonek, *Shoemakers in Northamptonshire, 1762-1911: a Statistical Survey*, Northampton (1971), for information about the development of the shoe industry in Northamptonshire (including statistics taken from the militia lists, 1762-86).

counties, but chiefly from the London market'.[17] 5 tanners were listed at Northampton, 2 each at Brigstock, Byfield and Wilby, and 1 each at Drayton by Daventry, Duddington, Kettering, Lowick, Middleton, Newnham, Oundle, Rushden and Wellingborough. At or near these places the presence of a tanyard may reasonably be assumed.[18] The 32 fellmongers and 1 skinner were concerned with the preparation and sale of hides and skins; 8 of these men lived at Daventry and 6 at Northampton, both of which had flourishing animal markets. Curriers, leather-dressers and tawers processed leather which had already been tanned. 33 men followed these occupations, 10 of them living at Wellingborough and 7 at Northampton, the two principal centres of shoe production in the county.

Also in 1794, James Donaldson calculated that 'in Wellingborough, and the neighbourhood, and towards the south-west corner of the county, from 9,000 to 10,000 persons, mostly young women and boys, are employed in lace-making'.[19] Only 28 men are recorded on the militia lists for 1777 as lace-makers. 11 of them lived at Bozeat and 7 at Grendon (neighbouring villages); of the rest, 3 lived at Ashton (Cleyley Hundred) and 2 at Stoke Bruerne (also neighbouring villages), 2 each at Raunds and Towcester, and 1 at Kettering. The commercial organization of lace-making was in the hands of men described variously as lace-buyers, lace-dealers and lace-men, 12 of whom were listed by the constables. 4 lace-men and 1 lace-buyer were recorded at Wellingborough, 2 lace-dealers and 1 lace-man a Northampton, 1 lace-dealer each at Wollaston and Finedon, and 1 lace-man each at Bozeat and Yardley Hastings.

Several occupations were limited to only a few places in the county, or had a special association with one town or village in particular. None of them gave employment to many men in comparison with widely-distributed occupations such as weaving, shoemaking, carpentry or tailoring; nevertheless, a number of them are worth mentioning in the context of this introduction.

Mat-making: there were 35 mat-makers, 15 of them at Earls Barton, 4 at Finedon, 3 each at Irchester and Stanwick, 2 each at Islip, Oundle and Thorpe Achurch, and 1 each at Higham Ferrers, Northampton, Wellingborough and Wollaston. All these places except Finedon border the River Nene; Finedon lies on the Ise, the Nene's principal tributary. Both these rivers provided a supply of rushes, from which the mats were made.[20]

Wood-turning: there were 22 turners, 10 of them at King's Cliffe, 4 at Northampton, 2 each at Towcester and Welford, and 1 each at Long Buckby, Daventry, Kettering and Oundle. Wood-turning is associated with King's Cliffe by John Morton in 1712,[21] and the craft remained a speciality of this village into the twentieth century.

Whip-making: there were 10 whip-makers, 8 of them at Daventry and

---

[17] Donaldson, p. 10.
[18] Sometimes confirmed by advertisements in the *N.M.*, e.g. tanyards at Grendon (23 Mar. 1778), Newnham (25 Nov. 1776), Oundle (1 Oct. 1770), Wellingborough (20 Nov. 1769, 11 Mar. 1776), and Wilby (1 May 1780).
[19] Donaldson, p. 10.
[20] Rushes in the River Nene at White Mills near Wellingborough were advertised for sale, *N.M.*, 7 Aug. 1769.
[21] Morton, p. 488.

2 at Northampton. This craft is mentioned in several sources, c.1790-1840, as a feature of Daventry.[22]

Paper-making: there were 15 paper-makers, 7 of them at Isham (described as 'tramping', i.e. itinerant workmen under the protection of their trade society, whose residence at Isham was probably only temporary), 5 at Northampton, 2 at Boughton, and 1 at Woodford (Huxloe Hundred).[23] One of the Northampton paper-makers (South Ward) was Francis Hayes, Mayor in 1804-5, who collapsed and died while dancing at the customary ball given in celebration of the appointment of his successor.[24]

Stone-quarrying: there were 9 quarry-men or stone-cutters—2 quarry-men and 4 cutters at Harlestone, and 1 cutter each at Kingsthorpe, Great Weldon and Wicken. Harlestone, Kingsthorpe and Great Weldon are all parishes which contain well-known quarries which have yielded much stone used for building purposes.[25]

Slate-quarrying: there were 40 slaters, 14 of them at Easton on the Hill, 10 at Collyweston, 4 at Oundle, 3 at Kettering, 2 each at King's Cliffe and Northampton, and 1 each at Deene, Deenethorpe, Duddington, Gretton and Wilbarston. Most of these men were engaged in quarrying, although some may have worked primarily at fixing slates on roofs (e.g. at Northampton, see also the entry for 'hilliard' in the glossary). The principal slate quarries in Northamptonshire are at Collyweston and Easton on the Hill, the former giving its name to the whole range of slates quarried there and at Easton.[26]

Gardening: there were 78 gardeners or garden-men, 11 of whom were listed at Northampton and 2 at Kingsthorpe. Gardeners and garden-men are, in fact, distributed fairly evenly throughout the county, although it is not clear how many were market gardeners and how many tended the gardens of a house. Market-gardening on the outskirts of the town was a feature of Northampton during the nineteenth century—175 gardeners or nursery men were enumerated there at the 1851 census—and thus it is significant that on the 1777 militia lists, 13 gardeners (17% of the whole) were recorded at Northampton or the adjacent parish of Kingsthorpe.

Woad-growing: there were 3 woad-men, 2 of them at Weston Favell, and 1 at Watford. According to the Rev. Robert Hervey Knight (Rector of Weston Favell, 1797-1842), the Rev. James Hervey, the celebrated Evangelical clergyman who was rector there from 1752 to 1758, raised money to rebuild the rectory 'by letting his land for the cultivation of woad, which always produces an extraordinary rent for a time.' Knight adds that 'my father [rector, 1760-97] had, I believe, to finish the interior. He too was a considerable benefactor to it, by building in 1777, a large room or parlour adjoining to it, for the sake of convenience . . . This he

---

[22] e.g. *Universal British Directory of Trade, Commerce & Manufacturing* . . . (1791), entry under 'Daventry'; Samuel Lewis, *Topographical Dictionary of England* . . . , 3rd ed. (1835), Vol. 2, entry under 'Daventry'.

[23] *N.M.*, 25 Nov. 1782 (paper-mill at Boughton), 14 July 1783 (paper-mill at Northampton). For 'tramping' see E. J. Hobsbawm, 'The Tramping Artisan', *Economic History Review*, 2nd ser., iii (1950-1), pp. 299-320. Mr. Hobsbawm states that 'Tramping arrangements among . . . paper-makers . . . were so well advanced at the turn of the century [1800] that they must have flourished for quite a while before then' (p. 300).

[24] *N.M.*, 10 Aug. 1805.

[25] *Victoria History of the County of Northampton*, Vol. 2 (1906), pp. 293-302 ('Stone').

[26] *Ibid.* pp. 302-3 ('Slate').

was enabled to do by letting his land for woad also.'[27] It is satisfying to have Knight's account of woad-growing at Weston Favell so neatly confirmed by evidence from the militia lists.

Two more of the entries appearing in Table 6 deserve special mention in this introduction: the 2 newsmen at Wootton and the 17 students at Daventry. The former would have been distributors of the *Northampton Mercury*, the important newspaper which was published at Northampton and circulated through a wide area of the East Midlands. Possibly the 'folio of four pages, happy work!', which William Cowper read with such relish over his evening cup of tea, had been brought to Olney by one of the newsmen living at Wootton.[28] The students at Daventry were attending full-time instruction at the nonconformist academy in that town. After the death of Dr. Philip Doddridge in 1751, the academy which he maintained in Sheep Street, Northampton, was moved to Daventry where it continued until 1789 when it returned to Northampton.[29]

One of the most interesting aspects of the militia lists is the wide range of occupations recorded in the larger villages of Northamptonshire, and in many of the smaller ones also. Holcot had a population of only 343 persons when the first national census was taken in 1801, yet in 1777 its constable listed the names of 7 farmers or farmers' sons, 7 labourers, 8 servants, 2 shepherds, 4 wool-combers, 4 weavers, 6 shoemakers, 1 horse-dealer, 1 miller, 2 carpenters, 1 joiner, 1 tailor, 1 blacksmith, 2 bakers and 1 butcher. Welford, two and a half times the size of Holcot in 1801 (931 inhabitants), listed 11 farmers, 2 graziers, 17 labourers, 17 servants, 2 shepherds, 1 gardener, 1 miller, 38 weavers, 1 mason, 3 fellmongers, 1 currier and 1 leather-dresser, 7 carpenters, 11 wool-combers, 1 butcher, 5 victuallers and 1 innholder, 2 turners, 1 tallow chandler, 1 carrier, 6 shoemakers, 2 bakers, 1 cooper, 2 tailors, 2 wheelwrights, 2 blacksmiths, 3 apprentices, 1 licensed teacher (a nonconformist), 1 naval officer and 14 men with no occupations stated (including the 'boarder'). No doubt many of the men whose names were recorded by the village constables were, like Joshua Ringrose and John Trestler at Naseby, highly-skilled craftsmen, of whose activities, however, all trace has now passed into oblivion. But sometimes a few tantalizing scraps of information do survive; so let us conclude this introduction by setting down the ambitious claims made on his own behalf by Samuel Beal, a London-trained tailor listed at Orling-bury, who, in 1782, announced that he was continuing to make 'in the newest and genteelest fashions, French and other stays, negligees, Polanese, Italian gowns, robe gowns, Stormont dresses, etc., on reasonable terms.'[30] Beal must have drawn his clientele from a wide area, and perhaps served ladies in Kettering, Wellingborough and Northampton; even so, he is surely a remarkable man to be found in 1777 living and working in a small and somewhat isolated Northamptonshire village, which had only 268 inhabitants in 1801.

---

[27] John Cole (comp.), *Herveiana; or, graphic & literary sketches illustrative of the life and writings of the Rev. James Hervey, A.M.*, Part 2 (Scarborough, 1823), pp. 18-19.

[28] William Cowper, *The Task*, Book IV ('The Winter Evening'), line 50.

[29] Thomas Arnold and J. J. Cooper, *The History of the Church of Doddridge* (Northampton, 1895), p. 165.

[30] *N.M.*, 27 May 1782, in which Beal styles himself 'stay and mantua maker'. ('Mantua', a corruption of 'manteau', was the general term for the loose upper garments worn by women at this period.) Another Beal advertisement will be found, *N.M.*, 20 May 1776.

Table 6:   complete list of occupations or status.

Apothecary/druggist	10	Cow keeper	1
Attorney/'law'	17	Cutler	7
Attorney's clerk	7		
		Dairy-man	1
Bailiff	1	Dealer/jobber/chapman	
Baker/gingerbread baker	198	& dealer	13
Barber/hairdresser	23	Dealer/jobber in hogs	
Baronet/earl	3	*or* swine	5
Basket-maker	10	Dissenting minister	3
Besom-maker/broom-		Distiller	1
maker	2	Doctor/surgeon/surgeon	
Blacksmith/smith	220	& apothecary	18
Boat-wright	1	Draper	31
Book-binder	3	Drover/cow drover	4
Book-keeper/clerk	5	Dyer	4
Bookseller	1		
Brazier	10	Engraver	1
Breeches-maker	18	Esquire	21
Brewer/ale-brewer	5	Excise	7
Bricklayer	7		
Brickmaker	9	'Farmer'	1332
Butcher	213	'Farmer's son'	224
Butler	7	Farrier	7
Butter merchant	1	Fiddler	1
		Fishmonger/fish-man	3
Cabinet-maker	2	Flax-dresser	21
Cake-man	1	Footman	3
Carpenter/joiner	398		
Carrier	6	Gamekeeper/keeper	21
Carver	3	Gaoler/turnkey	2
Chair-bottomer	1	Gardener/garden-man	78
Chair-maker	1	Gelder/'culer'	3
Chandler/tallow chandler	17	Gentleman	39
Cheese-factor	1	Glazier	25
Chimney sweep	3	Glover	44
Clergyman/curate/rector	15	Grit-maker	1
Clock-maker/watch-		Grocer	61
maker	15	Groom/under groom/	
Coach driver	1	groom's man	7
Coach-maker/carriage-		Gun-smith	2
maker	4	Gun-stock maker	1
Coachman	8		
Collar-maker	24	Haberdasher	2
Collector of taxes	1	Harness-maker	1
Compositor/printer	3	Hatter	2
Confectioner	1	Hawker	1
Cooper	34	Hedger	1
Coppice keeper	1	Hemp-dresser	9
Cork-cutter	2	Hilliard/hillier	7
Costermonger	2	Hog-man	1
'Cotther'	1	Horse-breaker	2

Horse-dealer	6	Roper/rope-maker	5
Horse-keeper	7		
		Saddler	6
'Inn-keeping'	214	Sawyer	15
Ironmonger	7	Schoolmaster/master of	
		free school/teacher	24
Jockey	1	Scuttle-maker	1
		Servant	2481
Knacker	3	Shepherd	160
		Sheriff	1
Labourer	2291	Shoemaking	705
Lace-buyer/lace-dealer/		Shopkeeper	20
lace-man	12	Shopman	1
Lace-maker	28	Sieve-maker	3
'Leather'	86	Sizer	1
Lime-trimmer	2	Slater	40
Locksmith	1	Snead-maker	1
		Soap-boiler	3
Maltster/maltman	50	Stable-boy	1
Mason	189	Stationer	2
Mat-maker	35	Stay-maker	25
Merchant	4	Steward	4
Militia (other counties)	20	Student	17
Militia (sergeant)	1	Surveyor/land surveyor	6
Miller	127		
Millwright	5	Tailor	281
Mole-catcher	2	Thatcher	4
		Tinker	1
Naval officer/seaman	2	Tripe-man	1
Newsman	2	Turner	22
Outrider/rider	2	Upholsterer	5
Painter	7	Wagoner	6
Paper-maker	15	Weaving & framework-	
Parchment-maker	5	knitting	1164
Peruke-maker	3	Wheelwright/wheeler	92
Pin-maker	1	Whip-maker	10
Pipe-maker	3	Whitesmith/tinman	21
Plasterer	7	Wine-merchant	3
Plough-wright	1	Woad-man	3
Plumber/plumber		Wood-man	1
& glazier	10	'Wool'	317
Porter	1	Total of those whose	
Poulterer	2	occupation or	
Pump-maker	1	status is given	11,955
Quarreyman/stone-cutter	9	Apprentice	49
		Boarder	1
Rag-man	2	Constable	18
Rake-maker	1	Drawn man	11
Reed-maker/slay-maker	3	*Illegible*	6

Infirm	1	Trade/tradesman	103
No details	1519	Workhouse	1
Not inhabitant	5	Total of those for whom	
Out of business	1	no occupation or ———	
Pauper/poor man	4	status is given	1786
Parish clerk	2		
Served last time	1	Total number of	
Single/single man	64	men listed	13,741

GLOSSARY

This glossary includes explanations of technical terms, and a few of the many variant spellings which will be found in the lists.

Ale draper.   Ale house keeper.
Attoy.   Attorney.
Backer; beacker.   Baker.
Beasomaker.   Besom-maker; maker of brooms.
Beley brock; broken; bussen.   Ruptured.
Blackth.   Blacksmith.
Cake-man.   A dealer in cattle-cake (?).[1]
Cardwinder.   Cordwainer (q.v.).
Carpainer.   Carpenter.
Carver.   Stone carver; sculptor.
Clother.   Clothier; master weaver.
Comber.   Wool-comber.
Comer; cummer.   Comber (q.v.).
Cordwainer.   Shoemaker.
Culer.   Gelder (?); culler.[2]
Dareman.   Dairyman.
Decenting.   Dissenting.
End holder.   Innholder.
Farrer.   Farrier.
Felmoner.   Fellmonger.
Flat-maker.   Shoemaker. (Flats = low-heeled shoes).[3]
Framar.   Farmer.
Giner; goynor.   Joiner.
Gobar; goblar.   Jobber.
Grecher.   Grocer (?).
Grit-maker.   Meaning unclear.[4]
Harrateen.   A kind of worsted cloth.
Headborough.   Deputy Constable.[5]
Hilliard.   Hillyer; 'one who covers houses with slate or tile'.[6]
Horsler.   Ostler.
Jaroser.   Grocer (?).
Jarsey.   Jersey; jersey wool.
Jienor.   Joiner.
Jorman.   Journeyman.

---

[1] A reference to 'oyl-cakes' for cattle occurs in J. Morton, *The Natural History of Northamptonshire* (1712), p. 491.

[2] In this form the late Alderman W. J. Penn, who was born at Wootton in 1890, and who farmed for nearly fifty years in Northamptonshire, recognized the word as soon as it was shown to him.

[3] Information from Miss June M. Swann, Assistant Curator, Northampton Museum.

[4] Grits are oats used for porridge; for local use of this word see J. M. Steane, 'The Poor in Rothwell', *Northamptonshire Past & Present*, iv, pt. 3 (1968-9), p. 146.

[5] In some districts this term was used as synonymous with that of constable: W. E. Tate, *The Parish Chest* (1960), p. 307.

[6] A. E. Baker, *A Glossary of Northamptonshire Words and Phrases*, i (1854), p. 324.

Larbra. Labourer.
Macon; marson; masoner.   Mason.
Malster. Maltster.
Millow. Miller.
Nettir. Knitter.
Non conpesments.   *Non compos mentis;* unsound mind.
Outride. Outrider; probably he was the travelling agent for a merchant or manufacturer.
Parsons. Persons.
Phthsical. Consumptive.
Plush. A kind of cloth, made of silk or wool, having a nap longer and softer than velvet.
Reed-maker. Maker of reeds or slays for looms.
Sart; savant; savront. Servant.
Serge. As manufactured in Northamptonshire, this was a kind of worsted cloth.
Shag. A kind of cloth, usually worsted, having a velvet nap on one side.
Shay. Chaise.
Silley. Silly; unsound mind.
Slatter. Slater.
Slay-maker. Maker of reeds or slays for looms.
Snead. Shaft or pole of a scythe.
Spiner. Spinner.
Soyor. Sawyer.
Stokiner. Stocking weaver or knitter.
Tawer. Whittawer (q.v.).
Tealer. Tailor.
Thirdborough. Tithing man or deputy constable.
Third brug. Thirdborough (q.v.).
Tithing man. Constable or deputy constable.
Unfermd. Deformed (?).
Vicr; victur; vinter. Victualler.
Wear. Weaver.
Whittawer. A man who taws skins into whitleather.
Whitesmith. Tinsmith.

CHIPPING WARDEN HUNDRED

Aston-le-Walls	18	Eydon	55
Lower Boddington	17	Greatworth	14
Upper Boddington	36	Sulgrave	55
Byfield	73	Woodford	61
Chipping Warden	38		___
Edgcote	9		376

Ale-draper	2	Groom (under)	1
Baker	8	Joiner	2
Blacksmith	8	Labourer	73
Brazier	1	Maltster	2
Butcher	9	Mason	6
Carpenter	6	Miller	3
Chandler	1	No trade given	16
Coachman	1	Schoolmaster	1
Collar-maker	2	Servant	106
Cooper	2	Shoemaker	19
Cutler	1	Shopkeeper	1
Dealer	1	Surgeon	1
Farmer	45	Tailor	6
Farmer's son	10	Tanner	2
Farrier	1	Weaver	14
Gardener	1	Wheelwright	3
Glazier	1	Wool-comber	8
Glover	1		___
Grazier	8		376
Grocer	3		

ASTON-LE-WALLS

A list of all the mility men of the parish of Asston Lee Walless in the county of Northampton made by me, William Cowper, constable of the said parish.

William Johnson, farmor	Thomas Amos, do.
James Page, do.	Thomas Jacock, do.
Edmund Fairbrother	Benjeman Gubbins, do.
Isaac Allett	William Aries
John Willkens, shou maker	Steepen Gee, laberor
William Lovell, sarvent	⟨John Harries, do.⟩
John Roberts, do.	Robert Askeu, do.
Samuell Shearsby, do.	Joseph Gubbins, do.
Richerd Hartcher, do.	John Tompkens, do.

William Cowper, constable.

BODDINGTON

1777 Decem. 4th. A list of the names of all such persons that are liable to serve as militia-men in the parish of Bodingtons for the county of Northampton being between the age of 18 and 45 years.

In UPPER BODINGTON

Job Draper, labourer
Benjamin Pointer, servant
William Bassett, taylor
Samuel Branson, sernt.
John Gibert, sernt.
George Southam, labr.
William Ladd, farmer
John Eliman, taylor
William Rainbow, sernt.
John Reynolds, farmer
Thomas Tucky, labr.
James Allen, farmer
John Izzard, farmer
John Garret, sernt.
John Payne, farmer
Thomas Jeffs, dealer
Richard Vigours, labr.
John Dawkins, baker
Samuel Russel, weaver

John Luckcuck, blacksmith
John Ley, weaver ⟨infirm⟩
Thomas Staunt, weaver
Thomas Clews, cutler
Thomas Smith, cordwainer
⟨John Butlin, cordwainer, infirm⟩
⟨Daniel Green,
    cordwainer, infirm⟩
⟨John Hartwell, butcher, infirm⟩
George Bradshaw, grazier
John Smallbone, labr.
⟨James Smallbone, labr.⟩
Thomas Allibone, labr.
Thomas Watts, farmer
    Dos. servant
James Bloxham, sernt.
John Wimbush, sernt.
William Wimbush, sernt.

In LOWER BODINGTON

⟨John Hawkins, labourer, infirm⟩
John Pollard, servant
John King, servant
Thomas Izzard, labr.
Robert Izzard, labr.
Joseph Frost, cordwainer
George Creed, labr.
William Goodwin, grocer
William Budd, butcher

Giles Ladd, farmer
Samuel Izzard, sernt.
James Mander, sernt.
Robert Keartland, labr.
William Miller, weaver
Abraham Baseley, grazier
William Haynes, blacksmith
John Stonton, sernt.

N.B.   The day of appeal for those that think themselves hereby aggrieved is held at Thorp Mundville on the eighth day of this instant December; no appeal afterwards will be received.

Silvester Harris ⎫
John Weston   ⎬ constables.
               ⎭

BYFIELD

A list of all the men in the parish of Byfield capacitated to serve in the militia.

William Cox, tanner
William Boote, servant
Joseph Muddyman, servant
William Hiron, labourer
William Coates, farmer
Samuel Batcheldore, servant
William Bucknill, servant

William Bloxom, maltster
Humphry Shotton, tanner
Edward Lawrence, labourer
James Haustin, servant
Richard Dodd, farmer
William Marriott, servant
Jno. Bush, junr., labourer

Samuel Lawrence, mason
Thomas Reynolds, junr.,
    carpenter
Richard Reynolds, carpenter
Richard Higham, servant
James Coates, farmer
Joseph Marriott, servant
Edward Thornton, surgeon
Jno. Bilson, woolcomber
Richard Harris, farmer
Jno. Wyatt, servant
James Smith, farmer
Jno. Smith, do.
William White, servt.
George Fessey, woolcomber
Edward Lawrence, mason
Thomas Cox, farmer
Robt. Burbidge, farmer
John Wimbush, cordwainer
Joseph Varney, servant
Jno. Causbrook, servant
William Adams, farmer
William Thornton, farmer
Thomas Orton, farmer
Edward Harris, schoolmaster
Thomas Gee, labourer
Robt. Coleman, woolcomber
Daniel Boote, do.
⟨Samuel Cox, butcher⟩ mistake
Jno. Wilcox, servant

Thomas Bonham, weaver
Jno. Spicer, collarmaker
Thomas Lawrence, junr., mason
William Basely, taylor
Richard Eyles, collarmaker
Jno. Fowkes, junr., glazier
Jno. Saull, cooper
William Nobles, labourer
Charles Allen, labourer
Thomas Gibbins, baker
Joseph Gibbins, miller
William Whorley, farmer
William Turner, servant
George Wells, farmer
William Brookes, labourer
Thomas Richards, brazier
Robert French, farmer
William Harris, servant
Jno. Turner, labourer
Jno. Hopper, farmer
Jno. Brookes, labourer
William Batcheldores, servt.
Thomas Boote, farmer
Jno. Cadd, servant
Richard Eyles, farmer
Thomas Bromley, farmer
George Mayo, servant
⟨Thomas Boote, servant⟩
William Saull, junr., cooper
⟨Thomas Newberry, cordwainer⟩

Wm. Chambers, constable.

CHIPPING WARDEN

December ye 3rd. 1777.   A list of the inhabitants of the parish of Chipping warden qualified to serve on militia to the best of our knowledge made by

George Douglas ⎫
Edward Hawks ⎬ constables.

George Hitchcock, grasier
George Hancock, servt.
William Thomas, servt.
Jonas Brown, servt.
Benjamin Douglas, farmer
William Friend, servt.
Richard Hawks, miller
Samuel Allen, servt.
John Petifer, servt.
⟨George Waters, labourer⟩
Edward Parker, servt.
William Smalbone, servt.
Richard Allen, servt.
Henry Bucknill, labourer
Richard Knib, labr.

John Stockley, farmer
William Phillips, farmer
William Witmill, servt.
Robert Clark, servt.
Richard Batchlor, servt.
William Douglas, baker
Richard Garret, carpenter
Thomas Ward, labr.
John Lines, labr.
Henry Basset, labr.
John Wilson, carpenter
William Wilson, wheelright
Thomas Hortin, labr.
William Lines, labr.
Joseph Garret, labr.

Thomas Garret, labr.
Benjamin Lines, servt.
Thomas Turner, servt.
William Garret, grocer

James Lines, servt., deaf
⟨John Smith, labr., deaf⟩
James Lovell, labr.
William Archear, labr.

N.B.   All persons that think themselves aggrieved in this list must appear att the Three Conies in Thrup Mandivill on the eight day of this instant December and make their appeal otherwise they will not be heard.

EDGCOTE

Northamptonshire to witt.   A true list of all men usually and now dwelling within the parish of Edgcott in the said county betwen the age of eighteen and forty-five which are fit to sarve as milita men.

Sarvants to
Wm. Henry
Chauncy, esqr.
⎰ Nathaniel Gardner, grazier
⎱ Benjamin Burling, gardner
⎱ John Lines, cothman
⎰ William King, under groom

William Horn, sarvant to Mr George Hithcock
Henry Jones, sarvant to Mr George Hitchock
William Wyatt, sarvant to Mr Jonathan Hancock
John Batman, sarvant to Mr Jonathan Hancock
Thomas Newman, sarvant to Mr James Hantley,
    miller

If any one be agrived by reason of the said list you are to make your complaint on Monday the eight day of December next ensuing at the Three-Conis in Thrup Mandevill whare your appeal will be hard. This list made by me, William Gardner, constable, December 4th. 1777.

EYDON

Northamptonshier to witt, December 4th. 1777.
A militerrey lisst for the pariesh of Eydon made by James Ward, constable.

William Ward, farmer
John Willabe, sarvant
Kurten Bronfield, labourer
William Smith, weaver
Edward Smalbone, labourer
William Willabe, labourer
Edward Tue, mason
James Burbidg, labourer
Linen Bull, sarvant
Thomas Willabe, labourer
⟨Samuell Hiam, weaver⟩
Thomas Brightwell, farmer
John Aderson, tayler
John Wills, cummer
Thomas Aderson, tayler
⟨Thomas Thornton, sarvant⟩
Thomas Hiam, weaver
John Maret, cummer
William Amas, cord winder

Jasha Gibs, sarvant
Richard Egle, all draper
Thomas Brightwell, juner
Charles Bree, cord winder
Thomas Bull, labourer
John Dodd, carpenter
John Dalton
Samuell Dalton
Thomas Dodd, sarvant
Marten Ivens, farmer
Samuell Haddon, sarvant
William Grimes, labourer
Robard Souel, all draper
Thomas Ward, sarvant
Richard Goldbey, mason
        ⟨Warwick⟩
⟨John Berrey, cord winder⟩
William Brightwells, sarvant man
John Lines, weaver

Mikel Dolly, chandler
Thomas Allen, sarvant
⟨Richard Nidel, sarvant⟩
William Ratnit, weaver
William Bush, sarvant
Thomas Mayo
Richard Mayo, blacksmith
⟨John Bagnell, cord winder⟩
Daniel Ward, butcher

Josef Jackson, labourer
Josef Blackwell, farmer
Thomas Malen, sarvant
Richard Rainbo, sarvant
John Grimes, cord winder
Benjamin Maud, labourer
Edwd. Kee, sarvt.
Joseph Tompson, coomber

The day of a peal will be the 8th. day of December wich is on Monday next at the Three Coneys at Thrupmandeveill and thear will be no a peal hereafter.

GREATWORTH

A true list of all persons proper to serve as militia men in the parish of Gritworth in the county of Northampton by Jno. Chester, constable.

Wm. Welsh, graizer
Geo. King, graizer
Thos. Castle, graizer
Wm. Cherry, blacksmith
Thos. Horrod, blacksmith
Wm. Franklin, farmer
Jno. Jarvis, labour

Richd. Rose, labour
Thos. Chamberlin, labour
Robt. Castle, labour
Jno. Sides, servant
Jno. Golsby, servant
Richd. Pain, servant
Richd. Bull, servant

The day of appeal will be held at Throp Mandevile on Monday the 8th day of December and no appeal will be afterwards received.

SULGRAVE

A list of persons capable to serve in the militia in the parish of Sulgrave in the county of Northampton.

Jas. Brown, labrour
⟨Jno. Brown, do.⟩
Ricd. Lamb, do.
Jno. Humfrey
Wm. Haycock, backer
Ricd. Rite, cordwinder
Walg. Moore, farmer
Wm. Whadops, servant
Nichls. Jackman
Robt. Kilby, farier
Jas. Stuchfield, malster
⟨Jno. Broocks, servant⟩
Thos. Jarvis, do.
Jno. Smith, labrour
Jos. Pawmer, do.
Jno. Allcock, wheelright
Jno. Barret, servant
⟨Ead. Cooper, joiner⟩
Wm. Brockliss, grazier
Jorg. Whadman, labrour

Ricd. Linel, cordwinder
⟨Jno. Taylor, lame, servant⟩
Jno. Willcox, butcher
Jos. Petifor, weaver
Jno. Jiles, labrour
Thos. Petifor, marson
Jos. Wisman, labrour
Jas. Paige, farmer
Jno. Timson, servant
Jno. Atton, do.
Sam. Treadle, do.
Wm. Jarviss, blacksmith
Aron Abbot, cordwinder
Jno. Willcox, labrour
Thos. Garner, do.
Jas. Dagley, backer
Wm. Moore, grocer
Wm. Bayliss, servant
Jno. Broackliss, miller
Jno. Smith, backer

Jno. Tame, servant
Wm. Jeffs, do.
Robt. Whiot
⟨Evins Mills, infurmed⟩
Stivon Abbot, cordwinder
Thos. Bishop, servant
Jno. Russel, do
⟨Jno. Simonds, butcher⟩

Jos. Willcox
Wm. Cooper, labrour
Jas. Willcox, butcher
Wm. Abbot, labrour
Wm. Wisman, do.
⟨Jno. Kilbey⟩
Jas. Cooper, joiner

Jos. Castle, cunstable.

WOODFORD

A list of all the names of persons that are liable to serve in the militia for the parish of Woodford in the county of Northampton, 1777.

William Hunt, farmer
George Brey, servant
William Beerey, servant
Thomas Tew, glover
William Tew, farmer
Benjamin Beere, servant
Joseph Higham, labourer
William Scriven, weaver
Richard Cleaver, baker
Henry Scriven, weaver
David Gibbs, labourer
William Seaton, farmer son
Thomas Eyles, butcher
John Blackwell, farmer son
James Blackwell, farmer son
Samuel Blackwell, farmer son
Edward Smith, taylor
Thomas Claridge, farmer son
Thomas Stanton, farmer
William Smith, labourer
Thomas Harris, farmer son
John Harris, farmer son
Joseph Bull, labourer
Robert Gibbs, weaver
John Hutchings, servant
William Claridge, farmer
Joseph Jerroms, labourer
Richard Smith, servant
John Fathers, servant
John Daniel, servant
William Daniel, farmer

⟨George Taylor, wheelwright⟩
Richard Marriott, servant
⟨John Mountfort, shoemaker
   & grazier⟩
William Mountfort, shoemaker
Richard Daniel, butcher
James Brooks, carpenter
⟨Thomas Sewell, blacksmith⟩
William Sewell, blacksmith
William Meacock, labourer
Thomas Meacock, labourer
Hattil Checkley, farmers son
John Clark, servant
Edward Checkley, farmer
John Aires, farmer
John Ward, woolcomber
Thomas Reynolds, farmer son
William Reynolds, farmer son
Edward Cleaver, shoemaker
Thomas Wilson, servant
Thomas Reynolds, servant
Thomas Busswell, baker
Thomas Webb, labourer
Matt. Smallbone, servant
John Rainbow, servant
John Mountfort, farmer
⟨Thomas Rainbow, servant⟩
Robert Tomalin, shopkeeper
William Price
John Marrlow
Daniel Plester, servant

This is to give notice that the day of appeal is on Monday next the 8th day of December 1777 at Thorp Mandeville where all persons that are aggrieved must to and appeal as no appeal will be heard afterwards.

Saml. Blackwell,
his X mark, constable.

CLEYLEY HUNDRED

Ashton	26	Potterspury	50
Cosgrove	40	Roade	28
Furtho	2	Shutlanger	23
Grafton Regis	11	Stoke Bruerne	34
Hartwell	40	Wicken	35
Hulcote	10	Yardley Gobion	36
Passenham &			
Denshanger	41		458
Paulerspury	82		

Ale-seller's son	2	Maltster	1
Baker	9	Mason	8
Baker's son	1	Mason's son	1
Blacksmith	9	Miller	3
Brickmaker	1	No trade given	15
Butcher	6	Sawyer	2
Butler	1	Schoolmaster	1
Carpenter	16	Servant	105
Coachman	1	Shepherd	6
Collar-maker	1	Shoemaker	15
Cooper	1	Shopkeeper	1
Dealer & chapman	1	Snead-maker	1
Dealer in hogs	2	Stableboy	1
Farmer	44	Stay-maker	1
Farmer's son	19	Stone-cutter	1
Framework-knitter	1	Tailor	9
Gardener	2	Victualler	6
Grazier	2	Weaver	8
Grocer	1	Wheeler	2
Hemp-dresser	1	Wheelwright	4
Horse-dealer	2	Wool-comber	2
Keeper	1		
Labourer	136		458
Lace-maker	5		

ASHTON

Decbr. ye 13th 1777.   A true list of all the men now dwelling in the parish of Ashton in the county of Northampton between the ages of eighteen and forty five years by me, John Hodgkens, constable.

Robert Cook, farmer	Robert Waite, farmer
William Webb, servant man	John Welch, labourer
William Linnel, farmer	John Penn, labourer
Jasper Blunt, servant man	William Morris, labourer
Thomas Wickens, dealer &	James Sturdidge, labourer
chapman	Robert Smith, lace maker
William Wickens, lace maker	Henry Linnel, farmer
Edward Clark, labourer	James Chrouch, servant man

William Ferne, lace maker
William Goodridge, senr.,
   blacksmith
William Goodridge, junr.,
   blacksmith
John Marriott, farmer
Daniel Dencher, servant man

Henry Ferne, labourer
Robert Raws, servant man
William Dunsby, farmer
⟨Thomas Marris, servant man⟩
Thomas Bull, labourer
Edward Blunt, famers sun

If any person in this list shall think himself agrieved you may appeal on Wednesday next at the White Horse Inn in Towcester being the 17 day of this instant December.

COSGROVE

1777 Cosgrove Northampton Shire to witt. A list of the names of all the persons in the said parish to be returnd to the Deputy Lieutenants and his Magesties Justices of the Peace of and for the said county to serve as militia men Decbr. 17.

Wm. Wilkison, farmer
John Symons, farmer
Wm. Calvert, farmer
Ead. Elliot, farmer
John Tombs, sert.
John Linnell, sert.
Wm. Helles, sert.
Thos. Numan, sert.
Wm. Hicks, sert.
Thos. Harris, sert.
Jeames Curtis, sert.
John Swift, lab.
Danel Travil, lab.
⟨Henry Branson, mason⟩
⟨Jos. Branson, mason⟩
John Meacham, sert.
Wm. Southam, sert.
⟨Wm. Jones, carpenter⟩
Wm. Clark, sert.
Jos. Burl, lab.
John Durrant, lab.

Wm. Sprittle, lab.
Ricd. Harris, black smith
Wm. Hollis, coard winder
⟨Ricd. Peacefer, lab.⟩
Cole Ratley, sert.
John Cox, taylor
Wm. Bloxham, carpenter
Charles Mabley, carpenter
Nat. Yearl, wheelrite
Wm. Blake, lab.
Jeames Hodges, gardener
Jeames Froggett, coller maker
Ricd. Scrivner, juner, graser
Wm. Battams, sert.
John Harris, sert.
John Jarves, lab.
⟨Sir Willoughby Astons—
   butler
   coachman
   stableboy⟩

FURTHO

The parish of Furtho. A list of men between ye age of forty five & eighteen.

  Gorge Ingram, horsedeler
John Pittam, headboro.

John Harvey, servant

GRAFTON REGIS

A list of the names of Grafton Regis. Decbr. 13 1777.

Joseph Gallard, farmer
Thomas Gallard, farmer
Saml. Adckens, sarvent

William Pell, sarvent
Richard Dawson, sarvent
Jonathan Hodkins, sarvent

William Blunt, laber.
Thoames Meakings, laber.
Thoames Ray, laber.

Thoames Adington, laber.
James Clare, farmer sun

The day of appeal will be on Wednesday the 17th and that no appeal will be afterwards receved.

James Clare, constable.

HARTWELL

A list of all the persons names in the parish of Hertwell in the county of Northamptonshire that are fitting to serve in the millitia betwen the ages of eighteen & forty five years for the three years ensuing. Made this 15 day of Decr. 1777.

John Stimpson, farmer
Willm. Denton, servant
John Church, servant
John Goodgridge, farmer's son
Willm. Goodgridge, farmer's son
Robert Goodgridge, farmer's son
Richard Webster, servant
Richard Church, servant
George Stimpson, farmer's son
James Foddy, servant
John Carvell, miller
Edward Mills, servant
Richard Fielding, servant
Thos. Smith, servant
⟨John Tite, servant⟩
⟨Richard Laurence, labourer, lame⟩
Daniel Geary, labourer
Daniel Fillips, taylor
John Fillips, taylor
Stephen Clarke, labourer

John Green, servant
Richard Trusler, carpenter
Samuell Briley, labourer
Willm. Brice, labourer
John Church, servant
John Hillyer, labourer
John Concous, labourer
Richard Winmill, farmer
Willm. Webster, servant
Willm. Gibbins, baker
⟨John Richardson, shopkeeper⟩
Thos. Richardson, labourer
Willm. Richardson, labourer
Willm. Spriggs, labourer
Richard Harris, carpenter
Richard Hines, blacksmith
Willm. Addams, labourer
Edward Aldridge, labourer
Shem Travell, labourer
Thos. Marriot, labourer

Willm. Odell, constable.

HULCOTE

Hulcott. A list of the malitia.
viz.

William George, butcher
John Trifin, servant
James Cross, laborow
⟨Willam Basford, cordwainer⟩
George Wooton, labro.

Joshep Claridge, sernt.
Thos. Pittam, sernt.
Humpherey Cook, servant
⟨Jiles Hall, laborow⟩
John Ward, junier, laborow

N.B. You are hereby required to return to the Deputy Lieutenants & Justisses of the Pease for the said county at there meeting for that purpose to be held on Wednesday the 17th day of this instant December at the White Horse in Towester.

That if any of you think your selves a grieved may then apeal & that no apeal will be after riceived. Here in fail you not.

David Cross, constable.

PASSENHAM AND DENSHANGER

A list of the mens names between the ages of eighteen and forty five that are liable to sarve in the militia in the parish of Perssingham come Denshenger in the county of Northampton.

William Clarke, farmor
John Bayley, labrour
Thomas Benson, farmor
Edmand Davis, Davice, sarvt.
Thomas Bates, sarvt.
William Goad, sarvt.
Matthew Hobs, sarvt.
John Littlford, labourer
John Clarke, do.
Thomas Garnor, do.
William Massom, do.
John Clarke, farmor
Thomas Arnold, carpenter
William Scarr, labourer
Richard Littlford, shoe maker
William Clarke, sarvant
Thomas Clarke, labourer
Crissmus Parsons, labourer
⟨John Bignill, labourer⟩
Henry Jackman, labourer

George Dickins, baker
John Woard, labrour
Thomas Jarvice, carpenter
Samuel Foocks, labourer
Bengiman Robinson, labourer
⟨William Clarke, labourer⟩
William Dickins, farmor
Jarvec Conquest, malster
⟨Thomas Pointer, labourer⟩
William Beamon, labourer
Thomas Durrant, labourer
William Foxley, brick maker
Henry Jarroms, sarvant
Thomas Church, farmour
George Taylor, keeper
James Wills Row, sarvant
Robert Shaw, blacksmith
John Bruff, sarvant
Joseph Bruff, servant
Thomas Woodward, labourer
John Garrit, servant

Hary Dickins, constable.

PAULERSPURY

Decr. 1777. A list of the names of persons from the age of eighteen to forty-five, liable to be drawn in the militia for the parish of Paulerspury in the county of Northampton.

John Hewes, servt.
Edwd. Williams, cordwainr., 3 childr.
Jno. Linnell, carpenter
⟨Wm. Linnell, carpentr, 3 childr.⟩
Robt. Blunt, farmer
Jno. Scott, butcher
Thos. Causby, taylor
⟨Wm. Crow, carpentr, 3 childr.⟩
Thos. Smith, victualer
Wm. Baldwin, labr.
Thos. Tarry, baker
Saml. Norton, labourer
Edwd. Poynter, labourer
Richd. Kirby, labr.
Jno. Long, labr.
Jno. Robbins, taylor
Wm. Ratliff, labr.
Joseph Tarry, farmer

Jno. Glinn, servt.
George Blundell, labr.
Wm. Jones, labr.
Neal Newman, farmer
Jno. Leech, taylor
Jenkins Inwood, wheeler
Jno. Horton, victualer
⟨Nathl. Jackson, sawyer, 8 childr.⟩
Jno. Ashby, labr.
Thos. Lepper, mason
Wm. Jackson, sawyer
Jno. Bitcheno, sneadmaker
Isaac Lovel, grazier
William Collins, weaver
Jno. Hill, framework knitter
Thos. Jones, weaver
Charles Cockeril, cordwainr
Wm. Mayo, labr.
George Scott, labr.

Jno. Norton, labr.
James Smith, woolcomber
Elisha Smith, weaver
James Gordan, labr.
James Burges, weaver
Richd. Taylor, weaver
Jno. Burton, servt.
Humphrey Poynter
Charles West, miller
Joseph Fowkes, weaver
Wm. Peasland, sheppard
Thos. Labram, servt.
Robert Norriss, servt.
Wm. West, farmer
Jno. Fielding, labr.
⟨Jno. Poynter, wheelr., 3 childr.⟩
Thos. Pettifer, woolcomber
Jno. Treen, labourer
Benjn. Poynter, weaver
John Hillyer, servt.
Wm. Hawley, farmer
Robt. Curtis, labr.
Edwd. Caporn, farmer

Jno. Rainbow, servt.
Wm. Brown, cordwainer
Thos. Storey, mason
Nathaniel Webb, labr.
Stephen Orsborn, labr.
Thos. Denny, labr.
Francis Mayo, butcher
Wm. Frost, servt.
Jno. Forster, cordwainr.
Thos. Ship, servt.
Thos. Vann, servt.
Wm. Ross, servt.
Saml. Laughton, servt.
Paul Hinds, servt.
William Smith, shepherd
Robt. Pettifer, servt.
Benjn. Ratlidge, labr.
Henry Pettifer, victualer
Saml. Holland, servt.
Wm. Smith, servt.
Jno. Foxley
Richd. Linnell, labr.

Samuel Canish, constable.

N.B. The day of appeal will be on Wednesday the seventeenth day of this instant Decr. at the White Horse Inn, at Towcester, where all persons who shall think themselves aggriev'd must then appeal, as no appeal will afterwards be heard.

POTTERSPURY

Decbr. 12th 1777. A list of the persons residing in Potterspury in the county of Northton that are between the ages of eighteen and forty-five years to serve as militia men viz.

Henry Onan, baker
John Onan, do.
Tho. Wise, wheell-right
Samuel Marriott, labourer
Richard Griffen, do.
Daniel Homan, labourer
George Cook, servant
Wm. Mayo, do.
Daniel Packer, do.
Charles Cockrill, cordwainer
Edward Albright, shepherd
James Mapley, blacksmith
Francis Abraham, do.
John Robinson, hemp-dresser
Joseph Stanton, servant
William Gray, labourer
William Church, dealer in hogs
Joseph Church, labourer

Tho. Williams, do.
Tho. Bason, mason
John Wise, junr., victualer
William Toombs, baker
Tho. Webster, carpenter
Robt. Ratlif, labourer
Francis Malard, do.
Tho. Toombs, junr., baker
Richard Adams, carpenter
Charles Woodard, labourer
John Woodard, do.
William Bason, junr., victualer
John Robinson, do.
John Colvert, taylor
Jos. Sanders, senr., carpenter
Jos. Sanders, junr., do.
Tho. Bignal, servant
John Jones, gardener

William Keeves, butcher
Bampr. Sanders, carpenter
Henry Banks, grocer
William Meakens, butcher
Tho. Ratlif, labourer
John Jones, labourer
Tho. Bliss, do.

Richard Henson, do.
William Henson, do.
John Tarrey, junr., do.
⟨Tho. Druce, do.⟩
John Emberley, do.
Richard Gunn, servant
Samuel Webb, do.

Joshua Wood, constable.

ROADE

Decmr. 12 1777. Road list of the militia in the hundred Clely.

William Fielding, farmer
Charls Longstaff, farmers son
Robert Paggett, black smith
William Paggett, farmers son
Robert Travil, farmers son
Thomas Marriett, farmers son
William Blunt, farmers son
William Caves, farmers son
William Travil, farmers son
Gorge Caves, farmer
Gorge Caves, farmer son
Robert Stimeson, shepard
Morriss Dent, bakers son
⟨Charls Sargent, labourer. Lally [*lately ?*] cut 2 of his fingers, a poor man⟩
Timothy Lightman, labourer
Jesper Hillyard, labourer
William Shipp, ale selers son
Samuel Shipp, ale selers son
John Webster, cooper
William Hedge, mason son
Samuel Walker, sarvent
Francis Farrin, sarvent
Gorge Joans, labourer
⟨William Caves, privet man son, lame in his toes⟩
John Larance, had his leg broke a little lame
⟨John Atterbury, labourer, one eie a mis his left thum out of jint⟩
⟨John Hedge, mason, 6 children got of apeared himself⟩
Thomas Hillyard, labourer, says he has one eie a mis has fits

John Warwick, constable.

SHUTLANGER

Cleyley Hundred, Northampton Shire. Alist of the inhabitance of Shut-langer in the parish of Stoke Bruen lyable to serve in the militia.

Jno. White, laborour
Jno. Warde, servant
Charles Hands, cordwinder
Thos. Buttris, weaver
Abnr. Inwood, wheelwright
⟨Jno. Iwood, wheelwright⟩
Robrt. Travil, sheepherd

Bartmw. Charke, farmer
Edmond Warring, servant
Willm. Linnil, servant
Willm. Smith, servant
Samul. Smith, servant
Danl. Bass, farmer
Jos. Going, laborour

Thos. Simkens, laborour
Willm. Curtis, servant
Jos. Chrimes, farmer
Jno. Bayles, servant
Richd. Tew, servant

Benjm. Whitlock, servant
Willm. Robinson, laborour
James Adams, sheepherd
Willm. Carter, laborour

All persons who think them selves agrived may appeal at the White Horse Inn in Towcester on Wednesday the seevententh day of December next as no appeal will hereafter be received.

Jno. Clarke, constable.

STOKE BRUERNE

Cleley Hundred. Northamptonsheere. A list of the inhabintants of Stoke Bruen that are liable to sarve as militia men.

Gorge White, farmer
Thomas White, farmer
Samuel Clif, sarvant
William Abbey, macon
William Brittan, farmer
Bengaman Brittan, farmer
William Jeffery, miller
William Gillit, shomaker
Thomas Martin, laber.
William Martin, laber.
Mark Martin, lacemaker
Thomas Parrish, farmer
William Hill, sarvant
John Wlford, laber.
Thomas Welford, laber.
Charles Welford, lacemaker
William Sturges, sarvant
John Valantine, farmer

Thomas Frost, sarvant
John Smith, scolmaster
Thomas Smith, shomaker
John Joanes, laber.
John Battams, shomaker
Thomas Tew, laber.
⟨William Tew, laber.⟩
Nathanel Glin, shomaker
William Black, shomaker
John Jeffery, laber.
John Malcher, laber.
Bengaman Tite, sarvant
⟨Samuel Hillier, laber.⟩
Robert Wattson
⟨William Evines, laber,
   lame of one hand⟩
⟨Jeames Martin, servant,
   lame of one knee⟩

This is to give notice that all persons who shall think them selves aggrived are to appeare at the White Horse Inn in Toweseter on Wednesday the seventeenth day for thare will be no appeal day after ward.

John White, constable.

WICKEN

A true list of the names of the men in the parish of Wicken liable to serve on the militia.

William Turpin, constable.

Edward Underwood, farmer
Thomas Foxley, farmer
Thomas Adams, farmer
Thomas Hickinbottom,
   farmer son
Mathew Hickinbottom,
   farmer son
John Hickinbottom, farmer son
John Dickins, farmer son
Edward Green, labourer
Joseph Tirrel, servant

Thomas Webb, carpenter
William Kemp, labourer
⟨Thomas Bandy, labourer⟩
⟨John Bandy, labourer⟩
Thomas Goode, servant,
Thomas Bason, mason
Thomas Foddey, labourer
Edmund Pipkin, labourer
William Caves, servant
John Hooar, cordwiner
Richard Turvey, labourer

John Smith, labourer
William Bavin, labourer
Reubin Webb, labourer
William Hillier, servant
John Bason, stone-cutter
James Foddey, staymaker
John Burt, labourer
⟨Thomas Smith, servant⟩

William Caudle, servant
Thomas Church, servant
John Cook, servant
John Adams, servant
Thomas Atkins, servant
John Hunt, labourer
John Benson, blacksmith

The day of appeal being the 17th of this instant December, if any person thinks himself aggrieved, may then and there appeal; at the White Horse Inn at Towcester, and that no appeal will be afterwards received.

YARDLEY GOBION

The names of the persons liable to be drawd to searve as militia men in the constable wick of Yardley Gobion ye 17 of Decemr. 1777.

Mr. Thos. Wood ⎫
Mr. Fisher Clark ⎪ farmers
Mr. Thos. Horton ⎬
Mr. Wm. Edward ⎭
Mr. Jno. Hawley ⎫ farmers
Mr. George Hawley ⎭ sons
Saml. Marritt ⎫ bakers
Peek Hobson ⎭
Edwd. Risley ⎫ taylers
Jno. Smith ⎭
Wm. Garritt, butcher
Joseph Johnson, horsedealer
Saml. Kenning, hogdealer
Wm. Warr ⎫
Richd. Brown ⎪ searvants
Jno. Pettifer ⎬
Peter Tilly ⎭
Wm. Sreve, harde of hereing
Jno. Smith ⎫ say thay have
Danl. Carr ⎭ been drawd

Thos. Lamburn ⎫
Wm. Punn ⎪
Wm. Sturdige ⎪
Saml. Lyman ⎪
Jno. Mason ⎬ labourers
Adam Dawks ⎪
Arthur Harris ⎪
Thos. Borton ⎪
Henry Packer ⎭
⟨Wm. Holman, very neare sited⟩
⟨Wm. Swain, very little site in
   one eye⟩
⟨Thos. Onan, has fitts⟩
⟨Thos. Bignell, very bow leged⟩
⟨David Rockingham,
   rheumatick pains⟩
⟨Robt. Philpott, has had a
   hurt in is head⟩
⟨Wm. Robinson⟩ saith he has fitts

CORBY HUNDRED

Ashley	52
Blatherwycke	20
Brampton Ash	13
Brigstock	83
Bulwick	40
East Carlton	6
Corby	73
Cottingham	57
Deene	31
Deenethorpe	23
Dingley	16
Fineshade	4
Geddington	83
Gretton	57
Harringworth	43
Laxton	21
Middleton	48
Newton	9
Great Oakley	31
Little Oakley	15
Rockingham	17
Stanion	22
Stoke Albany	40
Sutton Bassett	24
Wakerley	14
Weekley	26
Great Weldon	38
Little Weldon	40
Weston by Welland	34
Wilbarston	98
	1,078

Baker	13	Keeper	5
Blacksmith	11	Keeper's servant	1
Breeches-maker	2	Keeper's son	4
Bricklayer	1	Jobber	1
Butcher	17	Joiner	3
Butler	2	Labourer	138
Carpenter	32	Landlord	1
Carrier	1	Maltster	2
Chandler	1	Mason	16
Coachman	1	Miller	7
Collar-maker	3	Miller's servant	1
Cooper	2	Millwright	2
Curate	1	Mole-catcher	1
Esquire	1	Mole-catcher's son	1
Farmer	56	No trade given	291
Farmer's servant	7	Plasterer	1
Farmer's son	27	Publican	2
Fish-man	1	Ragman	1
Gamekeeper	3	Rake-maker	1
Gardener	7	Serge-maker	2
Garden-man	2	Servant	123
Gentleman	1	Servant in husbandry	5
Gentleman's service	3	Shepherd	12
Glover	3	Shoemaker	24
Glover's son	1	Shopkeeper	1
Grazier	9	Skinner	1
Grazier's son	2	Slater	4
Grocer	2	Smith	1
Groom	1	Stay-maker	2
Horse-dealer	1	Steward	1
Husbandman	4	Stone-cutter	1
Innholder	1	Tailor	26
Innkeeper	2	Tanner	3

Tawer	1	Wool-comber	16
Victualler	2	Wool-comber's	
Victualler's son	2	apprentice	1
Waggoner	2	Wool-stapler	1
Weaver	143		——
Wheelwright	4		1,078

ASHLEY

Ashley. Decr. ye 10th 1777.   A list of the names of all men usually and at this time dwelling within ye parish of Ashley between ye ages of eighteen and forty five years.

George Corolishaw, gent.
Edwd. Kemp, farmer
John Munton, servt.
Robt. Wilford, farmer
John Spencer, farmer
Leonard Clow, servt.
Henry Bent, servt.
Joseph Clifton, weaver
John Clifton, weaver
Daniel Clifton, weaver
John Clifton, mason
William Ward, shoemaker
John Ward, weaver
Edmund Berry, farmer
James Stiles, servt.
William Warmsly, servt.
Thos. Stafford, shoemaker
William Harrison, weaver
Richard Noon, weaver
James Kendall, blacksmith
William Timson, weaver
Thos. Scott, farmers son
John Scott, carpenter
Thomas Berry, farmers son
Thomas Tebbatt, servt.
Joseph Wilford, servt.

Thomas Kirby, weaver
John Kirby, weaver
Joseph Fryar, wooll comber
Thomas King, mason
Thomas Timson, weaver
James Timson, weaver
Robert Colman, farmer
George Colman, farmer
Thomas Colman, farmers son
John Goodman, farmers son
John Fox, servt.
Samuel Thorp, weaver
Thomas Frewton, labourer
William Crain, farmers son
Thomas Crain, farmers son
Zachary Stafford, weaver
Samuel King, labourer
William Bates, weaver
Joseph Bates, servt.
John Edgley, farmers son
Edwd. Edgley, farmers son
Thomas Noon, weaver
William Noon, weaver
John Skellon, labourer
Thomas Taylor, labourer
Thomas Edgley, weaver

Wm. Whiteman, constable.

BLATHERWYCKE

Northamptonshire, Blatherwick, Corby Hundred. December the 10th 1777. A just and true list of the men's names in our said parish of Blatherwick, who is able to serve in the militia which is as follows.

Men's names and their occupations.

Lucius O'Brien, esq.
Lawrence Gilbert, butler
Luke Holmes, gardener
John Pickurin, servant

Joseph Whyman, servant
Thomas Ludgate, servant
William Dewey, servant
Daniel Nichols, shopkeeper

GUILSBOROUGH HUNDRED

Long Buckby	183	Hollowell	25
Clay Coton	20	Lilbourne	27
Cold Ashby	55	Naseby	62
Coton	20	Stanford	8
Cottesbrooke	40	Thornby	16
Great & Little		Watford	62
Creaton	68	Welford	158
Crick	188	Winwick	18
Elkington	7	Yelvertoft	94
Guilsborough &			
Nortoft	65		1,254
West Haddon	138		

Apothecary	3	Labourer	162
Apprentice	8	Leather-dresser	1
Attorney	1	Maltster	1
Baker	6	Mason	9
Baronet	1	Miller	12
Blacksmith	16	Naval officer	1
Butcher	7	No trade given	265
Carpenter	22	Schoolmaster	1
Carrier	1	Servant	167
Chandler	2	Shepherd	19
Clergyman	2	Shoemaker	32
Clock-maker	1	Soap-boiler	2
Clothier	1	Stay-maker	2
Collar-maker	2	Surgeon &	
Cooper	2	apothecary	1
Currier	1	Tailor	18
Esquire	2	Tallow-chandler	1
Farmer	132	Teacher (licensed)	1
Farmer's son	20	Turner	3
Fellmonger	3	Victualler	6
Flax-dresser	1	Weaver	189
Framework-knitter	8	Wheelwright	7
Gardener	2	Whitesmith	1
Gentleman	1	Whittawer	1
Glover	4	Woad-man	1
Grazier	13	Wool-comber	71
Grocer	5	Writer	1
Hog jobber	1	Yeoman	2
Husbandman	2		
Innholder	1		1,254
Joiner	6		

LONG BUCKBY

County of Northampton (to wit).   A list of all men usually and at this time dwelling in Long Buckby in the said county between the ages of eighteen and forty five years made this 27 day of November 1777 by us, William Coleman and Thos. Marriott, constables.

Farmers
Edw. Sabin
⟨Thos. Burbridge, lame⟩
Wm. Abbott
Saml. Marriott
Thos. Wadsworth
Wm. Haynes
Wm. Clark
⟨Jno. Andrew, lame⟩
Joshua Cure
⟨Jos. Wills⟩ ⎫
⟨Jos. Morris⟩ ⎬ thurdboroughs
⟨Jno. Hodges⟩ ⎪
⟨Wm. Bland⟩ ⎭

Farmers' sons
Thos. Haynes
Jno. Robinson
Robt. Tebbitt
Jno. Sabin
Wm. Sabin
⟨Jno. Wadsworth⟩ ⎫ drawn and
⟨Jos. Haynes⟩ ⎬ found
            ⎭ substitutes

Woolcombers
Jno. Robinson, junr.
Jno. Porter
Jno. Tomalin
Jno. Lee
Andrew Allin
Jno. Smith
Thos. Mabbitt
Houseson Newitt
Jno. Robinson, senr.
Wm. Dunkley
Jno. Matcham Coleman
Thos. Marriott
Jos. Sabin
Wm. Marriott
Jos. Tomalin
Jno. Smart
James Hanwell
Daniel Pool
Thos. Coleman
Edw. Pool
Wm. Manning
Wm. Haddon
Robt. Andrew
Thos. Reeve
Stephen Smith
James Cole

Thos. Bunting
Richd. Bunting
Jos. Fretter
Wm. Eyre
Jos. Hanwell
Wm. Birch
Richd. Reeve
Wm. Mawby
⟨Hail Marriott, thurdborow⟩
⟨Jos. Lee, drawn, found
    substitute⟩
⟨Wm. Spencer, lame⟩
⟨Wm. Mackinley, infirm⟩
⟨George Allin, lame⟩
⟨Thos. Green, lame⟩

Weavers
Wm. Muscutt
Wm. Fennell
Jos. Boswell
Wm. Eales
Thos. Rushel
Wm. Muddiman
Jos. Muddiman
Benjamin Tomalin
Wm. Lee
Wm. Muddiman, junr.
Thos. Chater
Jos. Groom
Wm. Cross
Wm. Daniel
Thos. Shepherd
Geo. Whyat, served in ye
    regulars
⟨Wm. Wells⟩ ⎫ drawn and
⟨Thos. Groom⟩ ⎬ found
          ⎭ substitutes
Jno. Bennett
Edw. Clark, infirm
Saml. Holt

⟨Revd. Doctor Freeman⟩
Geo. Freeman, his son, esqr.
Wm. Denny, attorney at law
Jno. Osborn, writer
Edw. Swinfin, appothecary
Anthony Floyer, appothecary
Jno. Nixon, turner
Thos. Harbidge, flax dresser
Robt. Coleman, blacksmith
Thos. Townsend, blacksmith

Wm. Johnson, mason
Simon Norris, mason
⟨Jno. Letts, one eye⟩
Wm. Cole, grocer
Jno. Watson, miller
Jno. Jillis, miller
⟨Joseph Boreman⟩ ⎤ drawn and
⟨Ben. Goodman⟩ ⎬ found
 ⎦ substitutes
Thos. Teeve, served in ye
 regulars
Jno. Newitt, carpenter
Harden Jarvis, carpenter
Richd. Kimbel, carpenter
⟨Jno. Wilson, lame⟩

Labourers

Thos. Dunkley
Jos. Bennitt
Wm. Marriott
Wm. Cooper
Richd. Garlick
Robt. Rushell
Thos. Baily
Abraham Abbott
Jno. Bradshaw
Jno. Green
Jno. Higgason
Jno. Adams
Wm. Smith
Jno. Paggett
Edw. Paggett
Wm. Battison
Jno. Froast
⟨Jos. Green, one eye⟩

Servants

Jno. Rushell
Jno. Davis
Richd. Buckingham
Jno. Hollis
Thos. Kinch
Thos. West
Jos. Welch
Ephraim Boswell
Saml. Hodges
Wm. Carr
Thos. Murdin
Edw. Ward
Thos. Muscott
Ben. Brown
Edw. Robinson
Jno. Humphry

Jno. Wright
Thos. Buttling
Thos. Howe

Cordwainers

Jos. Wright
Thos. Burton
Jno. Dickens
Wm. Dickens
Jno. Kennell
Charles Luck

Taylors

Matw. Murdin
Wm. Wilson
Jno. Warwick
Thos. Blencowe
Matw. Stanger
⟨Saml. Wilson, lame⟩

Apprentices

⟨Jno. Smith⟩
Jno. Lea
Jno. Wadsworth
⟨Saml. Darlow⟩
⟨Wm. Luck⟩

Poor men having three children	
or more	*Children*
⟨Jno. Bunting⟩	6
⟨Joshua Walden⟩	7
⟨Thos. Watts⟩	7
⟨Jno. Groves⟩	4
⟨Jos. Tebbitt⟩	4
⟨Edw. Earl⟩	4
⟨Jno. Haynes⟩	5
⟨Jno. Hanwell⟩	6
⟨Wm. Bunting⟩	6
⟨Thos. Mitchell⟩	3
⟨Jos. Lee⟩	3
⟨Wm. Newitt⟩	4
⟨Jno. Smith⟩	3
⟨Jno. Eales⟩	6
⟨Jno. Groom⟩	5
⟨Daniel Merroll⟩	5
⟨Wm. Eales⟩	6
⟨Wm. Porter⟩	3
⟨Richd. Fennel⟩	6
⟨Wm. Townsend⟩	3
⟨Jno. Dodd⟩	3
⟨Thos. Luck⟩	3
⟨Thos. Hennell⟩	6
⟨Wm. Kimbel⟩	5
⟨Wm. Collins⟩	5

CLAY COTON

A fair and true list of all the men capable of serving for the militia for the parish of Clay-Coton from eighteen to forty five. John Maggott, constable.

Bassett Burrows, grazier
John Muson, weaver
Richard Reeve, sheppard
John Johnson, carpenter
John Reeve, weaver
William Smith, weaver
William Elkington, weaver
William Murcott, joiner
Samuel Reeve, labourer
John Riley, weaver
William Ward, labourer

Thomas Johnson, weaver
Richard Seamark, servant
Henry Pebbody, servant
Nathaniel Harper, servant

Drawn by ballott & infirm
⟨Wm. Billing⟩
⟨Wm. Smith⟩
⟨Willm. Page⟩
⟨Jno. Murcutt⟩
⟨Richd. Johnson⟩

COLD ASHBY

A list of the names of all the men at this time dwelling in the parish of Cold Ashby and county of Northampton between the ages of eighteen and forty five years distinguishing their ranks and occupations.

William Lovell, gent.
Thomas Pratt, labourer
John Stafford, cordwainer
Thomas Fretter, labourer
Edward Astell, woolcomber
Ebenezer Wormleighton, labourer
Thomas Parbery, labourer
John Rogers, labourer
John Wykes, weaver
⟨John Fox, labourer⟩ past age
Thomas Wykes, farmers son
William Moss, cordwainer
Daniel Dickins, shepherd
Edward Cave, master woolcomber
Thomas Tomlin, woolcomber
George Leeson, servant
Nathaniel Turner, servant
William Jones, servant
William Whale, servant
William Bosworth, servant
John Askew, cordwainer
Roger Astell, weaver
James Cowley, labourer
Thomas Cave, labourer
William Walden, taylor
Edward Vernon, carpenter
William Smith, weaver
Richard Bosworth, weaver
George Daws, weaver
John Clay, whitesmith

Christopher Palmer, farmers son
George Skillet, master woolcomber
John Freer, labourer
John Smith, servant
George Haddon, farmer
William Hern, servant
Robert Carr, farmer
Benjamin Dunn, servant
Thomas Swingler, labourer
Samuel Leatherland, servant
Benjamin Marlow, servant
John King, butcher
John Day, labourer
Matthew Perkins, labourer
⟨Edward Launsbury, servant, drawn last time⟩
⟨Edward Fleckna, servant, drawn last time⟩
⟨William Haynes, weaver, three children⟩
⟨John Wardle, labourer, three children⟩
⟨Richard Brown, labourer, three children⟩
Henry Garnet, labourer
⟨John Wykes, farmers son, but one hand⟩
⟨John Astell, labourer, dull of hearing⟩
⟨Thomas, labourer, three children⟩

⟨Joseph Kinney, labourer,
　　three children⟩

⟨Richard Kinsman, drawn
　　9 years since⟩

⟨Roger Ruskin, constable.⟩

COTON

1777 Dem. 2.　A list of the hamlet of Coaten betwen eighteen and forty five years of age.

John Moor, miller
John Tebbet, farmer
Willm. Dames, juner, famer
Thomas Biggs, dt., farmer
Willm. Biggs, dt., farmer
Henery Chrutchley, cordwainer
Willm. Horten, weaver
John Barfoot, labor and
　　one child
Willm. Hammans, labor and
　　one child
John Tomkin⟨g⟩s, labor and
　　two childeren

John Jorns, labor and two
　　children
Willm. Palmer, servant
George Palmer, servant
Willm. Baker, servant
John Goldby, servant
⟨John Jorns, tailor⟩
⟨James Horn, labor one⟩ eye
　　and on child
⟨Darwed men⟩
⟨Richard Biggs⟩
⟨Richard Wright⟩
⟨Wm. Healey⟩

William Biggs, cunstabel.

COTTESBROOKE

A list of the men of Cottesbrook betwixt the age of eighteen and fortyfive to serve as militia men.

⟨Sir James Langham⟩ bart., leiutenant cornal
⟨Thos. Packwood⟩ graser & drawd
Thos. Smith, servant
Thos. Seamark, servant
Steaven Powers, shepard & clark
⟨Thos. Martin⟩ farmers son, infirm & insane
⟨Michel Packwood⟩ infirm, quite a criple
Thos. Moll, blacksmith
Thos. Clark, farmer
Wm. Gamble, servant
⟨Benjamin Pain⟩ laberor, 3 childeren
John Packwood, farmer
Joseph Tipler, servant
Jeremiah Perrin, carpender
⟨Thos. Tipler⟩ laberor, poor man & lost ye use of part of his right hand
John Sanderson, garderner
James Manton, farmer son
John Manton, farmer son
Edward Eaton, graser
⟨John Chester⟩ laberor, infirm
Edward Benet, weavor
Edward Sherman, grasor
⟨John Green⟩ laberor & 3 childeren
⟨Joseph Green⟩ shepard & 3 childeren & drawd
Wm. Willson, laberor

Samuel Tomalin, laberor
Wm. Hobson, laberor
⟨Thos. Willson⟩ carpender & 3 childeren
Richerd Collins, weavor
Wm. Ducket, laberor
⟨Henery Starke⟩ servant & drawd.
Joseph Puser, servant
George Roberson, servant
Thos. Holmes, servant
Thos. Hodges, servant
Boley Lavender, servant
Wm. Radford, sarvant
Charls King, laberor
Wm. Tomons, laberor

⟨Jams. Manton⟩ constable.

CREATON

A list of the mens names to serve in the militia of Great and Little Creaton within the said county.

Ed. Farndon, servant
John Hollick, servant
Clement Arnold, husbandman
Michael Willson, weaver
Robert Herrington, apothecary
Frances German, labourer
John Francis, labourer
Joseph Homan, mason
Saml. Clefton, mason
Thos. Cornish, woolcomer
Thos. Parbery, woolcomer
John Brown, servant
Thos. Clark, servant
John Boyes, servant
James Goodman, servant
John Tarry, famer
Thos. Smith, servant
Ed. Curtchly, servant
William Colings, labourer
Thos. York, taylor
Joseph Lettes, labourer
Saml. Chrisp, weaver
Frances White, labourer
Thos. Smith, husbandman
Thos. Darker, servant
Teatt James, weaver
Steven Nailer, labourer
William Wykes, weaver
George Clark, shoumaker
William Dunn, butcher
John Chrisp, weaver
Thos. Barker, servant
Thos. Kenney, labourer

John Deacon, labourer
William Corsford, labourer
Thos. Wykes, weaver
Benjamen Buttling, woolcomer
William Orland, miller
Thos. Abor, servant
William Smith, servant
Ed. Allard, labourer
Joseph Smith, shepherd
William Harden, labourer
William Smith, shepherd
John Rose, labourer
John Webb, servant
John Wills, servant
Henery Brown, labourer
⟨John Day, inferm⟩
William Lansbury, servant
Richard Reeve, baker
Richard Clever, servant
George Dison, labourer
⟨John Chrisp, 3 children⟩
⟨William ffrancis, 3 children⟩
⟨James Dunkley, 3 children⟩
⟨John Wykes, 3 children⟩
⟨John Smith, 3 children⟩
⟨James Hadden, 3 children⟩
⟨William Dunkley, 3 children⟩
⟨Saml. Kilpack, 3 children⟩
⟨John York, 3 children⟩
⟨Thees are all poor men⟩
⟨James Humphry, inferm⟩
⟨Solomon Morgan, inferm⟩
⟨George York, inferm⟩

⟨John Streaton, inferm⟩ ⟨Will. Chrisp, inferm⟩

⟨Jams. Francis, constable.⟩

CRICK

County of Northampton to wit: parish of Crick. By an order from the Lieutenant and Depety Lieutenants of the Militia for the said county made at their general meeting. I am to return a true and fair list on Tuesday the 9th day of this instant December 1777 of the names of all the men usually and at this time living within our resepective parish of Crick between the ages of 18 and 45, as follows.

Farmers and Farmers Sons
John Ashwell
Thomas Ashwell
Thomas Watts, junr.
Edward Bucknell
William Edmunds
John Edmunds, son of S. E.
Thomas Mawby, junr.
William West, junr.
Thomas Sabin
John Knight
Joseph Clark
Thomas Whitmell
Thomas Clapham, offr. in exe.
John Furn
John Lee
Samuel Lee
Thomas Marson
John Marson
Thomas Wedding
William Pike, junr.
Thomas Draper
John Edmunds, sen.
James Wedding
Thomas Redgrave
Valentine Redgrave
Slynn Whitmell
William Smith
Thomas Smith
John Killworth
John Cupell
Thomas Watts, senr.
John Smith
John Baker
Thomas Cooper
Thomas Clark
⟨Thomas Harriss⟩ constable

William Newitt, wever
John Iliff, hog-gobler
William Dicey, weaver
Jeremiah Vans, weaver

John Wills, weaver
John Weekston, weaver
Richard Mole, miller
Edward Leatherland, weavr.
Packer Gudgin, glover
Thomas Stuckley, woolcomber
John Barnett, woolcomber
John Satchell, woolcomber
Samuel Carter, woolcomber
William Ange, weaver
Thomas Perkins, weaver
David Ange, weaver
Samuel Muscott, weaver
William Robinson, shepherd
John Lucas, weaver
William Dunkley, weaver
John Langford, weaver
Joseph White, weaver
William Killworth, weaver
Thomas York, collarmaker
Thomas Maggitt, weaver
John Butlin, weaver
John Baush, glover
John Cave, weaver
William Knight, staymaker
John Dollon, staymaker
James Cole, weaver
William Cave, weaver
John Towers, cordwainer
Thomas Vans, jun., weaver
William Vans, weaver
Thomas Brown, weaver
William Billington, weaver
William Cowley, blacksmith
Roger Cowley, blacksmith
Thomas Vans, senr., weaver
William Tew, butcher
Richard Smith, butcher
Samuel Lucas, weaver
Thomas Green, weaver
Thomas Wills, cordwainer
Nath. Muscott, weaver

William Armstone, baker
⟨Samuel Beal⟩ miller, 3 childn.
Charles Carter, weaver
John Pool, weaver
Samuel Powell, weaver
John Palmer, junr., weaver
William Vans, taylor
William Thornton, wheelright
Jeremiah Bullock, mason
Thomas Lord, wheelright
John Norriss, jun., mason
Joseph Billing, cooper
Thomas Lucas, weaver
John Smith, weaver
William Norton, weaver
William Cotsbrook, weaver
Joseph Ange, weaver
Thomas Ange, weaver
⟨Benjamin Button, joiner⟩
⟨John Maggitt, weaver, 4 childn.⟩
⟨John Tomalin, glover, 5 childn.⟩
⟨Samuel Crisp, weaver, 7 childn.⟩
⟨William Bromage, wer.,
    3 childn.⟩
⟨Saywell Bucknell, glover
    3 childn.⟩
⟨William Irons, weaver,
    6 childn.⟩
⟨Thomas Irons, weaver, 6 childn.⟩
⟨James Coral, weaver, 7 childn.⟩
⟨Thomas Bradshaw, weaver,
    3 childn.⟩
⟨James Bradshaw, weaver,
    5 childn.⟩
⟨Thomas Newitt, wheelright,
    4 childn.⟩
⟨Joseph Swingler, weaver, drawn
    for Yelvertoft in the year
    1769⟩

Labourers
William Norton
Samuel Fretter
Nath. Fennell
John Gee

Benjamin Webb
Edward Bennett
John Coleman
Richard Malmsburry
Thomas Walton
John Moore
Richard Luck
Richard Wilson
Thomas Hewitt
James Sale
Joseph Witherbed
Benjamin Bradshaw
James Elkington
⟨John Archer, 4 childn.⟩
⟨Richard Capell, 6 childn.⟩
⟨Richard Sale, 3 childn.⟩
⟨Thomas Iliff, 5 childn.⟩
⟨William Fox, 4 childn.⟩
⟨William Palmer, 5 childn.⟩
⟨Thomas Slynn, 3 childn.⟩

Servants
Bejamin Dicken
John Warwick
Richard Grim
Edward Dunkley
Aaron Yarn
Thomas Muscott
Isaac Wood
John Crofts
Joseph Jannis
William Hall
James Ward
John Wright
William Bucknell
Thomas Capell
Matthew Kinning
Edward Shilman
Thomas Wilson
William Jordan
Robert Dunkley
Robert Heifford, wheelwright,
    an apprentice
Benjamin Button, joiner,
    an apprentice

Infirmities
⟨John Newitt, non compos mentis⟩
⟨John Vans, non compos mentis⟩
⟨Thomas Marson, farmer, disabled in the thigh by being broke⟩
⟨William Boys, woolcomber, hard of hearing⟩
⟨Jonathan Vans, blind of one eye⟩
⟨Jonas Watts, cordwainer, infirm⟩
⟨William Lucus, soap boiler, disabled by his leg being broke⟩

⟨Robert Pettefer, lame on the left hand⟩
⟨John Muscott, weaver, rheumatic⟩
⟨William Muscott, deaf and dumb⟩
⟨Joshua Crock, servt., blind of an eye⟩
⟨John Marshall, woolcomber, infirm⟩
⟨Daniel Underwood, joiner, 5 children, deffective in his eye sight⟩
⟨Aaron Vans, hard of hearing⟩
⟨Edward Clark, labourer, near sighted⟩
⟨John Clark, vict., deffective in his eye sight⟩

Drawn to serve in the militia as under
    In the year 1763
⟨Samuel Marriott⟩ served by substitute
⟨James Ange, weaver⟩ served in person
    In the year 1766
⟨George Jundkin⟩ gror., by a substitute
    In the year 1769
⟨Thomas Killworth, farmr., by a substitute⟩
⟨William Robins, mason, by a substitute⟩
⟨William Leatherland, weavr., by a substitute⟩
    In the year 1772
⟨John Swingler, weaver, by a substitute⟩
⟨William Hopkins, labr., by a substitute⟩
⟨John Perkins, farmr., by a substitute⟩
    In the year 1775
⟨Thomas Bucknell, farm., by a substitute⟩
⟨William Clark, farmr., by a substitute⟩
⟨Willm. Sedgely, woolcombr., by a substitute⟩
⟨Edward Humphry, farmr., by a substitute⟩
⟨John Norton, weaver, by a substitute⟩

⟨Thos. Harris⟩ constable.

GUILSBOROUGH

Northamptonshire, Novr. 29, 1777.   A list of names of the persons liable
to serve as militiamen for Guilsborough and Nortaft between the ages of
eighteen and forty-five years.

Henery Bullivant, surgeon
    and apoticary
Thos. Comfield, English
    school master
Thos. Powell, servant man
John Nichols, carpenter
Richard Nichols, carpenter
William Darcus, labourer
⟨William Wills, butcher⟩
William Roberts, cloather
William Butlin, blacksmith
William Hollick, cordwainer
Arnold Abbott, tayler
Joseph Louke, labourer
John Smith, shephard
Richard Hollick, cordwainer
Thos. Jeays, blacksmith

Samuel Jones, blacksmith
Thos. Pell, chandler
Andrew Pell, chandler
Richard Dawes, cordwainer
William Wheately, weaver
William Tarry, comber of wool
John Matcham, labourer
Edward Ashby, farmer
John Darcus, butcher
John Willson, labourer
John Evans, farmer
Joseph Evans, farmer
Thos. Evans, farmer
James Bird, labourer
Henery Evans, farmer
William Hollis, servant man
Thos. Heally, servant man

Joseph Dent, servant man
John Johnson, farmer
Samuel Johnson, farmer
Thos. Browen, servant man
William Harris, weaver
Thos. Mold, labourer
George Smith, labourer
Thos. Holiday, farmer
⟨John Mitchel, labourer⟩
  lame hand

Robert Goodman, juner, farmer
William Green, mason
William Muscut, weaver
Thos. Heanes, weaver
William Mathews, farmer
John Haddon, shephard
William Payne, weaver
Robert Darcus, labourer

⟨James Dawes, constable of the parish.⟩

A list of the inferm and drawd men of Guilsboro. and the hamlet of Nortaft.

⟨Edward Letts, juner, drawd man⟩
⟨Jackson Payne, a lame man⟩
⟨William Gibbs, a drawd man⟩
⟨Edward Turner, a drawd man⟩
⟨Soloman Johnson, a poor man,
  three children⟩
⟨Samuel Wormleton, a drawd
  man⟩ quary
⟨John Underwood, a drawd man⟩
⟨William Pell, a drawd man⟩
⟨John Hollick, a drawd man⟩
⟨John Smith, a drawd man⟩
  quary

⟨William Cave, inferm, with
  fitts⟩
⟨Robert Walker, a drawd man⟩
  quary
⟨Samuel Towensend, a poor man,
  three children⟩
⟨Joseph Ashby, a drawd man⟩
⟨Thos. Good, a poor man,
  three children⟩
⟨James Harris, a drawd man⟩

WEST HADDON

West Haddon list of all the male inhabitants residing there between the age of 18 and 45 years to be laid before his Majesty's deputy lieutennants & others the justices of the peace in & for our said county of Northampton at a meeting to be held at the **Sarazen's Head Inn** on at Daventry on Tuesday the 9th. day of December 1777.

George Miller
Benjamin Vaus
Charles Heygate
Wm. Page (alias) Walton
John West
Robt. Killworth
Wm. Burbidge.
Wm. Capel
Nathl. Reeve
Thos. Gibbons
Thos. Ward
Wm. Buxhell
James Johnson
Edwd. Thompson
John Thompson
Thos. Newton
Richd. Bromwich

Richd. Hall
Thos. Cox
James Manning
Jonathon Wallis
John Foster
John Smith, farmer
Wm. Page, junr.
John York
Wm. Newton
John Newton
John Payne
George Taylor
Wm. Beal
Wm. Dunkley
Thos. Tavener
Wm. Goode
John Garrett

John Haycock
Wm. Gulliver
Richd. Worster
Richd. Harris
John Gibbons
Thos. Onely
Thos. Boys
Mark Lord
Thos. Parnell, senr.
Saml. York
Robt. Heygate
John Barker
Wm. Smith
Jacob Worster
Stephen Sheppard
Edwd. Cave
John Linnett
Thos. Palmer
Henry Robins
John Earl
Robt. Earl
Wm. Robins
John Abbott
Starkey Abbott
Thos. Abbott
Thos. Peck
Robt. Price
Thos. Dams
John Smith, blacksmith
Matthias Stanton
Wm. Adams
Wm. West
Josh. Buswell
John Robins
John Adams
John Bennett
Wm. Goodman
Edwd. Hipwell
John Earn
Charles Lovell
John Curtis
John Clerk
John Boys
John Facer
Wm. Facer
Saml. Ley
Thomas Fenell
Francis Burton
Saml. Perkins
Chs. Abbott
Harris Manton
Thos. Parnell, junr.
John Heygate
Josh. Smith

Poor men with 3 or more
children
⟨Nathl. Manning⟩
⟨John Vaus⟩
⟨Edwd. Linnett⟩
⟨Wm. Woodford⟩
⟨Clerk Eyre⟩
⟨Thos. Naseby⟩
⟨Saml. West⟩
⟨Andrew Reeve⟩
⟨Henry Newton⟩
⟨John Page⟩
⟨John Walton⟩
⟨John Killworth, labr.⟩
⟨John Killworth, weaver⟩
⟨Richd. Robins⟩
⟨John Dunkley⟩
⟨Nehe. Facer⟩
⟨James Robins⟩
⟨Jesse Cook⟩
⟨John Hensman⟩
⟨Wm. Hipwell⟩

Infirm
⟨Ephraim Walton, phthsical⟩
⟨Daniel Pring, wounded⟩
⟨Thos. Thompson, rupture⟩
⟨Saml. Pool, very lame⟩
⟨Richd. Palmer, consumptive⟩
⟨Richd. Turner, ditto.⟩
⟨Maurice Ward, near sighted⟩
⟨Wm. Gamage, wry neckd.⟩

Apprentices
⟨Thos. Collis, shoemaker⟩
⟨Wm. Reed, sope boyler⟩
⟨Wm. West, taylor⟩
⟨Thos. Rogers, ditto.⟩
⟨Wm. Rogers, weaver⟩
⟨Thos. Mabbott, woolcomber⟩

Drawn men
⟨James Vaus⟩
⟨John Hipwell⟩
⟨Thos. Norton⟩
⟨Job Payne⟩
⟨Wm. Page, senr.⟩
⟨Job Eaglestone⟩
⟨John Bosworth⟩
⟨Thos. Baucutt⟩
⟨Thos. Wikes⟩
⟨John Buswell⟩
⟨John Castell⟩
⟨Henry Russell⟩

Thirdboroughs
⟨Chs. Line⟩
⟨Wm. Martin⟩
⟨Richd. Baucutt⟩
⟨Richd. Collins⟩
⟨Jno. Underwood⟩ constable

Elkington list
George Gee, grazer
John Hobson, grazer
Thomas Michel, shepherd
Thomas Lee, shepherd
John Elkington, servant
Nathaniel Perkins, servant
John Packwood, laberour

⟨Robert Newton, constable.⟩

HOLLOWELL

1777 Novembr. 22.   A list of persons liable to serve as militia men for the hamlet of Hollowell.

William Lucas, esqr.
William Atterbury, yeoman
William Bates, yeoman
William Parnell, single man
John Haslock, labourer
John Hern, labourer
William Hern, labourer
William Knowles, wool comber
James Letts, farmer
Stephen Willmott, wheelwright
John Jelliss, miller
Thomas Arnold, servant
Richard Hern, son of
    Richard Hern, weaver
Richard Hern, son of
    Aaron Hern

Robert Flecknow, weavor
John Harriss, farmer
William Allard, wool comber
Solomon Bray, servant
Joseph Castle, servant
James Welling, travelling
    wool comber
John Chapman, glazier,
    single man
Have servd. ⟨Thos. Chester⟩
            ⟨Edward Middleton⟩
            ⟨Richard Watson⟩
            ⟨William Whale⟩

The day of appeal is on the 9 of Decembr. 1777.

John Haslock, constable.

LILBOURNE

Lilbourn, Northamptonshire, to wit.   Names of all the persons resideing within our parish of Lilbourn aforesaid between the ages of eighteen and forty five that are liable to be drawn to serve as malitia men for the said parish.

Edwd. Bennett, framework-
    knitter
Frans. Bennett, framework-
    knitter
Joseph Garner, framework-
    knitter
Willm. Garner, framework-
    knitter
John Tew, weaver
Robt. Nichols, framework-
    knitter
Francis Nichols, framework-
    knitter

Joseph Dunn, weaver
Henry Hobley, weaver
Thos. Allen, grasier
Jonathan Read, junr., labourer
John Smith, grocer
Wm. Smith, weaver
Samuel Cockerill, carpenter
Wm. Gardener, servant
Richd. Lee, junr., weaver
Wm. Marson, junr., cordwainer
John Kirkham, junr., framework
    knitter
Wm. Kirkham, junr., do.

Joseph George, weaver
Thos. Higgs, weaver
Wm. Hefford, carpenter
Robt. Langham, grasier

John Lee, weaver
Thos. Green, labourer
Thos. Haycock, servant
Wm. Mullings, servant

⟨John Garner⟩ cunstable.

If any of the above persons shall think themselves aggrieved by being in inserted in this list, the day of appeal for such will be on Tuesday the 9th. of December 1777 at the Saracens-Head Inn Daventry——and no appeal will be heared afterwards.

NASEBY

A list of the names between the ages of eighteen years and fortyfive in the parish of Naseby liable to serve in the militia 1777 by James Clark, constable.

Mr. Richard Herbert, farmer
Samll. Bosworth, servant
Thos. Henson, farmer
Thos. Wilford, servant
Samll. Frisby, farmer
Henry Frisby, farmer
Willm. Chester, farmer
John Chester, farmer
Daniel Phigeon, servant
Charles Wilford, weaver
John Cheney, cordwainer
⟨John Frisby, farmer⟩
Elisha Ringrose, farmer
John Wilford, weaver
John Hadden, labourer
James Clark, farmer
Thos. Garret, farmer
Edward Cheney, weaver
John Gibbs, weaver
John Hadden, farmer
Richard Wheatley, farmer
Samuel Landon, collarmaker
⟨Richard Hadden, farmer⟩
⟨Samuel Gill, labourer⟩
Moses Wright, servant
Willm. Everard, farmer
Robert Burdit, farmer
Willm. Burdit, shepherd
Moses Burdit, farmer
Willm. Gill, farmer
Joshua Gibbs, shepherd
John Page, cordwainer
John Swingler, labourer
Thos. Moody, labourer
George Everard, farmer

Moses Cox, weaver
William Chapman, labourer
Thos. Chester, servant
Joseph Warpool, weaver
Joseph Carvell, labourer
John Wright, taylor
Walter Harris, taylor
Mr. George Cowdel, farmer
Willm. Wallis, servant
Willm. Waldin, shepherd
⟨Willm. Martin, servant⟩
Robert Wilford, labourer
Robert Watts, farmer
John Adnit, carpenter
Willm. Cook, servant
Joshua Ringrose, joiner
James Cave, farmer
John Opherd, servant
Willm. Wilford, weaver
John Trestler, blacksmith
Richard Bale, servant
Joseph Wilford, servant
Thos. Linnit, servant
Henry Napp, labourer
⟨Isaac Martin, drawn man⟩
⟨John Hall, drawn man⟩
⟨George Adnit, infirm'd.⟩
⟨Willm. Wilford, senior,
  infirm'd.⟩
⟨John Bott, labourer, 3 children⟩
⟨Willm. Haines, labourer,
  3 children⟩
⟨Henry Fretter, shepherd,
  3 children⟩

STANFORD

Stanford list.

Bret Right, carpenter, 4 children
Edward Johnson, carpenter,
    5 children
⟨John Powell, laburer⟩ 3 children
Robart Jordan, shapard

⟨Thomas Walker, 4 children⟩
Abrham Dunn, infirm
⟨Samuel Thomson, infirm⟩
John Gudman, 3 children

Jos. Jurden, constable.

THORNBY

Novembr. 26th .1777.   A list of the militia of the parish of Thurnby.

Thos. Gulliver, farmer
Thos. Gee, farmer
John Swingler, molster
Benjaman Smith, cordwinder
Miah Ilson, miller
Esaw Ilson, beaker
John Martin, servant
John Vann, servant

Thos. Vann, servant
William Feacer, servant
Thos. Feacer, servant
John Miller, servant
Thos. Midelton, servant
Johnathan Chapman, servant
Richard Hickman, servant
Thos. Hall, servant

Edwd. Fellows, constable.

WATFORD

1777.   A list of the persons names now dwelling and residing within the parish and constablewick of Watford in the hundred of Guilsborough and county of Northampton between the ages of eighteen and forty-five; for raising the militia in the said county.

William Clark, farmer
Thomas Wiggins, farmer
John Wiggins, servant
Joseph Cross, servant
Samuel Howard, labourer
Thomas Payne, farmer
William Wright, servant
Thomas Leeson, servant
Richard Abbey, farmer
John Abbey, farmer
Thomas Packard, servant
John Mobbs, servant
Valentine Adams, woadman,
    the rheumatism
Thomas Parker, servant
John Coleman, blacksmith
George Cook, blacksmith
John Embery, weaver
John Hanbury, woolcomber
Christopher Bateman, labourer
John Butlin, cordwainer
James Green, junr., weaver
William Wood, junr., weaver

Nathl. Pebody, labourer
Richard Currin, weaver
John Currin, weaver
Thomas Johnson, labourer
John Frost, taylor
Joseph Butlin, cordwainer
John Lee, farmer
John Bennet, servant
John Mutton, servant
William Clifton, servant
John Bateman, weaver
Richard Reeve, farmer
Thomas Reeve, farmer
Samuel Butlin, weaver
Joseph Mawby, weaver
James Gilbert, junr., farmer
William Gilbert, farmer
Thomas Needle, servant
William Gare, labourer
Roger Haynes, weaver
Samuel Butlin, weaver
⟨Nathl. Fox, weaver⟩ infirm

Thomas Matthews, grazier, drawn in the Leicestershire militia but
does not say in which raising
⟨Thomas Pool, servant⟩ hard or dul of hearing
Thomas Wright, carpenter
John Clarke, shepherd, sayth he is subject to fits.
⟨Puliston Mawby, shepherd⟩ lame having lost his great toe off his
right foot
⟨John Morris, farmer⟩ drawn the last raising the militia.
⟨Thomas Butlin, weaver⟩ drawn 2d. raising, 3 children
⟨Robert Hunt, weaver⟩ drawn 3d. raising, 3 children
⟨John Seal⟩ weaver, drawn in the last militia

Poor men, 3 children and upwards

⟨Valentine Hanbury, clockmaker⟩ 3 children
⟨William Kenning, labourer⟩ 3 children
⟨Thomas Seal, labourer⟩ 3 children
⟨John Wingrove, labourer⟩ 6 children
⟨Richard Pebody, labourer⟩ 3 children
⟨John Mobbs, labourer⟩ 3 children
⟨Thomas Slynn, labourer⟩ 6 children
Richard Hanbury, weaver ⎫
⟨Richard Butlin, weaver⟩ ⎭ apprentices

Note. A copy of the above list hath been affixed on the door of the
parish church, and notice given in writing at the bottom of the day of
appeal, and that no appeal will be receivd after 9th. day of this instant
December.

James Gilbert, constable.

WELFORD

A list of the inhabitants of Welford in the county of Northampton liable
to be ballotted to be drawn to serve in the malitia for the said county
taken the sixt. day of December in the year of our Lord 1777 by me, John
Abbott, senr., constable.

William Wood, junr., farmer
Francis Wood, farmer
William Hassel, weaver
John Hassel, weaver
Thomas White, junr., mason
Thomas Wilson, weaver
Thomas Neal, shepherd
Jonathon Underwood, weaver
Thomas Kingston, weaver
John Abbott, junr., farmer
John Bosworth, servant
John Manton, servant
Thomas Bennett, felmonger
Benjamin Bennett, currier
Currer Wright, leather dresser
Francis Warring, felmonger
John Biggs, junr., farmer
Thomas Biggs, farmer
Joseph Chaplin, farmer

Thomas Seaton, weaver
Joseph Wilson, carpenter
Francis Bennett, farmer
Edward Aldridge, servant
Thomas Allard, wool-comber
Lewis Beatley, wool-comber
William Harrald, junr., weaver
William Skerral, weaver
Thomas Woodford, felmonger
William Day, labourer
Thomas Veasy, junr., labourer
Benjamin King, butcher
William Hardin, weaver
Benjamin Buckland, weaver
John Skerral, weaver
⟨John Hefford, weaver, infirm⟩
John Palmer, junr., shepherd
John Blawr, servant
John Butlin, victular

Samuell Sudborough, weaver
John Goodfellow, turner
⟨John Bilson, tallow-chandler⟩
Thomas Murden, weaver
James Harrald, senr., weaver
Peter Spencer, carpenter
Joseph Clay, grasier
Thomas West, weaver
Benjamin Cave, baker
Thomas Lucas, weaver
Henery Bamford, victular
William Billin, cooper
John Wilson, taylor
John Ward, weaver, junr.
Joseph Palmer, grasier
Thomas Toseland, weaver
Richard Millington,
    wool-comber
Francis Ponsford, wool-comber
Joseph Brokehous, wool-comber
⟨Nathaniel Nutt, weaver⟩
James Harrald, junr., weaver
Edward Bates, labourer
John Townley, weaver
Thomas Collins, weaver
Thomas Randle, junr.,
    wool-comber
Thomas Bennett, junr., weaver
William Ward, senr.,
    wool-comber
William Ward, carpenter
William Chapman, carpenter
William Palmer, victular
John Seaton, weaver
James Bassett, weaver
William Neal, weaver
Samuell Paul, a boarder
Thomas Hill, servant

Samuell Kilburn, wheelright
Jonathon Richards, labourer
John Woodford, labourer
John Martin, servant
John Spencer, inn-holder
William Oliver, farmer
John Reeve, servant
Thomas Digby, servant
Joseph Marlow, servant
John Hamlet, blacksmith
William Bennett, weaver
John Welton, wool-comber
Thomas Ducket, labourer
John Clark, servant
William Biggs, carrier
Thomas Jorden, cordwainer
James Ashton, baker
Richard Moor, junr., weaver
William Burr, cordwainer
George Vials, cordwainer
Philip Bliss, victular
Jonathon Hutchins, servant
Joseph Day, labourer
William Sprigg, labourer
John Hurst, carpenter
John Harrald, miller
Job Garner, servant
John Green, servant
John Gittus, servant
Thomas Giles, servant
James Crew, servant
Thomas Cox, servant
⟨Samuell Newitt, labourer, a poor
    man⟩ lame
John Letherland, labourer,
    a poor man
William Lucas, now a substitute
Thomas Line, now a substitute

⟨William Leatherland, now a substitute and a poor man with three
    children⟩
George Robinson, now a substitute
⟨William Biggs, weaver, drawn in the year 1775 and served⟩
⟨Jeremiah Wright, drawn in the year 1772 and served⟩
⟨Benjamin Palmer, drawn in the year 1772 and served⟩
⟨John Payne, esqr., officer in the navy⟩
⟨John Hill, licence teacher⟩
⟨William Butlin, junr., apprentice⟩
⟨John Moor, apprentice⟩
⟨John Law, apprentice⟩
⟨John Blockley, drawn in the year 1775⟩
⟨Francis Peck, farmer, drawn in the year 1775⟩
⟨John Kingstone, farmer, drawn in the year 1775⟩
⟨Mark Hancock, labourer, served in the army 3 years⟩
⟨John Davis. farmer, lame and infirm with illness⟩

⟨John Hefford, carpenter, lame and infirm with illness⟩
⟨John Hefford, weaver, infirmed by having a misfortune of a fall and
   broke part of his ribs⟩
⟨John Chambers, non compos mentis⟩
⟨Edward Seaton, a poor man with four children⟩
⟨John Manning, a poor man with three children
⟨Francis Hewitt, a poor man with eight children⟩
⟨John Holman, junr., a poor man with six children⟩
⟨William Astill, waever, a poor man with four children⟩
⟨Benjamin Wilford, weaver, a poor man with three childrn⟩
⟨Lawrance Crisp, weaver, a poor man with three children⟩
⟨Moses Goodfellow, turner, a poor man with seven childn⟩
⟨Benjamin Burges, weaver, a poor man with four childrn⟩
⟨Robert Butlin, cordwainer, a poor man with five children⟩
⟨John Croo, gardener, a poor man with three children⟩
⟨John Goode, tayler, a poor man with four children⟩
⟨John Adderson, labourer, a poor man with three children⟩
⟨William Durrad, labourer, a poor man with four children⟩
⟨John Patch, weaver, a poor man with four children⟩
⟨Thomas Ward, wool-comber, a poor man with four children⟩
⟨John Ward, senr., weaver, a poor man with four children⟩
⟨Thomas Wilson, wool-comber, a poor man with
⟨William Herbert, labourer, a poor man with three children⟩
⟨Lawrence Goodman, labourer, a poor man with three children⟩
⟨Thomas Page, wool-comber, a poor man with five children⟩
⟨Joseph Jeys, labourer, a poor man with five children⟩
⟨John Hefford, junr., carpenter, a poor man with four children⟩
⟨Thomas Medbourn, cordwainer, a poor man with three children⟩
⟨William Woodford, blacksmith, a poor man with six children⟩
⟨William Bliss, cordwainer, a poor man with six children⟩
⟨John Looe, labourer, a poor man with four children⟩
⟨Robert Hewitt, wheelwright, a poor man with six children⟩
⟨John Lucas, weaver, a poor man with four children⟩
⟨John Lucas, victular, a poor man with four children⟩

WINWICK

Winwick in the hundred of Guilsborough and county of Northampton.
A true list of the mens names between the age of eighteen and forty five
to save as militia men in the said parish of Winwick.

Thomas Lovell
   the younger
George Jackson ⎬ grazers
   the younger
William Walpole, milier

Laboures
Thomas Archer
⟨Benjamen Gurney, infermn⟩
⟨John Carvel, infermn⟩
John Brown

Sarvents
Joseph Garret
John Brumage
William Packwood
John Kinney
John Barker
William Collier
⟨John Chamberlin, infermn⟩
John Gurney
Edward Clifin
John Hollond
Edward Boyson

⟨Thos. Burnham⟩ constable.

YELVERTOFT

A list of all men in the parish of Yelvertoft in the county of Northampton between the ages of eighteen and forty five liable to serve as militia men taken and made this twenty ninth day of November 1777 by Richard Cattell, constable for the said parish.

⟨The Revd. Mr. Cooper⟩
Sam. Watson, farmer
⟨Edw. Underwood, farmer, chosen by lot and served by substitute at
    Westhadden⟩
Jos. Norton, farmer
Jno. Cattell, farmer
Robt. Matthew, farmer
Wm. Reeve, farmer
Thos. Bosworth, farmer
Jno. Linnitt, farmer
Robt. Cleaver, farmer
Jno. Cleaver, farmer
Geo. Smith, farmer
Jno. Townsend, farmer
Geo. Watkin, farmer son
Robt. Cattell, farmer son
Steph. Bolton, farmcr son
Geo. Bolton, farmer son
Jno. Hedley, farmer son
Jos. Hedley, farmer son
Thos. Malin, farmer son
Edw. Clark, farmer
Wm. Lidall, blacksmith
Jon. Ashby, black smith
Edw. Burbidge, grocer
Jno. Page, cordwinder
Abraham Page, cordwinder
Wm. Sivins, joiner
Wm. Castell, weaver
Geo. Billing, weaver
⟨Jos. Billing, weaver, infirm⟩
Edw. Walding, weaver
Wm. Garrett, weaver
Jno. Ward, weaver
Robt. Bodinton, weaver
James Willson, weaver
Jno. Lee, weaver,
James Griggory, weaver
⟨Jno. Willson, weaver, infirm⟩
Jno. Wilkins, weaver
Jno. Ringrose, weaver
Edw. Robins, weaver
Jno. Burbidge, grocer
Wm. Reeve, shephard
James Cleaver, miller
⟨Siman Cleaver, miller, chosen⟩ by lot and servd by substitute Long
    Buckby
Wm. Sturman, baker

Robt. Carter, labourer
Thos. Mawby, labourer
Wm. Sherwood, labourer
Wm. Willson, labourer
Wm. Stafford, labourer
Edw. Kendrick, labourer
Jno. Willson, labourer
Jno. Elson, labourer
Jno. Bolard, labourer
Jno. Tailor, labourer
Jos. Smart, labourer
Stepn. Hollick, servant
Jno. Crofts, servant
Thos. Pebady, servant
Wm. Wardell, servant
Jno. Clark, servant
Danil. Simans, servant
Wm. Brown, servant
Thos. Willson, servant

Poor men with 3 children
⟨Robt. Willson⟩
⟨James York⟩
⟨Edw. Minor⟩
⟨Sam. Wolton⟩
⟨Jos. Dunkley⟩
⟨Wm. Eales⟩
⟨Jno. Herbert⟩

⟨Geo. Ward⟩
⟨Jno. Eales⟩
⟨Wm. Facer⟩
⟨Wm. Cave⟩
⟨Wm. Hearbard⟩
⟨Wm. Matthew⟩

Infirm men
⟨Mr. Wm. Ensby, lost one hand⟩
⟨James Page, lost one leg⟩
⟨Robt. Stafford, near sighted⟩
⟨Thos. Reeve, lame⟩
⟨Geo. Matthew, hard of hearing⟩
⟨Jno. Clark, paralytick⟩
⟨Richd. Bodinton, lame⟩

*Men that have all redy been
chosen by lot and servd by
substitute*
⟨Thos. Matthew⟩
⟨Sam. York⟩
⟨Sam. Ward⟩
⟨Humphery Elson⟩
⟨Robert Willson⟩
⟨Jno. Matthew⟩
⟨Wm. Cowley⟩
⟨Thos. Fletcher⟩
⟨Thos. Claridge⟩

⟨Richard Cattle, constable.⟩

Notice is hereby given that there will be a day of appeal at the Saracens Head in Daventry on Tuesday the 9 of December, and all persons who shall think them selves agrieved may then appeal, and that no appeal will be hard afterwards.

HAMFORDSHOE HUNDRED

Great Doddington	30	Sywell	26
Earls Barton	83	Wellingborough	456
Ecton	68	Wilby	22
Holcot	48		
Mears Ashby	51		784

Attorney	1	Lace-man	4
Baker	16	Law	1
Barber	4	Maltster	3
Basket-maker	1	Mason	12
Blacksmith	9	Matmaker	16
Bookseller	1	Merchant	3
Brazier	1	Militia service	19
Breeches-maker	1	Miller	12
Brewer	1	Millwright	1
Butcher	18	No trade given	33
Carpenter	23	Ostler	5
Chaise-driver	3	Parchment maker	2
Chandler	1	Pipe-maker	1
Chimney-sweep	1	Plasterer	1
Clergyman	2	Poulterer	1
Collar-maker	3	Rider	1
Cooper	2	Schoolmaster	3
Costermonger	1	Servant	84
Currier	10	Servant (personal)	8
Cutler	1	Shepherd	6
Dissenting minister	2	Shoemaker	133
Draper	5	Shoemaker & currier	1
Dyer	1	Shopkeeper	5
Esquire	2	Smith	7
Excise	4	Stay-maker	2
Farmer	36	Surgeon	4
Farmer's son	4	Surveyor	1
Flax-dresser	6	Tailor	20
Gardener	7	Tanner	3
Gentleman	1	Tapster	1
Glazier	4	Thatcher	1
Glover	8	Tinman	1
Grocer	7	Victualler	7
Heel-maker	2	Waggoner	1
Horse-dealer	1	Waiter	1
Husbandman's son	6	Watchmaker	3
Innholder	3	Weaver	35
Ironmonger	1	Wheelwright	3
Joiner	1	Wool-comber	6
Keeper	1	Workhouse	1
Knacker	1	Yeoman	13
Labourer	116		
Lace-buyer	1		785

GREAT DODDINGTON

A list of the men of Great Doddington in the county of Northampton shire fhrom the age of eighteen to forty five.   Novbr. 29th., 1777.

Thos. Lovell, farmer
Rich. Chaloner, dt.
Thomas Petitt, dot.
William Knight, dt.
John Barns, dt.
John Townly, carpenter
⟨Anthony Townly, sarvent⟩
Thomas Townley, carpenter
Richard Pitts, shop keeper
John Rowkins, miller
William King, dt.
William Corby, blaksmith
Ralfph Geary, sarvant
Jonathon Dikx, dt.
John Howkins, dt.

Joseph Gooding, dt.
John Roberson, dt.
James Roberson, dt.
Robert Coalman, dt.
John Owen, dt.
John Chapman, bucher
William Carter, labor
Freman Corby, dt.
John Pettit, dt.
Robert Nutt, dt.
Joseph Jonson, dt.
⟨William Fhanton, dt., lame⟩
William Purkins, dt.
⟨Richard Piner, dt.⟩
⟨Henery Piner, dt., lame⟩

T. Blundel Kilsby ⎫
Joseph Powell   ⎬ constables.
                          ⎭

EARLS BARTON

A list of all the men in Earls Barton that are qualified to sarve in the militia from 18 yeares of age to 45 yeares of age, 1777.

Wm. Whitworth, gent.
Thos. Plackit, labr.
Thos. Sharag, sarvent
⟨John Abraham, labr.⟩
Robt. Whitworth, scl. master
Wm. Black, sarvent
Thos. Renals, servant
Wm. Tooky, officer excise
Adam Coock, servant
James Church, servant
John Austin, matmaker
Gabrel Kemhead, yeoman
Isaac Dodson, yeoman
Wm. Kemshead, yeoman
Thos. Austin, victlor
Samuell Austin, coardwindr.
⟨Wm. Hornsy, matmaker⟩
George Hornsy, matmaker
Daniel Sutton, coardwinder
Joph. Bywaters, blacksmith
John Hensman, baker
Wm. James, coardwinder
James Clark, matmaker
John Barker, matmaker
John Purkins, tayler
Robrt. Whitworth, yeoman
⟨Thos. Whitworth, yeoman⟩

Henry Lorton, labr.
Spencer Morris
Richd. Morris
Thos. Warren, yeoman
Henery Smith, blacksmith
Wm. Garner, labr.
Wm. Smart, labr.
Edmond James, yeoman
Joph. Abraham, coardwinder
Thos. Ayliff, labr.
George Jobson, tayler
Samuell Mathess, cordwinder
John Barker, yeoman
George Abraham, yeoman
Charles Sikes, sarvant
Henery Charmbers, yeoman
George Barker, yeoman
George Jordan, blacksmith
Abraham Jordan, carpenter
James Jordan, cordwinder
John Muddymore, labr.
Samuell Gariatt, labr.
Wm. Palmer, mattmaker
Thos. Bradshaw, laber
Wm. Cornish, matmaker
Wm. Tebbut, matmaker
Joph. Clark, weaver

George Powell, carpenter
⟨John Parnall, tayler⟩
Morrias Farow, tayler
Joph. Parnall, tayler
John Smith, butcher
Richd. Smith
John Berell, mason
⟨Wm. Molton, matmaker⟩
Thos. Cornish, matmaker
John Knight, cordwinder
John Mayse, sarvant
Joph. Bradford, cordwinder
John Gibbs, labr.
Joph. Tebbut, matmaker
Thos. Barker, matmaker
Wm. Donkley, coardwinder

Wm. Berell, matmaker
⟨Charls Hodge, matmaker⟩
Eelly Tebbutt, matmaker
Henery Mayes, coardwinder
Edward Sheffield, sarvant
Ellij James, labr.
Japhat James, yeoman
⟨Joph. Rodgers, parchment
　maker⟩
⟨Richd. Rodgers, parchment
　maker⟩
⟨Isaac Powell, yeoman⟩
Peter Cradock, miller
James Clark, sarvant
⟨James Hornsby, coardwinder⟩

The appeal day will be the eight day of December at the Hind Inn in Wellingborough.

Richd. Morris ⎫
Wm. Smith 　 ⎬ constables
　　　　　　 ⎭

John Simson 　 ⎫
George Groser ⎬ headboroughs.
　　　　　　　 ⎭

ECTON

County of Northampton and ⎫
division of Wellingborough ⎬ to wit. A true and perfect list of per-
　　　　　　　　　　　　 ⎭
sons usually and now dwelling in the parish of Ecton in the county aforesaid between the age of eighteen and forty-five.

Samuel Isted, esqr.
William Gaudern ⎫
John Brown 　　 ｜ servants to
Richard Marston ⎬ Ambrose
William Blason 　｜ Isted, esqr.
Thos. Clark 　　 ⎭
James Hern 　　 ⎫ servants to
William Muskee ⎬ the Revd.
　　　　　　　 ⎭ Mr. Whalley
John Slatter, husbandman's son
Jonathan Howkins, butcher
John Langley, carpenter
William Langley, labourer
James Ingram, ditto.
Edward Wheeler, victuler
John Blason, servant
⟨Joseph Knight, do.⟩
Allen Lovell, husbandman's son

Anthony Childs, do.
Jonathan Childs, do.
Peter Lovell, do.
Jonathan Lovell, do.
Ruben Abbot, servant
Thomas Pinny, do.
John Yooul, do.
Robert Garret, do.
William Cox, cordwainer
Stephen Langley, carpenter
John Norris, mason
Robert Nichols, cordwainer
John Johnson, butcher
William Morris, blacksmith
Anthony Clark, baker
William Maine, do.
John Simmons, cordwainer

Names of persons that have upwards of three children.

⟨John Van, schoolmaster⟩
⟨John Bayes, carpenter⟩
⟨Thomas Thompson, keeper⟩
⟨James Thompson, gardener⟩

⟨William Johnson, labourer⟩
⟨William Jolley, do.⟩
⟨Edward Jolley, parish clerk⟩
⟨Edward Goodwin, labourer⟩

⟨Thomas Collins, do.⟩　　　　⟨John Kemp, do.⟩
⟨Henery Morris, do.⟩

Names of persons that have served by substitute.

⟨Stephen Prentice, servant to　　⟨Jonas Thompson, servant⟩
　　A. Isted, esqr.⟩　　　　　　⟨James Barret, servant⟩
⟨Edward James, labourer⟩　　　⟨Samuel James, labourer⟩
⟨Henery Norris, mason⟩　　　　⟨Thomas Hart, do.⟩
⟨Thomas Robinson, labourer⟩　　⟨Richard Luck, servant⟩

Liable to serve.

John Luck, gardener　　　　　　Samuel Orlebar, do.
John Brown, servant　　　　　　Edmond Hensman, cordwainer
John Wilson, do.　　　　　　　John Collins, labourer
John Baizley, do.　　　　　　　William Pinny, do.
William Robinson, do.　　　　　John Pettit, do.
John King, carpenter　　　　　　Bartholemew Naberry, do.
Lovell Stonebanks, do.　　　　　John Hensman, do.

Note, the meeting of the Justices and Deputy Lieutenants is fixt for Monday the 8th. day of December next at eleven o'clock in the forenoon, at which all persons who think themselves aggriev'd at their names being put into this list may attend and appeal; the meeting to be held at the Hind Inn in Wellingborough in the said county.

Thomas Walton ⎫
Arthur Childs 　⎬ constables.
　　　　　　　⎭

Novemr. 30th. 1777.

HOLCOT

Holcutt list of all persons who are lyable to serve in the militia between the age of eighteen and forty-five for the parish of Holcutt, 1777.

Aldern. Houghton, farmer　　　Wm. Treslove, servant
Stepn. Dickins, farmer's son　　Wm. Murdin, farmer's son
Wm. Brown, wool-comber　　　John Day, taylor
Saml. Hills, servant　　　　　　Wm. Faulkner, labourer
John Wallace, do.　　　　　　　Wm. Wright, cordwainer
Thos. Burdit, weaver　　　　　　Wm. Houghton, farmer
Richd. Wright, cordwainer　　　Heny. Ward, farmer's son
Thos. Clark, labourer　　　　　John Brown, carpenter
Josh. Hull, wool-comber　　　　Nathl. Lansberry, shepherd
Wm. Wright, weaver　　　　　　Nathl. Ager, do
Binyn. Drage, horse-dealer　　　Saml. Marriot, woolcomber
Wm. Sargin, servant　　　　　　Saml. Dickins, blacksmith
John Pool, cordwainer　　　　　Wm. Wright, baker
Saml. Mabbutt, labourer　　　　Wm. Turland, labourer
Thos. Spokes, miller　　　　　　Heny. Campion, cordwainer
Geoe. Spokes, servant　　　　　Josh. Wright, baker
Wm. Lucas, weaver　　　　　　Wm. Powel, labourer
Thos. Lack, servant　　　　　　Heny. Page, butcher
Underwood Denton, joiner　　　⟨Robert Howes, servant,
Wm. Sharp, carpenter　　　　　　　lame foot⟩
Thos. Houghton, farmer

⟨Thos. Turland, servant,
    lame legs⟩
⟨Wm. Campion, weaver,
    lame arm⟩
⟨Wm. Peach, cordwainer, deaf ⟩
⟨Edwd. Smith, wool-comber,
    one eye⟩

⟨Robt. Ekins, farmer, lame leg⟩
⟨John Wright, cordwainer,
    lame arms⟩
Wm. Goodman, labourer
Josh. Goodman, labourer

John Dickins, constable.

MEARS ASHBY

A list for the militia for the parish of Mears Ashby, Novr. 29, 1777.

John Pate Lister, esqr.
Samuel Pell, farmer
Robert Luckas, sarvant
James Pratt, labour
Thomas Lack, sarvant
⟨John Jeley, labour, served⟩
⟨James Sturges, labour, served⟩
William Bradshew, taylor
William Allen, sarvant
Palmer Pratt, labour
Robert Pratt, labour
Robert Murdin, labour
Barker Hewett, sarvant
William Underwood, farmer
⟨Thomas Brown, sarvant, sarved⟩
John Childs, sarvant
Rodger Grove, labour
John Solsbery, labour
William Mundin, carpenter
John Hewett, blacksmith
Thomas Mundin, labour
John Willding, taylor
Thomas Willding, baker
John Haddon, labour
Thomas Gillitt, labour
James Gillitt, labour

William Roberson, labour
Thomas Miller, labour
William Church, farmer
⟨William Pratt, farmer, served⟩
John Patridge, sarvant
Samuel Kerby, weaver
⟨William Gillitt, labour, lame⟩
⟨Richard Gillitt, labour, lame⟩
⟨John Wollstone, labour, fitts⟩
William Tarry, butcher
Samuel Pratt, nacker
Charles Pratt, baker
John George, sarvant
William Fowkes, farmer
John Mobs, labour
William Robords, labour
Thomas Pratt, farmer
Thomas Pratt, malster
⟨John Pratt, shepard, searved⟩
William Price, sarvant
James Palmer, sarvant
⟨William Row, sarvant, sarved⟩
⟨William Haddon, labour⟩
⟨William Bays, labour, sarved⟩
⟨William Tebbut, labour⟩

All persons that think themselves aggrieved may then appeal on Monday the eight day of December at the Hind in Wellingborough. Thomas Gillitt, constable, and Charles Barker and William Pratt, senor, headborough.

SYWELL

A list of the names of such as are liable to to serve as militia men in the parish of Sywell.

Geo. Worly, farmer
John Pell, farmer
Wm. Allgood, farmer
Wm. Bauctut, miller
John Marriot, blacksmith

Wm. Lack, labourer
John Houghton, servant
Wm. Richardson, servant
Saml. Bryant, carpenter
Thos. Bignal, labourer

John Cox, labourer
John Allen, butcher
Wm. Brown, labourer
John Hensman, servant
Robert Dauks, servant
James Brown, servant
Thos. Faulkner, servant
Joseph Wymont, servant

John Darker, taylor
Wm. Sumerling, taylor
Richd. Warwick, servant
John Brown, servant
Richd. Knight, servant
John Hitchcock, labourer
Thos. Dauks, labourer
Richd. Hewitt, labourer

Decr. 8th. 1777.   Edward Ward, constable.

WELLINGBOROUGH

A list of the names of persons in the parish of Wellingborough liable to
serve in the Northamptonshire militia made out November 28th. 1777.
John Tilly, Thos. Mee, constables.

Alicock, Gregory, taylor
  & shopkeeper
Adams, Willm., tapster
Allen, Stephen, glazier
Allen, Willm., do.
Ashton, John, cordwainer
Ashton, Thos., do.
Arnold, Joseph, surgeon
Addington, Willm., cordwr.
Allen, John, mason
Adson, Frans., cordwr.
Allen, Daniel, do.
Ayer, John, labourer
Allen, Willm., mason
Allen, Isaac, do.
Abraham, Robt.
Attwood, Charles, mat-maker
Abraham, James, labor.
Barker, Lucas
Bradly, Lewis, farmer
Baily, Thos., lace-man
Benson, Willm.
Bradshew, Watson, grocer
Brightwel, Thos., gardiner
Baily, James, labor.
Blunsum, Wm., smith
Broughton, Thos., book-seller
Briant, Benjamin, weavr.
Butlin, Jno., cordwr.
Buthy, Francis, labr.
Bulivant, Thos., grocer
Brigstock, Roger, labr.
Briant, Willm., weavr.
Barron, James, mill-wright
Brown, Willm., cordwainer
Bays, Saml., do.
Bently, Thos., weaver.

Birchin, Willm., cordwr.
Bowen, Willm., do.
Belamy, John, shepherd
Bletsoe, Richd., wheel-wright
Beeby, John, breechis-maker
Brown, Jas., miller
[Burton, pauper]
Chapman, Tresham, servant
Cowlishaw, Edward, inn-holder
Crafts, Willm., brewer
Church, John, cordwr.
Coalman, Henry, miller
Clark, Fleetwood, watch-maker
Cross, John, smith
Cherry, John, carpenter
Coles, Willm., cordwainer
Clay, John, do.
Corrie, Willm., mercht.
Corrie, Richd., mercht.
Chamberlin, Willm., cordr.
Chapman, Thos., servant
Crane, Joseph, weaver
Croxon, Benjamin, do.
Chester, Thos., cordwr.,
Coles, Richard, smith
⟨Clayson, Thos., victualr.⟩
Cooper, James, cordwr.
Cornfield, John, smith
Coles, William, cordwr.
Cooper, Willm., do.
Croxon, John, weaver
Chettle, Thos., grocer
Cowper, Willm., surveyor
Clark, Joy, cordwr.
Darling, Thos., basket-maker
Davis, Daniel, cordwr.
Divine, John, currier

Drinkwater, Chas., heel-maker
⟨Davis, John, horsler⟩
Desborough, Sam., cordwr.
Durden, John, do.
Deton, Joseph, thatcher
Dunmore, Thos., taylor
Dunmore, John, cordwainer
Dunkly, Peter, do.
Draper, Willm., do.
Dunkly, George, servant
Dickins, John, smith.
English, Thos., horsler
Embry, Jno., miller
Elliott, Jno., carptr.
Foster, Saml., tin-man
Froggat, Francis, barber
Faulkner, Edwd., cordwr.
Fleming, John., do.
Gill, Edwd., collar-maker
Green, George, victulr.
Groome, Daniel, cordwr.
Goward, Richd., chimney
    sweepr.
Garner, Willm., cordwr.
Gent, Willm., labr.
Grove, Saml., cordwr.
Garret, Richd., shepherd
Green, Jno., school-master
Hawthorn, Jno., chaise driver
Hensman, Miles, servant
Hafford, Nathl., cordwr.
Horne, James, do.
Hartington, Willm., do.
    & currier
Hurry, Willm., in the excise
Hardwick, Quiller, taylor
Hurst, Henry, draper
Horne, Willm., taylor
Holland, Timy., carpenter
Holloway, John, labor
Hartwel, Willm.
Hawks, Thos., carpenter
Hawks, Saml., cordwr.
Hunt, John, servant
Harbridge, Jno., flax-dresser
How, George, labr.
Hull, George, labr.
⟨Houghton, Saml., weavr.⟩
Houghton, John., weavr.
Hopkins, Joseph, weavr.
⟨Hawley, Willm., cordwr.⟩
Henson, Joseph, do.
Hensman, Willm., do.
Hodgson, Jno., attorney

Horne, James, cordwr.
Hardwick, Edwd., butcher
Hardwick, Willm., do.
Hafford, Francis, weavr.
Hafford, Willm., do.
Hardwick, Jno., butcher
Hensman, Henry, wheel-wright
Hobey, Robert
Jones, Matthew Easton
Jervis, George, currier
Jordin, Willm., cordwr.
Ingram, Joseph, do.
⟨Jordin, Francis, carpentr.⟩
Ives, Thos., wool comber
Jeffery, Paul, weaver
Jackson, Thos., miller
Kately, Joseph, mason
Knight, Samuel, inn-holder
Keep, John, brazier
King, Isaac, cordwr.
Knight, Joseph, do.
Kemsit, Thos., glover
Kilbourn, Robt., miller
Langley, Thos., cordwr.
Love, Wm., stay-maker
Lilly, John, farmer
Lawton, John, cordwr.
Lomas, Willm., do.
Law, Willm., labr.
Lucas, Thos., do.
Lucas, Jams., do.
Lucas, Willm., cordwr.
Lee, Thos., senr., do.
Lee, Thos., junr., do.
Ley, Joseph, shop-keeper
Mynor, Bawcut, servant
Mariner, horsler at the Hind
Mee, Jno., in Sheep Street
Moss, Saml., collar-maker
Martin, John, taylor
Murphy, Willm., lace-buyer
Middleton, Benjmn., draper
Mather, Benjn., grocer
Moreton, Archbd., mercht.
Mee, Thos., junr.
Mee, John, in High Street
⟨Merry, Willm., labor.⟩
Meacock, Jno., do.
Mims, Daniel, servant
Matthews, Willm., laborr.
Mee, Thos., senr., baker
Marriot, John, labor.
⟨Manning, Willm., shop-keeper⟩
Mantle, Willm., cordwr.

More, Richd., do.
Maning, Thos.
Meadows, Willm., weaver
Meadows, James
Martin, Thos., taylor
Mallery, Willm.
Martin, Willm., taylor
Nobles, Willm., cordwr.
Newman, Richd., labor.
⟨Nobles, Willm., weaver⟩ Bed.
Neal, Willm., cordwr.
Nobles, John, do.
Neal, John, do.
Overal, Francis, watch-maker
Orlibear, Francis, mason
Overal, James, labourer
Osbourn, Anthony, horsler
Overal, Joseph, watch-makr.
Poll, Moses, waiter at the Hind
Pew, Richd., surgeon
Peach, Sanderson, butcher
Pack, Joseph, servant
Page, Willm., junr., cordwainer
Patridge, Francis, victulr.
Patridge, Thos., inn-holder
Porter, Thos., chaise driver
Philips, rider
Page, Thos., barber
Pack, Martin, lace-man
Plats, Richd., cordwr.
Palmer, Willm., at the work-
house
Page, Thos., cordwr.
Patison, Jno., farmer
Page, Jno., cordwr.
Page, Jno., carpenter
Pendred, Willm., flax-dresser
Patridge, Daniel, cordwr.
Page, Jno., farmer
Page, Willm., senr., cordwr.
Perring, Jno., servant
Paget, Gabriel, cordwr.
Page. Joshua, do.
Pattison, Joseph, farmers son
Riley, Wm., chaise-driver, Hind
Russel, Jno., collar-maker
Revel, Jno., currier
Roberts, Jno., cooper
Reynolds, Joseph, heel-maker
Rowkins, Thos., baker
Rutlidge, Francis, glazier
Rodick, Archibald, draper
Riley, Thos., do.
Robertson, Charles, farmer

⟨Reynolds, Benjamin, cordwr.⟩
Rowlidge, Thos., butcher
Robertson, James, farmer
Randel, Jno., cordwr.
Reynolds, Richd., taylor
Ripponer, Joseph, cordwr.
Reed, Ebenezer, do.
Roberts, Edwd., do.
Robertson, John, weaver
Robertson, John, farmer
Robertson, Joseph, do.
Robertson, Saml., do.
Sikes, Charles, servant
Sikes, John, do.
Sanders, Thos., currier
Sikes, Joseph, cordwr.
Smith, John, do.
Smith, John, victulr.
Stevens, Willm., barber
Sharman, Saml., cordwainer
Sloane, John, lace-man
Swales, Willm., labourer
Shipley, Richd., baker
Swetman, Willm., stay maker
Simons, miller
Smith, Willm., servant
Smith, Willm., glover
Stevens, Saml., do.
Simonds, Humphry, butcher
Spencer, Jno., cordwr.
Sayer, Simon, butcher
Stevens, Jno., servant
Sanders, Thos., weaver.
Somes, James, farmer
Skillit, Robt., labr.
Somerly, Wm., Ch. Coles's servt
Sanders, James, weaver
Sheffield, John, mason
Sikes, George, servant
Somerly, Wm., weaver
Simson, James, cordwr.
Stevens, Jno., do.
Trench, Jno., dyer
Taylor, Thos., cordwr.
Tewis, Jno., horsler
Tilley, Thos., cordwr.
Turland, Nathl., butcher
Turland, Francis, butcher
Tester, Jno., pipe-maker
Tewis, Jno., labr.
Trolley, Jno., shop-keeper
Trolley, Saml., lace man
Tewis, Edlock, weavr.
Tomlinson, Coles, currier

Richard Knowls ⎤
Steven Meares ⎥   farmers
Leonard Teer   ⎬   servants
Thomas Ruff   ⎥
John Godfrey   ⎦

James Tomlin, constable.

LOWICK

A list of persons liable to serve in the militia for the parish of Lowick, December 7th. 1777.

John Hodges, tanner
James Eaton, miller
⟨Smll. Morehen, servant, very short and very splaid footed⟩
Richard Walden, labourer
⟨Walter Bradly, disabled lost one finger⟩
Smll. Olive, mason
Smll. Knight, farmer
Thos. Crawly, servant
John Coleson, farmer
Chas. Bird, keeper
Ed. Barker, labourer
Thos. Barker, taylor
⟨Thos. Darnel, gardener⟩
Jno. Hodges, blacksmith
Thos. Baxter, labourer
Wm. Bird, labourer, has been a solger in the reagulers and has served
     as a subtute
⟨Wm. Watts, mason⟩
⟨Danll. Semak, shop keeper⟩
⟨Stephen Whitchurch, shopkeeper, he is not rite in his head⟩
Charles Bradly, carpainter
⟨Wm. Waples, thirdbarer⟩
John Wilding, baker
Thos. Cradock, labourer
Jno. Bradly, junr., carpainter
Wm. Simson, servant
Thos. March, labourer
Jno. March, ditto
Robt. March, ditto
Danll. Wells, thirdbarer
Gilbert Swiniset, servant
Wm. Newton, farmer
Wm. Sikes, servant
Robt. Danes, labourer
⟨Natt. Bales, lost a finger⟩
⟨Jno. Luck, thurdbarer⟩
Thos. Day, servant
Thos. Spencer, farmer
Joseph Coleson, Spencer's man
John East, Mark Day's man
⟨Jno. Bales, labourer, married a widow woman who has 3 children and
     one by him⟩
Robt. Bradly, blacksmith

⟨Robt. Elmer, prentice⟩
⟨Wm. Bradly, prentice⟩
Jos. Medows, labourer

Jno. Wells, constable.

SLIPTON

Slipton milita list.

⟨John Smith, famer son⟩
Joseph Battes, famer son
Samuel Battes, coard winder
Thomas Hervey, labour
⟨Thomas Fellows, labour⟩

Henery Ruff, labour
William Billing, servant
Robert Fox, servant
James Battes, servant

Wm. Billing, constabl.

SUDBOROUGH

December ye 10, 1777.   A list of men for the parish of Sudborough.

Mr. John Patirick, farmer
Mr. John Tebbutt, farmer and
    church wardin
Mr. Saunders Tebbutt, farmer
Mr. John Worthington, farmer
    and tax gather
Mr. Richard Lawford, farmer
Mr. Perkines, geame keeper
Jarves Worthington, farmer son
James Fox, millers son
John Jackson, shoemaker
William Jackson, shoemaker
Thomas Jackson, sheeperd

illegible Cook, labouror
John Day, mason
William Folkner, labouror
Thomas Smith, labouror
Simon Stevens, labouror
John Mears, labouror
Thomas Waldin, labouror
William Wadd, sarvnt
Thomas Ward, sarvent
Thomas Lee, sarvent
Jonathan Spriges, sarvent
Moses Aryes, singel man

William Haseldon, constable.

TWYWELL

Twywell millitta list.

John Eaton, grazer
Thos. Bulling, grazer
Wm. Percival, heelmaker
John Blackwell, blacksmith
John Coleman, labrough
Wm. Skempton, hempdresser
Robt. Peach, butcher
James Percival, shoumaker
Thos. Archer, baker
Wm. Abbot, plastrer
Wm. Abbot, carpenter
Saml. Hews, shoumaker
Edward Phips, labrough
John Cox, servant
Wm. Jacks, servant
Thos. Steevens, servant
John Foster, ale keeper
James Harford, servant

John Harley, servant
⟨John Scriven, rector⟩
⟨Thos. Knight, constable⟩
⟨John Harison, third brug⟩
⟨John Percival, lame⟩
⟨John Lancom, drawn the time
    before⟩
⟨Frances Skempton, drawn last
    time⟩
⟨James Abbot, a prentice⟩
⟨Mathew Baker, a prentice⟩
⟨Thos. Nobels, three children,
    poor⟩
⟨Frances Abbot, lame⟩
⟨Frances Eaton, three children.
    poor⟩
⟨Ritchard Bates, three children,
    poor⟩

⟨Joseph Duke, three children, poor⟩

⟨John Parker, not sharp⟩
⟨Joseph Crackstone, lame⟩

Thos. Knight, Twywell constable.

WARKTON

1777. A list of the names of them who are liable to serve in the militia for the parish of Warketon.

Gorge Cave, farmer
John Branson, servant
John Ward, miler
Thomas Routhon, servant
William Sturgis, farmers son
Thomas Tebat, shepard
Edward Panter, shepard
William Marshal, servant
John Kirk, farmer
Abraham Rawson, servant
Francis Stevns, carpintor
Thomas Meadows, wevor
John Craft, servant
William Wiliees, servant
John Beane, laberor

John Cave, farmor son
William Long, servant
Moses Groves, servant
William Burditt, farmor son
Henry Burditt, butcher
Joseph Wright, wever
Samuell Wright, servant
John Panter, shepard
Thomas Edis, servant
Joseph March, labror
John Tebot, servant
John Cox, servant
⟨Samuell Riminton, but one eye⟩
⟨Robert *illegible*, bad state of helth⟩

Samuell Cave and Thomas Kirk, hedbarows.
Edward Brampton, constable.

If any one thinks them selvs agrieved the may make thire apeal at the justis is meeting at the Whighthear in Kettring on Wensday next: 10th. of Decmbir. After wards no apeal will be heard.

WOODFORD

1777. A list of their names to serve as militia men in the parish of Woodford.

Will. Wells, servant
Richd. Britten, servant
John Amey, servant
Will. Dickence, servant
Will. Cosford, servant
Will. Barns, shue maker
Ephrim Brawn, servant
Danel Humpry, weaver
John Day, mason
Saml. Cheney, tealer
Richd. Beatles, labourer
Will. Ficher, inn keeper
John Abbut, capender
Will. Abbut, capender
George Hardick, servant
Will. Neler, black smith
Tho. Harise, black smith
Will. Musket, servant

John Ausbun, servant
Will. Hicks, baker
⟨John Wood, labourer⟩
Will. Wood, labourer
Will. Abour, tealer
Will. Gun, inn keeper
Will. Askew, capender
Tho. Teat, labourer
⟨John Cutbud, hard of hearing⟩
⟨Tho. Amey, single eye⟩
John Humpry, week eyes
Will. Simson, paper maker
James Bales, servant
James Marten, servant
Henry Richason, labourer
John Cuper, servant
Joab Sofard, labourer
Jacob Gun, sarvent

John Brawn, constable.

KINGS SUTTON HUNDRED

Astwell & Falcutt	8	Middleton Cheney	104
Aynho	76	Newbottle	38
Old Brackley	16	Radstone	10
Brackley St. James	65	Steane	3
Brackley St. Peter	53	Stuchbury	3
Chacombe	36	Syresham	39
Croughton	33	Thenford	17
Culworth	48	Thorpe Mandeville	10
Evenley	37	Warkworth	42
Farthinghoe	22	Wappenham	46
Helmdon	38	Whitfield	23
Hinton in the Hedges	18		
Kings Sutton	90		914
Marston St. Lawrence	39		

Apprentice	2	Grazier	8
Baker	19	Grocer	1
Barber	1	Hatter	1
Blacksmith	14	*Illegible*	2
Butcher	21	Joiner	6
Carpenter	22	Labourer	177
Chair-maker	1	Law	1
Chaise-man	1	Maltman	4
Chandler	2	Maltster	6
Cooper	4	Mason	13
Currier	2	Miller	5
Dairyman	1	No trade given	177
Dealer	2	Servant	186
Draper	1	Shepherd	5
Endholder	4	Shoemaker	20
Esquire	3	Stay-maker	3
Excise officer	1	Surveyor	1
Farmer	83	Tailor	14
Farmer's son	3	Weaver	18
Farrier	2	Weaver (plush)	5
Fellmonger	2	Weaver (shag)	6
Flax-dresser	3	Wheelwright	10
Framework-knitter	30	Whittawer	1
Gardener	1	Wool-comber	11
Gentleman	7		
Glover	1		914

ASTWELL and FALCUTT

A list of the mens names and their occupations for the hamlett of Astwell and Falcutt made by me John Edmunds, constable.

William Brown, farmer   John Jorns, sarvent

Bongeman Blackwell, labeour
Thomas Cad, labeour
Thomas Bayliss, labeour

Thomus Pollard, sarvant
⟨Thomas Jerroms, labeour⟩
Thomas Kilpin, sarvant

John Edmunds, constable.

AYNHO

A list of all men usually and at this time dwelling within the constable-wick of Aynho and Walton made December the 6th 1777.
bettwen ye age of 18 & 45 years.

Wm. Merry, miller
John Letch, farmer
Joseph Smith
Edward Smith
Peter Smith
⟨Mathew Borton, labour,
    7 children⟩
John Haynes, servant
Wm. Allcock, wheelwright
Sam. Goude, carpender, 1 child
John Howes, labour
⟨John Turvey, labour, 3 children⟩
⟨Edwd. Kelleridge, labour,
    6 children⟩
⟨Joseph Tarry, labour, 3 children⟩
Wm. Buckler, labour 2 children
James Betts, labour, 2 children
⟨Wm. Righton, labour,
    4 children⟩ past age
⟨John Watts, blacksmith,
    4 children⟩
⟨Saml. *illegible*, labour,
    4 children⟩
⟨John French, labour, 6 children⟩
⟨Wm. Seawell, mason, 4 children⟩
John Bridge, labour
Jethro Eelley
⟨Tim. Hall, labour, 4 children⟩
⟨Thos. Claydon, servant, hard
    of hearing⟩
⟨Thos. Gregory, labour,
    4 children⟩
Thos. Walker, wheelwright
⟨Thos. Marsh, shoumaker,
    bussen⟩
⟨Wm. Bull, labour, 3 children⟩
Thos. Steel, labour, 1 child
John Bailey, servant
⟨Wm. Wattson, labour,
    3 children⟩
⟨John Staple, servant⟩
John Handcock, taylour,
    2 children

⟨John Buckingham, labour,
    4 children⟩
⟨Richd. Chilton, labour,
    6 children⟩
⟨John Goude, carpender⟩
Robert Walton, servant
Thos. Miller, servant
Wm. Whidby, servant
⟨Tim. Halbird, baker⟩
⟨Thos. Silver, labour, 3 children⟩
Richd. Terry, labour, 1 child
⟨Zach. Dolton, labour,
    5 children⟩
Wm. Watts, blacksmith, 1 child
Wm. Simson, servant
Phillip Treadwell, servant
Richd. Hollier, servant
Thos. Treadwell, servant
⟨Edwd. Spires, carpender,
    4 children⟩
Henry Dry, cooper
Joseph Wagstaff, weaver
⟨Wm. Turner, labour, 3 children⟩
John Collins, labour, 1 child
John Taylour, servant
John Pollard, servant
James Coates, baker
John Endall, malster
George Wheatton, baker
James Snellson, labour
John Nickolls, labour
Edwd. Baylis, servant
John Merry, servant
⟨John Cosse, servant and heard
    of hearing⟩
Wm. Balding, servant
Chris. Shires, servant
Wm. Cross, servant
Thos. Goodyer, labour,
    2 children
Edwd. Bygrave, butcher
John Alday, servant

These have bean drawn:

⟨Thos. Bygrave, malster⟩
⟨Richd. Claridge, servant⟩
⟨Richd. Ansty, labour⟩

⟨Wm. Balding, labour⟩
⟨Wm. Callaway, labour⟩
⟨Fra. Collins, carpender⟩
⟨Wm. Knatt, blacksmith⟩

The day of appeal is on Monday the eight of this month at Throp and all persons who shall think themselves aggrieved may then appeal and that no appeal will be afterward received.

The Constable desire them who think to make an appeal to let him know to night and for them to be at Throp by ten o clock to morrow morning before the list is given in.

OLD BRACKLEY

December 5th 1777. A list of all the person in the constablewick of Old Brackley in the county of Northampton that are liable to serve for militia men are as follow.

James Bating, serv.
Edward Tanner, serv.
Henry Garett, serv.
David Corby, serv.
⟨John Billing, serv.⟩
Sam. Seckinton, serv.
Benj. Tanner, labr.
⟨Edward Beere, labr.⟩

Charles Nind, labr.
Wm. Pollard, labr.
George Buttler, labr.
⟨Wm. Kilby, labr.⟩
Wm. Archer, labr.
John Minnil, labr.
Tho. Watson, currier
Wm. Boneham, labr.

John Nichols, constable.

The day of appeal will be on Munday the eightth day of December next 1777 at Thorpe and all persons who shall think themselves aggrieved may then appeal and that no appeal will afterwards received.

BRACKLEY ST. JAMES

A list of all persons betwen the ages of eighteen and forty five years in the parish of Brackley St. James's to be drafted as millitta men &c.

Edwd. Jones, gent.
Edwd. Ridgeway
Thos. Durrant
John Lathbury
Richd. Howard
Joseph Grigery
Thos. Green
Ezrh. Norton
William Holloway
John Walton
Wm. Warner
Jonathan Carpenter
Richd. Blaby
Wm. Daniel
Edwd. Tuckey
Thos. Perrin
John Painter

Mr. John Yates
Wm. Paxton
Edwd. Wills
John Timbs
Robt. East
Thos. Layton
⟨Wm. Lamprey⟩
Mr. John Burrows
Mr. Oldfield, officr. of excise
Thos. Tuckey
John Wootton
Wm. Steedon
James Warr
John Jecock
Wm. Robins
Wm. Knibbs
John French

John Mobbs
Richd. Buckley
Wm. Savin,
John Neal
⟨Richd. Neal⟩
James Blackwell
John Blackwell
Daniel Langstone
Thos. Lathbury
Richd. Bannard
John Parrish
Mr. Robt. Olley
Wm. Stanley
James Wagstaff
Wm. Heath
Francis French

John Evans
Geo. Thompson
Wm. Whitehead
Wm. Parker
John Shelton
Wm. Whitmore, joynor
James Morris
Benjm. Morris
Thos. Hawkins
⟨Thos. Miller⟩
Wm. Durrant
James Lathbury
Saml. Boarman
⟨Wm. Whitmore, barber⟩
Henery Robbins

Wm. Cave, constable.

N.B. The day of appeal is on Monday the eighth day of December 77 at Thorpe.

BRACKLEY ST. PETER

December 5th 1777. A list of the names of all the persons in the constable-wick of the parish of St. Peters New Brackley in the county of Northampton that are liable to serve for militia men are as follow.

Thomas Mander, servant
Joseph Fenemore, staymaker
Tho. Stuchfield, servant
John Osborn, laberour
Obadiah Robbins, laborour
John Coles, labr.
James Coles, labr.
Robt. Carpenter, a carpenter
John Lock, labr.
Mich. Russel, surveyor
Thos. Blencowe, baker
Tho. Dawkins, labr.
Joseph Barrett, wheelwright
⟨Martain Barnfill, taylor⟩
⟨William Tuckey, servant⟩
Wm. Beck, blacksmith
Richard Bowerman, slatter
Paul Williams, law
Richard Carpenter, a carpenter
Edmd. Carpenter, a carpenter
George Minturn, labr.
⟨Joseph Pollard, labr.⟩
Saml. North, farmer
John Layton, joyner
Wm. Lathbury, butcher
Joseph King, blacksmith
John Wells, servant

Tho. Taylor, junr.
⟨Richd. Wootton, mason⟩
William Ridge, currier
John Nickinson, labr.
John Simpkins, servant
Thomas Toy, servant
John Butterfield, gent.
John Butterfield, junr., gent.
Charles Matthus, servant
Robert Bartlett, farmer
Tho. Bannard, carpenter
James Grove, labr.
Tho. Bedford, labr.
William Nichols, wheelwright
Wm. Bannard, carpenter
Wm. Vicars, shepherd
Wm. Tucker, labr.
Tho. Webster, labr.
Wm. Milwood, mason
John Bull, chandler
Wm. Bowton, servant
Tho. Bartlett, felmonger
Wm. George, journeyman do.
George Milwood, mason
John Hall, baker
Thomas Smith, farrier

James Walter, constable.

The day of appeal will be on Munday the eighth day of December next

1777 at Thorpe and all persons who shall think themselves aggrieved may then appeal and that no appeal will be afterwards received.

CHACOMBE

Northamptonshire Decemr. 6th 1777. A list of the malitia men in the parish of Chalcomb.

Alban Bull, gent.
Willm. Herbage, farmer
Charles Chinner, do.
Willm. Gibbard, do.
Jobe Sachwell, miller
Willm. Jessop, baker
Wyatt Hancock, framework
   nitter
Willm. Bazely, do.
Thos. Emery, do.
Richd. Reader, do.
Robert Shepherd, do.
Willm. Bradly, do.
Willm. Middleton, plushweaver
Nathanel Blencow, do.
Robert Jeffs, do.
Jno. Walker, do.
Thos. Rogers, do.
Joseph Warner, carpender

Jno. Warner, do.
James Jarvis, labourer
Michael Pratt, do.
Jno. Dale, do.
Willm. Wheeler, do.
Richd. Abbets, do.
Joseph Hertwell, do.
Walter Day, servant
Jno. Wilsdon, do.
Willm. Wesbury, do.
Jno. Stanley, do.
Samuel Bloxham, do.
Jno. Millnes, do.
Willm. Townsend, do.
Petter Taylor, do.
Willm. Perrey, do.
Edward Clifford, do.
Jno. Lampery, woolcoomer

Michael Bennet, constable.

CROUGHTON

A true list of all ye inhabitance of ye parish of Croughton, (to ye best of my knowledge) that are of age and capable to serve in ye militia.

Robt. Hopcraft, farmer
Richard Wakling, servant
Thos. Addams, servant
Richard Cox, servant
Richard Skilman, labourer
Thos. Thornton, taylour
Willm. Flowers, farmer son
John Flowers, farmer son
Mathew Hinton, baker
John Tayler, carpinter
Willm. Causbey, labourer
Willm. Wood, servant
Thos. Morris, blacksmith
Willm. Bazley, labourer
⟨John South, farmer son, hard
   of hearing⟩
Thos. Crow, servant
⟨John Lake, servant, inferm⟩

Joseph Dumbleton, labourer
Willm. Russel, gardiner
John Jones, carpinter
⟨Robert Addington, inferm⟩
Richard Arnold, labourer
⟨Henry Barton, shepherd, inferm⟩
Richard Allday, weaver
Thos. Wakling, servant
⟨John Nurding, servant, inferm⟩
Joseph Temple, labourer
James Lamberd, labourer
John Tappling, weaver
Richard Howse, labourer
Willm. Chambers, labourer
⟨Willm. Buckingham, labourer,
   inferm⟩
⟨Willm. House, labourer, inferm⟩

John Tibbits, constable.

CULWORTH

A list of the men of the parish of Culworth in the county of Northampton from 18 to 45 years of age taken the 7th of Decr. 1777.

John Mander, farmer
Thos. Roberts, labourer
Debroux Wall, butcher
Wm. Adams, cordwainer
⟨Thos. Wigson, labr.⟩
John Bourton, servt.
Christopher Needle, servt.
Thos. Jessop, baker
Samuel Gibbs, servt.
Wm. Belcheir, grasier
John Dean, groser
Wm. Walesby, cordwainer
Richd. Law, carpenter
Thos. Jessop, grasier
Moses Jessop, grasier
Richd. Lathbury, miller
John Jones, taylor
Edwd. Bateman, grasier
Moses Bateman, grasier
John Wheeler, cordwainer
Wm. Turrell, labourer
George Humfrey, labourer
⟨Thos. Wells, butcher, lame⟩
Thos. Daniel, labourer

John Abel, cordwainer
⟨Thos. Abel, cordwainer⟩
John Baylis, grasier
Daniel Dalton, cordwainer
Joseph Bloxham, servt.
John Humfrey, labourer
Thos. Jones, cordwainer
Samuel Jones, farmer
Richd. Neal, grasier
Wm. Seemish, servt.
Peeter Furnace, servt.
Thos. Needle, chairmaker
Thos. Thornton, butcher
Robt. Tucker, farmer
Samuel Judge, servt.
Wm. Ward, blacksmith
John Egleston, labourer
Samuel Piddington, farmer
⟨Richd. Thomas, *illegible*⟩
Jonas Hawks, blacksmith
Joseph Turner
⟨Samuel Douglas, *illegible*⟩
Wm. Smith, servant
John Ward, sarvant

Thos. Wimbush, cunstable.

EVENLEY

A list of the militia of Evenly.

Thomas Hopcraft
William Walton
William Hopcraft
Bengman Hopcraft
William Paintr
Henry Paintr
Samuell Hart
John Basset
John Pusel
Joseph Holton
Sill Hont
John Smith
George Smith
Thomas Bodenton
Robbard Abbots
Thomas Weaver
William Basset
Thomas Line, shopard
Henry East

Richard Smith
Thomas Weatly
William Weatly
Edward Moren
Joseph Cras
John Samons
Joseph Hivel
John Huse
William Burch
Jobe Lambord
James, Mr Walton shay man
John, Mrs Hopcraft shopard
⟨*illegible*⟩
William Mayho
⟨Henry Side⟩
⟨James Holton⟩
⟨George Basset⟩
William Palmer

Wm. Holton, constable.

FARTHINGHOE

Farthingoe Northamptom Shiear to wit. Decemr. ye 8th 1777. A list of persons from the aige of eighteen to forty five years.

John Right
Wm. Clarige
Nathanl. Clarige
Nathaniel Bowers
Wm. Right
John Austin
John George
Hantany Buttler
Samewel Baldwin
Wm. Hinton
John Barott

John Paige
Wadkins Paige
Joseph Truss
Daniel Petefer
Thos. Buttler
Richad. Jarvis
Wm. Hartwell
Danil Adams
Thos. Ralins
Thos. Hartwell
John Hiorns

John Brotherton, constabel.

HELMDON

A list of persons liable to serve as militia men for Helmdon ⟨lists⟩

Thomas Hinton, farmer
George Hinton, farmer
Willm. Camption, sarvant
Thomas Stevens, weaver
Josiah Drake, weaver
Willm. Gibbs, weaver
Willm. Hanson, juner, carpinter
Roberd Hindes, beacker
Thomas Branson, masoner
Uriah Gilberd, laberer
Richard Shortland, juner, famer
Edward Shortland, famer
John Coock, sarvant
John Blinckow, boocher
Willm. Thomason, boocher
John Hawkes, sarvant
John White, laberer
Thimothy Needle, sarvant
John Adkins, famer

⟨James Hindes, sarvant⟩
Joseph Stevens, laberer
⟨John Kinch, staymaker⟩
Thomas Edmunds, maltster
Luke Fairbrother, famer
Willm. Flowers, sarvant
Willm. Harris, sarvant
Thomas War, beacker
Willm. Caves, beacker
Nathell Blinckow, masonder
Willm. Pratt, farier
Willm. Powell, boocher
George Powell, dealer
Willm. Bailes, masonder
John Bailes, laberer
Thomas Fairbrother, famer
Willm. Lacey, shewmaker
⟨John Lacey, wheel rite⟩
Petter Warrin, famer

Anthony Drake, constable.

HINTON IN THE HEDGES

Decr. 5th 1777. A list of all men useally dwelling in the parish of Hinton to serve in the militia.

John Battes, farmer
John Arnol, servant
Edward Witton, servant
William Bazley, farmer
Lathy Bazley, farmer
John Wilson, farmer
Thomas Oliver, servant
Thomas King, servant

John Wilkins, laboure
Thomas Besseand, farmer
John Besseand, farmer
Richard Harris, servant
William Lines, servant
Henery Blincow, laboure
Thomas Hunt, laboure
⟨John Peach, farmer⟩

⟨James Mobs, black smit, lame⟩   George Seccinton, servant

Thos. Wilson, constable.

The day of appeal will be Decr. the eight a Thorpe.

KINGS SUTTON

A list of all the men in the parish of Kingsutton betwext the age of 18 & 45 years made by Joseph Sodon & Richard Jennengs constabls.

Willm. Goffe, farmer
Willm. Jurams, sarvant
Willm. Curnock, end holder
Willm. Tibbetts, molt man
John Hayns, blacksmith
Lo. Hall, labour
Tho. Side, labour
Sam. Walter, labour
Edwd. Wyatt, sheephard
⟨John Wyatt, labour⟩
John Sachwell, stay maker
Ben. Reeder, end holder
John Mobley, sarvant
Joseph King, labour
Willm. Sodon, blacksmith
⟨Jon. Brocklis, labour⟩
Tho. Thoms, farmer
⟨John Blincow, sarvant⟩
Robert French, bucher
Edwd. Watson, labour
Willm. Kerby, cooper
⟨Robert Grimby, molt man, bad eye⟩
Jon. Capenter, molt man
Tho. Lett, mason
John Cockshall, labour
Petter Pageter, labour
Willm. Clark, bucher
Tho. Ridgeway, farmer
Tho. Gibord, farmer
Willm. Parish, farmer
Willm. Higgs, capenter
Willm. Kerby, end holder
Tho. Tibbetts, molt man
James Paker, labour
Tho. Holding, labour
Willm. Weight, labour
Robert Pageter
Richard Jennengs, end holder
Nathanel Smith, labour
⟨John Higham, labour⟩
⟨Tho. Picher, labour, beley brock⟩
George Coles, labour

Henry Hockens, sarvant
Willm. Stanton, labour
Willm. Upston, sarvant
Willm. Combs, sarvant
Edwd. Johnson
Henery East, sarvant
Tho. Jeptes, sarvant
Jon. Molcher, sarvant
Robert Wyatt, farmer
Richard Tayler, labour
Richard Fathers, mason
Tho. Golby
Edward Densey
John Wootton, taylor
James Simson, miller
Elias Simson, miller
Willm. Blackwell, labour
Tho. Ward, labour
Tho. Pettefer, sarvant
Frances Blake
Jon. Wayman
John Packson, sarvent
⟨George Capenter, prentis⟩
⟨Willm. Pain, prentis⟩
⟨John Addington, 3 children⟩
⟨Willm. Templer, 3 children⟩
⟨Willm. Wilkins, 3 children⟩
⟨Wetter Hayns, 3 children⟩
⟨James Nevel, 3 children⟩
⟨Tho. Haddon, 3 children⟩
⟨Joseph Edwards, 3 children⟩
⟨Willm. Bucher, 3 children⟩
⟨Jon. Holton, 3 children⟩
⟨Richard Humfries, 3 children⟩
⟨George Swain, 3 children⟩
⟨Tho. Lambert, 3 children⟩
⟨Jon. Smith, 3 children⟩
⟨John Leak, 3 children⟩
⟨Tho. Blincow, 3 children⟩
⟨Willm. Sumerton, 3 children⟩
⟨James Garner, 3 children⟩
⟨Marten Dale, 3 children⟩
⟨Joseph Charmbling, 3 children⟩
⟨Sam. Betts, 3 children⟩

⟨Willm. Blackwell, 3 children⟩   ⟨Jon. Cooker, deaf⟩
⟨Willm. Mumford, 3 children⟩   James Witte, ⟨lame⟩

Joseph Sodon, constables.

December 8 a day of apeall at Thropmandvel.

MARSTON ST. LAWRENCE

A list of people propper to serve as militia men in the parish of Marston St. Lawrence in the county of Northampton, by Paynton Sharrock, constable.

Saml. Blencowe, esqr.			⟨Saml. Hanwell⟩
Farmers	Mr. Willm.		Jno. Handley
	Wamsley	Butchers	Thos. Whitton
	Thos. Cherry		⟨Jno. Stanton,
	Thos. Blencowe		senr.⟩
	Timothy		Jno. Stanton, junr.
	Blencowe	Wevers	Jno. Hands
	⟨Willm. Jeffs⟩		Jno. Jerves
	Richd. Chester	Bakers	Nathl. Blencowe
	Willm. Bannard		Willm. Cherry
Servants	Willm. Rhodes	Labourers	George Rogers
	Edwd. Brownsil		Willm. Brownsil
	Thos. Whilton		Thos. Gardner
	George Aris		Thos. Gee
	Thos. Brown		James Chester
	Jno. Horwood		Jno. Blencowe
Shewmakers	Simon Spires		Chas. Clements
	Thos. Barrott		Willm. Isham
	Thos. Brooks		Willm. Newman
Woolcomers	⟨Willm. Hall⟩		Jno. Humfris
	Richd. Evington		James Bull

The day of appeal will be on Monday the 8th day of Decr. 1777 at the Three Conies Inn in Thorpe, and no appeal will be afterwards receved.

MIDDLETON CHENEY

A list of proper persons to serve as militia men for the parish of Middleton Cheney.

John Arris, farmer
Robord Arris, farmer
John Cocks, sarvant
William Mold, sarvant
Jonathan Dumbleton, sarvant
⟨William Clark, sarvant⟩
Matthew Harrod, blacksmith
William Garner, jienor
Thomas Golby, whileright
John Righton, jienor
John Garnear, farmear
Richard Gaskins, sarvant

Thomas Buckingham, frame work nitter
⟨John Miller, sarvant⟩
Samuell Arbeg
Games Bull, masen
⟨Daved Barret, shag weaver⟩
⟨John Rodnight, glover⟩
Matthew Wise, frame work nitter
⟨Gorge Tuckey, frame work nitter⟩
William Lam, shag weaver

Samuell Burchal, shag weaver
Joseph Miller, frame work nitter
Thomas Prufe, whit taw
John Pettefer, frame work nitter
William Tomkins, farmer
Richard Pinfold, blacksmith
Robord Wille, flax drecr
Samuell Merivale, sarvant
Thomas Jufes, frame work nitter
John Jufes, frame work nitter
Joseph Garret, frame work nitter
Joseph Gresley, frame work nitter
John Warters, frame work nitter
⟨William Chamblen, shag weaver⟩
William Gaskens, frame work nitter
Joseph Grant, sarvant
Henery Flowers, sarvant
William Garner, shag weaver
Samuell Lock, shag weaver
William Bull, farmer
Samuell Lord, copper
Harrey Medos, laboar
Joseph Marren, frame work nitter
John Webster, jinor
Thomas Charles, laboar
Thomas Penn, farmer
William Penn, molster
Abarom Glover, sarvant
Thomas Pinfold, sarvant
Thomas Lock, frame work nitter
Thomas Bolton, flaxdresser
Games Cartear
Edward Hartlett, backer
Games Hobkins
John Watts, frame work nitter
John Falkinbridge, frame work nitter
John White, frame work nitter
Thomas Golby, frame work nitter
Robord Clemons, frame work nitter

Thomas Clemons, frame work nitter
Robord Penn, wool commer
Robord Charles, labor
Wolter Humpres, frame work nitter
John Middleton, weaver
Thomas Jinkens, weavor
Thomas Pettefor, cord winder
William Penn, weavor
Thomas Williams, whileright
William Flowers, sarvant
Robord Bricknell, sarvant
Richard Lock, frame work nitter
Thomas Braddley, frame work nitter
Richard Garret, malster
Matthew Neall, sarvant
Samuell Taylor, sarvant
Edward Cach, sarvant
Thomas Golby, farmer
William Shulwell, flaxdresser
Owen Buckingham, buchar
Richard Wise, farmer
Thomas Hornear, buchear
William Merivale, farmer
John Watts, sarvant
John Taylor, sarvant
Robord Penn, farmer
Nickles Yong, labor
⟨William Hornear, taylor⟩
William Williams, farmer
William Toay, sarvant
⟨James Lock, frame work nitter⟩
Thomas Eingram, sarvant
John Smith, woll commer
Samuell Smith, sarvant
Edward Humpris, weaver
William Giles, sarvant
John Penn, farmer
Humprey Penn, farmer
Samuell Wilkens, masen
Parcy Gaskens, frame work nitter
Gorge Stockley
Zacakariah Jordien, whelright
William Golby, savant
Games Trentom, sarvant

John Wise, constable.

This is to give you notice that the day of appeal his on Monday next at the sine of the Thre Cones at Throp Mamdifold, and that no appeal will be afterwards received.

NEWBOTTLE

December 8 1777 A list of militia men Newbottle parish, Northampton Shire.

Wm. Cox, servant
Wm. Raubuns, servant
Thomas Buckingham, servant
Thomas Howkins, servant
Aran Enock, servant
Wm. Elceton, labor
Thomas Wyat, farmer
Neley Wyat, farmer
Eward Wakelin, labor
Matthew Side, carfender
Wm. Side, carfender
Wm. King, carfender
Roberd Johnson, baker
Edward Howard, servant
John Franklin, servant
Wm. Jdge, servant
Edward Fathers, servant
Edward Wats, labor
Wm. Belcher, baker

Wm. Baker, labor
Wm. Cad, labor
John Soden, labor
James Kerry, labor
Thomas More, servant
Wm. Taylor, labor
Antoney Cross, labor
Roberd Web, servant
Richard Read, farmer
Richard Hall, farmer
Wm. Hoten, servant
John Shepperd, servant
John Sparrow, servant
Wm. Sparrow, servant
Gorge Gardener, servant
Thomas Pottenger, servant
John Tebe, labor
Thomas Tibets, servant
John Wills ⟨esqer⟩

Wm. Stockley, constable.

RADSTONE

A trew coppy of a list made of all the men between the age of eighteen and forty five that are able to sarve as militia men for the parish of Radston in the county of Northampton and in the hundred of Kingsutton.

William Painter ⎫
John Hadland   ⎬ farmers
Mordecai Wise   ⎭
Bengiman Brun ⎱ labours
Jobe Smith   ⎰

Jonnathan Umfris ⎫
Richard Yates   ⎪
Tho. Noris   ⎬ sarvants
Tho. Painter   ⎪
John Haynes   ⎭

Dec. 6 1777.
George French, constable.

STEANE

A list of all men usually and at this time dwelling in the constablewick of Stean in the county of Northampton, dated 4th day of December 1777, betwen the age of eaight teen & fortifive.

Mr. Saml. Gee, farmer
Richard Brain, sarvant

Willm. Court, sarvant

Fras. Collins, constable.

STUCHBURY

Kings Sutton Hunderd. A list of the militia for the parish of Stuchbury.

John Curtis, sarvent   ⟨William Edmonds⟩
⟨John Edmonds, subject to fitts⟩

                        Daniel Warren, constable.

SYRESHAM

Decr. the 8th 1777. Northamptonshire to wit. A list of all person residing within the constablewick of Syresham from the ages of eighteen to forty five years who are liable to serve in the militia of the said county.

James Kendal, farmer
James Allen, laber.
John James, ditto.
George Yates, ditto.
Robert Kendal, carpntr
Thomas Allen, laber
Richard Middleton, ditto.
William Middleton, do.
Henry Collison, mason
John Short, cooper
Stephen Pain, laber
John Rawlins, taylor
William Cowley, ditto.
Lawrence Pollard, ditto.
Samuel Southam, ditto.
Edward Jarvis, lunatick
William Wrighton, farmer
John Baldwin, gent.
James Baldwin, cordwainr
John Linnel, malster

Richard Fairbrother
William Bliss, baker
William Bull, butcher
John Flowers, farmer
John Badby, farmer
James Sewell, wheelwright
George Starkey, gent.
George Cowley, laber
James Cowley, carpenter
William Eldridge, farmer
Francis Thomas, cordwainer
William Collison, gent.
John Liddington, laber
Richard Liddington, ditto.
Thomas Wotton, laber
James Whitehead, ditto.
West Green, cordwainer
⟨Thomas Sayar, wheelwright⟩
Job Williams, laber

                        William Baldwin, constable.

THENFORD

A list of the militia in the parish of Thenford 77.

Michell Woodell, esqr.
William Kerred
John Phips
Matthew Habbits
John Fearn
Thomas Elston
John Bannard
John Ninds
Ritchard Law

William Thomkins
William Simson,
Benjeman Golby
George Trentom
Thomas Numan
John Franklin
Thomas Hall
John Broocks

Any person who shall think themselvs aggreved may appeal the eighth day of December nxt at the Three Conees in Thorp as no appeal will be afterwards receved, hearin fail you not.

                        Edward Buswell, constable.

THORPE MANDEVILLE

A list of the names of them that are capeble of sarving as militia-men in the parish of Thorp Mandevill by Edward Taylor constable.

John Golsby, farmer
Edward Golsby, farmer
Edward Carpenter, farmer
Richard Cave, laborer
John Matthews, blacksmith

William Kemp, goyner
William Crass, servant
John Smith, servant
Joseph Tue, servant
Samuell Basley, servant

N.B. This is to give notice that the day of apeal is on Monday, eighth day of this instant at the Thre Coneys and no apeal will be given after.

WAPPENHAM

Decr. 6 1777. A list of their names that are able to sarve in the militia betwen the age of eighteen an forty five in the pariesh of Wapenham in the county of Northampton.

⟨Mr. Charles Fairbrothers, farmer⟩
Mr. Giles Fairbrothers, farmer
John Vison, sarvent
Thos. Warwick, weaver
Thos. Stockley, butcher
Mr. Jno. Shepeard, farmer
Thos. Shepeard, butchear
Richd. Shepeard, butchear
Thos. Matin, sarvent
Wm. Bull, sarvent
Samuel Shepeard, farmer
Wm. Franklin, farmer
George Barnett, dealer
John Cockerill, farmer
Thos. Tolton, tailer
Richd. Maulsbury, coardwainer
Mr. Henry Cockerill, farmer
Joseph Pain, sarvent
⟨Wm. Adames, sarvent⟩
Wm. Pittom, sarvent
Wm. Reeve, labrour
Wm. King, labrour
Thos. Pursell, baker

Thos. Aries, butcher
Thos. Aries, sarvent
John Kingston, woolcomer
Wm. Eaben, coardwainer
John Cogbrock, labrour
James Midlton, mason
Wm. Bragins, tailor
Henry Button, labrour
Mr. Richd. Richardson, drapear
Richd. Bryan, sarvent
⟨Joseph Kingston, comear⟩
Francies Warwick, comear
James Webb, labrour
Richd. Tarrey, labrour
Richd. Spragett, farmer
John Montgomery, farmer
James Adams, labrour
Edwd. Adams, labrour
Wm. Adames, candlear
John French, sarvent
Thos. Giles, labrour, past age
James Witton, labrour
Charles Dyear, comear

John Jones, constable.

The day of appeal is on Monday the eight day of December an that no appeal will be afterward received. Hearin fail not.

WARKWORTH

Warkworth miliata between the ages of eighteen and forty five years.

Wm. Taylor, famer
Wm. Ariss, do.
Ed. Ariss, do.
Henry Hawtwin, greazer

Love Lovet, labour
James Smith, searvant
John Flowers, do.
Wm. Bagley, do.

John Neal, do.
Solomon Petyfor, do.
Samuel Barnes, do.
Wm. Barret, do.
Henry Neal, do.
Joseph Hodgkins, do.
Wm. Nevel, do.
John Trenton, do.
Thos. Nutt, do.
Wm. Hazelwood, do.
Thos. Hebdon, do.
John Crouch, do.
John Hartwell, do.
Henry Gordon, do., black
Wm. Golby, searvent
Wm. Rose, do.
Wm. Southan, do.

Michel Pratt, do., labour
Thos. Pargeter, do.
John Hartwell, do.
John Simkins, do.
Wm. Simkins, do.
Sabin Simkins, do.
Wm. Pain, do.
Richd. Righton, do.
Joseph Baker, do.
Wm. Cosbrook, do.
James Lock, teyler
Frances Wilsdon, weaver
Wm. Jackson, do.
John Adams, do.
Wm. Toy, do.
John Sawer, do.
Charles Esex, do.

Their will be a meeting at the Three Conies in Throp on the 8 day of December next that all persons who shall think themselves agrieved may then appeal and that no day appeal will be afterward received.

John Taylor, constable.

WHITFIELD

A list of the millisha in the parish of Whitfield.

Anthoney Cooper, a farmer
John Phillips, a farmer
Richard Morres, a labour
John Green, a sarvent
Edward Jarves, a cordwinder
John Brown, a tallor
Richard Goodin, labour
John Blackwell, a labour
John Wise, a sarvent
Edward Berrey, a bucher
Thomas Hakings, a sarvent
Bengiman Heretege, a sarvent

Richard Gaskin, a labour
William Allen, a sarvent
⟨West Green, a cordwinder⟩
Edward Fenemer, a labour
George Robens, a labour
Larance Bragins, a labour
William Berrey, a sarvent
John Turvey, a labour
William Hindins, a sarvent
William Kendel, dareman
John Starkey, a labour

Thos. Phillip, constable.

The day of appel is one Mondey the eight day of December at Thrope and after that day no appeal receved.

NAVISFORD HUNDRED

Clapton	6	Titchmarsh	77
Pilton	14	Wadenhoe	41
Stoke Doyle	14		——
Thorpe Achurch	24		247
Thrapston	71		

Apothecary	1	Mason	6
Attorney	1	Mat-maker	2
Baker	3	Miller	3
Barber	2	No trade given	13
Basket-maker	2	Ostler	2
Blacksmith	4	Postboy	3
Brazier	1	Scuttle-maker	1
Breeches-maker	1	Servant	51
Butcher	5	Shepherd	5
Carpenter	10	Shoemaker	13
Clerk	1	Shopkeeper	2
Farmer	25	Smith	1
Farmer & grazier	2	Stay-maker	1
Farmer's son	2	Tailor	4
Gardener	4	Watch-maker	1
Glazier	1	Wheelwright	1
Innkeeper	2	Whip-maker	1
Joiner	1	Wool-comber	3
Labourer	65		——
Maltster	1		247

CLAPTON

A list of ye persons names resideing in ye parrish of Clapton North'ton-shire that are a propper age to serve as militia men, taken by Thos. Todd, constable for ye said parrish, Decbr. 10th, 1777.

Thos. Chapman, gardiner	John More, servant
Francis Noble, sheepherd	John Gray, servant
John Pack, servant	George Hopkins, servant

PILTON

December 11, 1777. Pilton Northamtonshere.

A true lest of the milita men that are liable to sarve.

Benjamin Spencer, farmer	Tho. Jackson, do.
Wm. Richardson, do.	Samuel George, sarvent
James Tomblin, carpenter	John Higings, do.
Nathanael Blodworth, gardenor	Tho. Smith, do.
James Kirby, measson	Robert Stanyan, do.
Tho. Bream, labour	John Muns, do.

John Swale, 5 children, poor   Henry Hutton, 3 children, poor

By me Walter Stretton, constable.

STOKE DOYLE

A list of persons in the parish of Stoke Doyle in ye county of Northampton between ye ages of eighteen & forty five years.

Thos. Smith, junr., farmer &
 graizer
John Pywell, junr., do.
John Redhead, servant
Michael Pepper, do.
Owen Maning, do.
Thos. Perkins, do.
Geo. Rowell, do.

Thos. Petit, do.
John Adams, labourer
⟨Daniel Bries, do.⟩
Thos. Cole, do.
⟨Joseph Bettels, do., 3 children⟩
⟨Saml. Gore, do., 3 children⟩
⟨Thos. Pywell, do., 3 children⟩

If any one thinks themselves agreiv'd: the day of appeal is the 15 day of December instant at the Talbot Inn in Oundle.

THORPE ACHURCH

A list of the names of all persons within the parish of Thorpe Achurch in the county of Northampton that are liable to serve in the militia made this 12th. day of December 1777 by me Mathew Weed, constable.

⟨William Hitchcock, labourer⟩
Thomas Nichols, labourer
Charles Plowright, cordwainer
Samuel Corwain, cordwainer
John Willson, junr., labourer
⟨John Tibbs, baker⟩
William Howkins
Edward Howkins
Josiah Howkins
William Pheasant, junr.,
 shepherd
Thos. Fletton, servant
Edward Cunnington

Jeremiah Lee, junr., servant
Joseph Weed, farmer
John Harlock, labourer
⟨John Tee, labourer⟩
John French, junr., labourer
John Rands, severant
John Coaton, labourer
Joseph Saddington, servt.
Thos. Norton, gardener
William Fortiscue, labourer
Isaac Hubbard, mattmaker
John Hubbard, do.

THRAPSTON

A list of the inhabitance in the parish of Thrapston liable to searve in the militia in and for the county of Northampton.

Thos. Chapman, searvant to Jno. Bland
Richard Tosland, jorneman shooemaker
Mr. Bell, clark to Mr. Yorke
Thos. Smith, sarvent to Mrs. Drage
Wm. Smith, son to Jerimiah labourer
Jno. Adcock, basket maker
Jno. Bates, shooemaker
Mr. Wm. Yorke, aturney at law
Stephen Lockington, carpender

George Jackson, carpender
Richard Lockington, carpender
Jno. Bland, Dukes Head, mason *
Wm. Levart, baker
Henry Lenton, juner, glazer
Jno. Brwce, labourer
Saml. Gess, labourer
⟨Wm. Kendal, journeman blacksmith⟩
Wm. Green, labourer
Wm. Worlidge, basket maker
Richard Bland, mason
Thos. Webb, sarvent to the Revd. Mr. Willan
Thos. Box, journeman whip maker
Edward Swinshead, horsler to ye Queens Head
Robart Burrows, journeman baker
Thos. Bearnard, labourer
Henry Bearnard, labourer
Thos. Rippen, son to Jno. the frmer.
James Rippen, dto. to dto.
Jno. Sanchfeild, jorneman shooemaker
Wm. Griffen, shoemaker
Jno. Vourly, butcher
Jno. Sanderson, journeman blacksmith
Jno. Eaton, shopkeeper
Saml. Eaton, dto.
Jno. Buck, at ye George
Edward Wright, post boy at ye George
Jno. Tarrey, barbour
Henry Leet, apothecary
Rodger Woods, sarvant to Mr. Leet
Christpher Picket, sarvant to Barbour
Jno. Umphrey, watchmaker
Joseph Webbster, journeman joiner
Thos. Gilby, barbour
Jno. Read, at ye Swan
Thos. Britten, horsler to ye Swan
James Wells, stay maker
Charles Marrener, post boy
Wm. Jolley, sarvent to Philip Eaton
Philip Eaton, farmer
Thos. Freeman, son to Mrs. Sanderson
Jno. Wright, journeman shoemaker
Jno. Day, journeman wool cumber to Barbour
Isaac Sutcliff, dto. to dto.
Jno. Preston, dto. to dto.
Henry Langford, shepard to Mr. Collins

Poor men that has three children or more born in wedlock, and the lame [and] not able to sarve

⟨Jno. Hankins, gardenar⟩
⟨Thos. Sharman, labourer⟩
⟨Thos. Beaton, labourer⟩

* A public house named the Duke's Head existed at Thrapston in 1777, and John Bland was the landlord. I owe this information to Mr. P. I. King.

⟨Wm. Curtis, dto.⟩
⟨Thos. Campton, dto.⟩
⟨Danl. Coalman, scutle maker⟩
⟨Thos. Bratenal, labourer⟩
⟨Wm. Abbot, shoemaker⟩
⟨Edward Badger, journeman britches maker⟩
⟨Thos. Phesant, near sited⟩
⟨Jno. Robinson, taylor⟩
⟨Jno. Farrarah, brazor⟩
⟨Thos. Peacock, post boy at ye White Hart⟩
⟨Jno. Vorley, taylor⟩
⟨Wm. Usher⟩
⟨Jno. Scarborough, shepard⟩

Any person that thinks themselves a greeved are desired to appeal at the Talbat Inn in Oundle the 15 day of this instants December, for no appeal will be heard after.

TITCHMARSH

A list of the persons liable to serve for the milita in the parish of Titchmarsh in the county of Northampton.

⟨Mr. John Fowler⟩ farmer,
  drawn befere
Robert Austin
William Gray
John Knighton
Thomas Weed
Robert Coales
John Coales, miller
William Rippen, farmers
William Green
John Bolds
Richard Bolds
Daniel Coales, senor
Thomas Heaps
William Cooper
James Eaton
Thomas Barns
Joseph Dudley, junor
Daniel Coales, junor
Thomas Carley
Austin Eaton, bucher
James Mansell, mason
Edward Mansell, carpenter
Thomas Barfield, cordwinder
James Dyson, wheelright
William Coales, cordwinder
Thomas Davison, blacksmith
John Curtice, baker
⟨John Curwain, cordwinder⟩
Benjamin Blackwell, blacksmith
⟨John Freer, bucher⟩
Richardson Mansell, mason

William Maverslie, labrs.
John Preston
John Mayse
William Smith
Elias Poolley
William Salmon
⟨William Cradock⟩
⟨John Smith, drawn before⟩
Thomas Martin
⟨Robert Richardson⟩
William Tibbot
Lambert Hodson
William Sanders
Samewel Coalman
Thomas Boulton
⟨Joseph Johnson, drawn before⟩
John Dean
Robert Polhead
John Wright
William Smith, maltster
James Nuham, labours
William Adcock
Jonathan Godfrey
William Obey
James Hailes
Robert Martin
⟨James Richardson⟩
James Baker, servants
John Danner
⟨William Todd, not at age⟩
David Green
Richard Webb

William Pettit
John Titman
Edward Lettin
John Breadwel
John Carley
William Freman
Edward Titman

Thomas Preston
Daniel Busiell
Peter Peach
Edward Rippen
⟨Robert Boulton⟩ drawd before
Samewel Green
John Dicks

The day of appeal is the 15th of December 1777, att the Talbot in Oundle and that no other day of appeal will be afterward received.

WADENHOE

Wadenhoe list.

Thomas Chew, farmer
John Chew, ditto
Thomas Wright, labourer
Thomas Holles, butcher
William Nicholes, servant
Thomas Porter, carpenter
Isaca Trayfoot, labourer
Olever Bucket, mason
John Lee, servant
John Davison, labourer
Edward Gray, labourer
Edward Burde, labourer
Joseph Allen, miller
Philip Allen, farmer
William Nickson, servt.
William Stretton, butcher
William Briggs, sert.
John Wagstaff, cordwainer
John Willson, sert.
William Willson, carpenter
John Bell, cordwainer
Henery Eaton, taylor

Daneil Briggs, servt.
Joseph Cumberland, servt.
⟨John Heighton, mason⟩
⟨James Willson, carpenter, deaf⟩
⟨Wm. Smith, labourer, 3 children⟩
⟨James Emmerton, taylor,
   3 children⟩
⟨Wm. Clark, sheaperd, 4 children⟩
⟨William Porter, has served⟩
⟨Tho. Andrew, labourer, 6 child⟩
⟨Tho. Wells, labourer, 3 children⟩
⟨John Ruffe, labourer, 3 children⟩
⟨Thos. Cottingham, labourer,
   5 children⟩
⟨Will. Gray, labourer, 3 child⟩
⟨Will. Elles, carpenter, 3 child⟩
⟨Thos. Edinges, has served⟩
⟨Robert Gray, smith, has served⟩
⟨William Eagle, labourer,
   4 children⟩
⟨John Leader, has served⟩
⟨Will. Foard, carpenter prentice⟩

NOBOTTLE GROVE HUNDRED

Great Brington	101	Nether Heyford	25
Brockhall & Muscott	14	Upper Heyford	15
Bugbrooke	65	Holdenby	12
Chapel Brampton	25	Kislingbury	90
Church Brampton	34	Ravensthorpe	66
Dallington	32	Teeton	16
Duston	46	Upton	12
Flore	92	Whilton	44
East Haddon	58		
Harlestone	82		884
Harpole	55		

Apprentice	4	Husbandman	19
Bailiff	1	*Illegible*	2
Baker	12	Joiner	3
Blacksmith	9	Keeper	1
Blacksmith's servant	1	Labourer	158
Butcher	20	Maltster	4
Butter merchant	1	Mason	12
Carpenter	22	Miller	9
Chair bottomer	1	Miller's servant	1
Clergyman	3	No trade given	82
Cooper	1	Plough-wright	1
Earl	1	Plumber	2
Esquire	3	Quarrey-man	2
Farmer	68	Rag-man	1
Farmer &		Roper	1
churchwarden	1	Sawyer	2
Farmer & grazier	4	Schoolmaster	3
Farmer & overseer		Servant	193
of the poor	2	Shepherd	4
Farmer & surveyor		Sheriff	1
of the highways	1	Shoemaker	36
Farmer's servant	17	Shopkeeper	1
Farmer's son	8	Spinner	1
Framework-knitter	8	Stay-maker	1
Gardener	1	Stone-cutter	4
Gentleman	1	Surgeon	1
Gentleman's servant	3	Surveyor	2
Glover	1	Tailor	18
Grazier	2	Victualler	6
Grocer	2	Weaver	51
Harrateen-maker	1	Wheelwright	5
Harrateen-maker &		White-smith	2
farmer	1	Wool-comber	51
Hemp-dresser	1	Wool-sorter	1
Hilliard	1		
Hosier	1		884

GREAT BRINGTON

Taken by Jno. Walker & Richd. Butlin, constables. Great Brington, Novbr. 28, 1777.

A list of all the inhabitants of the above parish, that are of a proper age to serve in ye militia.

⟨The Revd. James Preedy, clergyman⟩
Thomas Russel, servant
⟨Joseph Elliott, lame⟩
⟨John Adams, labourer, 3 children⟩
Barnard Dunkley, weaver, 3 children
⟨Thos. Elliott, labourer, ditto.⟩
⟨Henry Jollens, labourer⟩
⟨Henry Bottrill, do.⟩
⟨Luke Hancock, do.⟩
⟨Saml. Fisher, do.⟩
⟨Thos. Write, do.⟩
⟨Thos. Dunkley, labourer, 3 children⟩
⟨John Russel, do.⟩
Thos. Jakeman, shoe maker
Richard Manning, labourer
John Webb, husbandman
George Manning, do.
Joseph Goodman, do.
Nathaniel Manning, do.
Tubal-Cain Taylor, do.

Philip Taylor, taylor
Thos. Hewes, labourer
⟨Robt. Maine, thurdborough⟩
Robt. Worley, maison, 3 children
⟨Jonathan Blencow, shoe maker, 3 do.⟩
Edward Wright, mason
Matthew Manning, labourer
⟨Thos. Maine, carpenter, 3 children⟩
⟨Henry Maine, carpenter, aprentice⟩
Thos. Jenkins, labourer
Wm. Claridge, black-smith
Benj. Henson, do.
Thomas Oakley, labourer
Edward Goode ⟨labourer⟩ servant
Edward Moss, servant
John Mailing, labourer
Thos. Mailing, do.
⟨Samuel Jakeman, thurdborough⟩

LITTLE BRINGTON

William Bosworth, servant
⟨Thos. Claridge, labourer (Great Brington) 3 children⟩
Jno. Sumerton, labourer
Wm. Dunkley, husbandman
John Maine, wool-comber
⟨Wm. Ball, carpenter & apprentice⟩
Wm. Hall, labourer
Willm. Gent, carpenter
Thos. Haynes, labourer
John Haynes, do.
⟨John Davis, shoe-maker, 3 children⟩
Thos. Billing, labourer
⟨John Marriott, weaver, 3 children⟩
⟨Thos. Treadgold, labourer, 3 do.⟩
John Billing, servant
Edward Manning, shoemaker

John Packwood, labourer
Nicholis Marriott, labourer
John Redley, do.
Wm. Treadgold, do.
George Treadgold, do.
Richar. James, servant
⟨Joseph Treadgold, labour, 3 children⟩
Wm. Botteril, labourer
⟨Thos. Goodman, woolcomber, 3 children⟩
⟨Geo. England, carpenter, 3 children⟩
⟨Thos. Gent, carpenter, disabled⟩
Thos. Pulley, shoemaker
⟨George Capel, do., 6 children⟩
Robert Brown, malster
Thos. Manning, labourer
⟨Richard *illegible*, shoemaker, 3 children⟩

NOBOTTLE

John Hawgood, husbandman
George Purkens, labourer
James Treadgold, do.
Thos. Chapman, butcher
Robt. Butlin, husbandman
John Russel, servant

Thos. Lummas, do.
John Wills, husbandman
Richard Faulkner, servant
⟨Jno. Payne, taylor, 3 children⟩
Luke Lucas, labourer

ALTHORP

⟨The Rt. Honble. Earl Spencer⟩
Mr. White, baily
⟨Nathaniel Wright, servant,
    3 children⟩
Saml. Dumbleton, servant
Robt. Haddon, do.
⟨Richd. Knight, servant,
    3 children⟩
Joseph Faithful, servant
Samuell Hopkins, do.
Willm. Horne, do.

Purser Ireland, do.
Thos. Ellis, do.
St. John Height, do.
Edward Morris, do.
⟨Richard Richardson, aprentice⟩
Francoes Poriz, servant
Richard Cherrington, do.
⟨Robt. Tebbut, labourer,
    3 children⟩
Lucas Butlin, keeper
Thos. Colledge, servant

BROCKHALL

November ye 27, 1777.   A true list of the names of all persons that are liable to serve as militia-men in the parrish of Brockhall with Muscutt in the county of Northampton.

John Dunckley, servant
Robert Chatter, servant
James Lovill, servant
Joseph Borman, farmer
John Hughes
⟨James Hughes, with an
    impediment in his eyes⟩
John Judkins
Thomas Judkins

James Dicks
William Dicks
Thomas Watson, servant
John Oandley, servant
⟨Thomas Deney, farmer, has
    served⟩
⟨William West, servant, has
    served⟩

The day of the said and appeall his the eight day of December next at the Peacock Inn in Northampton.

James Dicks, constable.

BUGBROOKE

A list of the milishou for the year 1777.

⟨William Francies, grasier⟩ dead
Edward Turland, servent
Amas Linnell, servent
John Ashby, farmer
⟨William Reeve, servent⟩ infirm
William Moore, wolcomer
Thos. Cock, wolcomer
Thos. Lines, servent
Sam. Harris, servent
Thos. Adkins, butcher

John Moore, malster
⟨Thos. Moore, tayler⟩ apprentice
William Wodin, wolcomer
William Parbey, plumer
John Reeve, labor
Richard Capel, drawed
John Croxford, servent
William Willes, baker
Benj. Willes, butcher
Sam. Garlick, labour

John Phipps, farmer
John Worick, servent
Henary Billingham, laborow
William Worley, mason
William Bason, labour
Thos. Nuckom, sarvent
James Phipps, giner
Nimrod Garner, servent
William Phipps, vitler
James Parbey, labour
William Johnson, farmer
Henary Johnson, farmer
Thos. Tibes, labor
Thos. Huet, servent
Sam. Pool, servent
Thos. Turland, farmer
John Turland, farmer
Sam. Ashby, servent
⟨John Muscott, drawed⟩
John Marret, servent
Richard Ashby, labour
Thos. Lee, servent
Thos. Pesnall, farmer

Thos. Pesenall, cordwinder
Richard Webester, servent
George Wilkins, servent
⟨Thos. Mudeman, drawed⟩
⟨William Billing, drawed⟩
Sam. Kingston, laberow
Maritt Whitlock, servent
⟨Henary Garner, cord winder,
   drawed⟩
William Ward, weaver
Richard Colines, laborow
⟨Daniel Fisher, drawed⟩
William Billing, shepard
Richard Wait, miler
William Grigrey, servent
William Tibes, juner, laborow
⟨Edward Willes, drawed⟩
Edward Barker, laborow
Thos. Billingham, laborow
⟨John Bailey, drawed⟩
William Brown, plumer
John Coles, servent
Nath. Dugless, talyler

⟨Thos. Billing, constable.⟩

Bugbrooke. Any person or persons that think them selves aggrieved may appeal at the Peacock Inn in Northampton, the eighth day of December.

CHAPEL BRAMPTON

A list of the mens names that are qualifi'd to serve in the militia of ye parissh of Chapple Brampton.

James King, grazier
Willm. Clever, farmer
James Cook, servant
Henry Judg's, servant
Bartlet Miller, farmer
Willm. Spencer, laberour
John Spencer, servant
Stephen Hadden, servant
John Hammon, laberour
Henry Maine, butcher
John Wissh, blacksmith
Benjamen Knight, shoemaker
Edwd. Tarry, shoemaker
Robert Litchfeild, farmer
Richard Bray, miller
Thos. Brewer, laberour

⟨Willm. Hammon, laberour,
   not sharp⟩
⟨Nathil. Green, shoemaker,
   drawn⟩
⟨James Morris, ragman, lame⟩
⟨Henry Crutchly, shoemaker,
   seven children⟩
⟨John Litchfield, farmer, very
   bad health⟩
⟨William Litchfield, farmer,
   drawn⟩
⟨Edwd. Hogden, labourer, four
   children⟩
⟨Thos. Moird, butcher, drawn⟩
⟨John Bradshaw, shoemaker,
   not sound⟩

Edwd. Sherman, constable.

CHURCH BRAMPTON

Church Brampton. A list of all persons between the ages of eighteen and fourty five lieable to searve in the millita —— 1777.

Edwd. Carr, farmer
⟨Willm. Baringer, do.⟩
Edwd. Baringer, do.
Willm. Pain, do.
Willm. Clarke, servt.
Willm. Cox, do.
Thos. Winter, do.
Vinct. Shortland, do.
Thos. Cruft, do.
Henry Summerfield, do.
Willm. Ashby, do.
George Walker, do.
Josh. Fancutt, labr.
John Tarry, labr.
Benjn. Rigby, do.
Robt. Ingram, do.
Thoms. Tarry, wool comber
Josh. Sharpe
Charles Fancutt, farmer

Henry Webb, do.
⟨Josh. Higason, labr., 5 childn.⟩
⟨John Bauldwin, do., 3 childn.⟩
⟨Wm. Brightman, do., 4 childn.⟩
⟨James Neeal, do., 6 childn.⟩
⟨Saml. Tarry, do., 3 child.⟩
⟨John Tarry, drawn once⟩
⟨Wm. Rigby, drawn once⟩
⟨Wm. Sharpe, drawn once⟩
⟨John Camp, drawn once⟩
⟨Wm. Roe, dischargd. soldier,
  lame, quit last time⟩
⟨John Webb, lame four finger⟩
⟨Wm. Bradshaw, taylor, hath
  fits, 5 child.⟩
⟨John Tutchinor, wool comber,
  hath the rumaties⟩
⟨Wm. Esom, weaver, one eye
  blemished, quit last time⟩

⟨Robt. Carr, constable.⟩

DALLINGTON

N.B. The meeting is on the 8th. of Decbr. at the Peacock Inn in Northampton.

A list of the names of persons in the parish of Dallington liable to serv in the militia of this county.

Joseph Jekyll, esqr.
James Spink, gardiner
James Shepheard, servant
William Bruce, servant
Robert Bruce, servant
William Plowman, servant
William West, farmer
Richard Earl, farmer
Samuell Day, baker
William Tresler, servant
William Dunkley, servant
William Brookes, servant
James Hall, carpinter
James Gore, carpinter
Thomas Brookes, carpinter
Heyford Farmer, servant

John Taylor, servant
John Freeman, servant
William Newill, servant
John Andrus, wooll sorter
Thomas Persivall, mason
George Freman, laberour
John Dickson, laberour
Nathan Mawby, hoseyer
John Holloway, servant
⟨James Labriam⟩
Sam. Smith
John Pilgrim
James Graham
John Moore
William Tear
William Jisop

John Paine, constable.

DUSTON

Northamptonshire, Nov. 29, Duston list, 1777, for the millita.

John Pickiring, gentn.   John Phipps, farmer

John Roberts, farmer
Robert Spencer, farmer
Samuel Hilliard, farmer son
John Whitsy, servant
William Rickit, servant
William Dawson, servant
William Cosby, servant
Thomas Tresler, larbour
⟨Thomas *illegible*, whill right, has
  3 children⟩
John Faser, labourer
⟨William Joans, shoe maker, has
  3 children⟩
Benjaman Clark, searvant
William Blewitt, mason
Joseph Smith, labourer
Benjaman Harris, labourer
Thomas Easton, hilliard
Thomas Arriss, sheperd
⟨John *illegible*, labourer⟩
Samuel Harris, labourer
Danil Harris, servant
William Easton, labourer
Richard Dove, labourer
Thomas Smith, labourer
John Claridge, farmer

Richard Farmer, servant
Richard Smith, labourer
⟨John *illegible*, labourer⟩
William Forster, labourer
William Phipps, miller
John Willson, servant
William Butcher, farmer
Charles Howen, servant
Rice Muliner, servant
William Neal, wheelright
John Harrison, wheelright
Richard Marller, labourer
James Whitsy, servant
William Ingrom, labourer
⟨Thomas Smith, carpenter, been
  drawn⟩
⟨John Page, carpenter, been
  drawn⟩
⟨Edward Pettet, labourer, been
  drawn⟩
⟨William Smith, labourer, been
  drawn⟩
⟨John Palmer, farmer, been
  drawn⟩
⟨William Robinson, sheperd,
  been drawn⟩

Robert Blewitt, constable.

EAST HADDON

25 Novr., 1777.   A list of all person liable to serve in the militia in the
parish of East Haddon in the county of Northampton.

Thos. Claridge, farmers son
Jos. Claridge, do.
Jno. Claridge, do.
Jno. Crutchley, surveyor
⟨Wm. Smith, weaver⟩ 3 childeren
Wm. Clark, farmer & grazier
Jno. Wagstaff, farmers servant
Wm. Johnson, do.
George Wilkins, maltster
Jno. Facer, blacksmith
Wm. Pen, blacksmiths servant
Fras. Facer, farmers son
Jerves Gregory, farmers servant
Fras. Chapman, carpenter
Edwd. Chapman, do.
Wm. Chapman, do.
⟨Thos. Billing, farmers son⟩
Thos. Hilles, grocer
Thos. Bottrill, labourer
Fras. Bottrill, do.
⟨Jno. Gudgeons, taylor⟩

Jno. Noon, labourer
Jno. Herbert, do.
Robt. Andrew, weaver
Joseph Chapman, wooll comber
Jno. Bosworth, surveyor
Danl. Simonds, weaver
John Sodin
Wm. Tebbott, weaver
Jno. Tebbott, do.
Jno. Archer, farmers servt.
Thos. White, farmers son
Wm. Russel, weaver
Tho. Billing
Saml. Coy, taylor
William Collis
James Garrett, farmer & grazier
Thos. Garrett, wooll comber
Wm. Garrett, butcher
Jno. Dunkley, labourer
Jno. Homan, farmers servant
Jno. Smith, labourer

Wm. Webb, do.
Barl. Clark, farmer & grazier
Wm. Clark, farmers servt.
Richd. Blakeman, do.
Richd. Smith, shoemaker
Jno. Chapman, weaver
Wm. Barfoot, farmers servt.
Richd. Roberts, do.

Richd. Smith, weaver
Thos. Watts, weaver
Richd. Soden, do.
Jno. Smith, shoemaker
Edwd. Marler, labourer
Jno. Tomson, farmers servant
Jno. Butlin, baker
Joshua Car, farmers servant

Fras. Stanley, constable.

FLORE

A list of such persons as are able to serve in the militia in the parrish of
Flower and Glassthorpe in the county of Northampton.

William Crabtree, servant
William Collins, servant
Daniel Billingham, servant
Samuel Roddiss, butcher
Robert Murcott, taylor
Richard Collitt, husbandman
Edward Collitt, servant
Thomas Horn, servant
Charles Meacock, labourer
John Dunkley, servant
William Emmery, weaver
Thomas Write, servant
George Jakeman, miller
Samuel Lee, servant
⟨William Letts, butcher (infirm)⟩
Henry Ramsey, servant
George Cockerill, servant
James Ayres, weaver
John Mellows, servant
⟨George Cross (infirm)⟩
James Brumage, servant
John Reynolds, weaver
William Roddiss, butcher
Edward Roddiss, butcher
Gabriel Hix, labourer
⟨William Rogers, labourer
   (infirm)⟩
John Rogers, labourer
⟨John Hadland (infirm)⟩
Thomas Hadland, labourer
Thomas Knight, frameworkniter
⟨John Knight, taylor (infirm)⟩
John Cuckson, frameworknitter
Samuel Goode, servant
Simon Knight, frameworkniter
John Dunkley, labourer
Joseph Roe, labourer
Thomas Marriott, husbandman
Richard Jones, servant

William Robbins, servant
Edward Hoare, husbandman
⟨Thomas Clarke, servant (infirm)⟩
John Wills, woolcomber
⟨Richard Wills, wool comber
   (infirm)⟩
Elias Hadland, woolcomber
John Muscott, cordwainer
Thomas Muscott, weaver
John Boote, glover
John Billinham, cordwainer
   (younger)
Thomas Dunkley, shepherd
Alexander Chapman, baker
⟨Joseph Shaw, labourer (infirm)⟩
Thomas Faulkner, weaver
William Faulkner, weaver
Samuel Davis, taylor
John Lummas, taylor
Joseph Elliott, butcher
John Darby, frameworkniter
⟨William Darby, frameworkniter⟩
Samuel Weymont, grocer
John Poole, carpenter
⟨Charles Shaw, servant (infirm)⟩
John Packer, stay-maker
William Cappell, husbandman
John Robbins, servant
Samuel Dunkley, servant
⟨William Adams (infirm)⟩
⟨John Billingham, cordwainer
   (infirm)⟩
⟨Thomas Letts, plough-wright
   (infirm)⟩
John Capell, husbandman
Robert Brown, frameworkniter
⟨William Liddy, frameworkniter
   (infirm)⟩
John Hopcraft, servant

⟨John Smith, school-master
   (infirm)⟩
John Collis, woolcomber
⟨Adam Shaw, servant (infirm)⟩
Thomas Packer, servant
Charles Hinkes, servant
⟨Thomas Manning, woolcomber
   (infirm)⟩
Robert Marriott, wheelright
Thomas Marriott, wheelwright
Thomas Webb, labourer

William Jones, frameworkniter
John Webb, servant
James Pickering, sawyer
William Watts, servant
William Dumbleton, taylor
William Simons, husbandman
William Crane, servant
William Garrett, servant
John Bricket, cordwainer
John Faulkner, cordwainer
William Cole, surgion

This is to give notice that all such person as think themselves aggrieved hereby are to appear at the day of appeal which will be held at the Peacock Inn in Northampton of on Monday, December 8 day 1777.

HARLESTONE

1777.   A list of persons residing in Harlestone between the age of eighteen and forty-five liable to serve in the militia.

⟨Robt. Andrew, esqr., sherriff⟩
Jno. Flavel, farmer
Thos. Moore, farmer
Jno. Moore, farmer
Robt. Clarke, labr.
Sam. Arden, labr.
⟨Laurence Peaciful, weaver⟩
Jno. Dillow, cordwainer
Thos. Gross, blacksmith
Richd. Simons, woolcomber
Edw. Murden, weaver
Dan. Eason, labr.
Heny. Smith, weaver
Rogr. Allen, labr.
Wm. Davis, farmer
Dan. England, carpenter
Heny. Saunders, butcher
Robt. Welch, cordwainer
Jno. Welch, stonecutter
Thos. Cox, do.
Jno. Worley, mason
Jno. Major, taylor
Geo. Dicey, do.
James England, woolcomber
Jno. Vials, farmer
Jno. Vials, junr., do.
Jno. Roe, sert.
Richd. Ellis, mason
Thos. Marson, cordwainer
Jno. Ager, sert.
James Corbett, sert.

Richd. Peasnall, do.
James Billington, do.
Wm. Battin, do.
Jno. Gee, do.
Thos. Lumly, quarryman
Morris Ward, sert.
Jno. Lumly, quarryman
Jno. Boswell, sert.
Thos. Cliff, joiner
Wm. Roe, mason
Thos. Cooch, farmer
Jno. Cooch, do.
Thos. Treslar, baker
Edw. Clarke, sert.
Wm. Cave, farmer
Thos. Allen, joiner
Sam. Bennet, sert.
Wm. Cross, do.
Sam. Horton, do.
Jno. Green, baker
Geo. Cox, labr.
Thos. Pool, do.
Mr. Wm. Andrew, farmer
Wm. Walton, do.
Wm. Preston, labr.
Chars. Whitting, stonecutter
James Rickett, do.
Jno. Bird, schoolmaster
⟨Jno. Cox, junr., thirdborough⟩
⟨Jno. Cox, constable⟩

Decbr. 5th. 1777.

ABINGTON

A list of all persons in the parish of Abington in the County of North-ampton at ages of eighteen and forty five years to serve as militia men.

Johanthan Collis, steward
John Geary, buttler
John Prestig
Thos. Wright
Richd. Cox
Nathanl. Jones
Mark Southwick, miller
Willm. Haddon, carpinter
Willm. Warrner
Richd. Nippin, servt.
John Maning, do.

John Nipping, do.
George Comefield, blacksmith
Joseph Gibson, servt.
Henry Gibson, do.
John Sterman, do.
James Holloway, do.
John Coalman, do.
James Jeffs, do.
Robt. Witworth, do.
Richd. Wright, do.

John Hawkes, constable.
Thos. Jones, headborough.

GREAT BILLING

The names of person's to serve as militia men in the parrish of Great Billing (Northamptonshire).

Mr. Jno. Faucutt, grazier
Willm. Parbery, farmer
Richd. Hodges, farmer
Matw. Drinkwater, miller
Willm. Willson, taylor
Willm. Campion, cordwinder
Anthony Hilham, servt.
John Busting, servt.
Jos. Smith, servt.
Wm. Tompson, shepd.
Ed. Robinson, labr.
Jno. Hensman, labr.
Jos. Smart, labr.
Thos. Clason, servt.
Thos. Clark, senr., weaver

Thos. Clark, junr., weaver
Willm. Wills, servt.
⟨Justinian Tebbutt, servd. in the militia⟩
John Turnall, labr.
Andrew Lattimore, servt.
Jas. Hodges, labr.
John Tompson, servt.
Thos. Curtis, labr.
⟨John Freeman, deformed⟩
⟨Wm. Hodges, servd. militia⟩
⟨Wm. Benn, lame⟩
Thos. Bollings, servt.
Jno. Barwick, servt.

The appeal day will be on Monday the 8th. day of Decr. at the Peacock Inn in Northampton.

LITTLE BILLING

A list of all persons inhabiting in the parish of Little Billing in the county of Northampton at the age of eighteen and forty five to sarve as mititia men.

Robr. Harris, searvant
Charles Daukins, dito
Stephen Gill, dito
Tho. Green, dito

Joseph Purkins, dito
Tho. Bennet, labours
Tho. Nite, dito
Tho. Harris, dito

⟨Richd. Hawkes, constable.⟩

BOUGHTON

Richard Faulkner, cunstuble of Boughton.

Robbert Fascutt, farmer
John Hollis, farmer
Robbert Rucill, sarvant
James Buttlin, cordwinder
⟨Benjaman Burton⟩ cordwinder
Benjamin Ivens, wool coomer
John Moore, wool coomer
Wm. Mathews, laberer
James Peasifill, laberer
John Tarry, laberer
Thos. Smith, farmer
Jonas Parrot, sarvant
Tebbot Allen, paper maker
Thos. Allen, paper maker
Richd. Allen, baker

⟨Wm. Tarry, taylor⟩
Benjaman West, laberer
Richard Worick, laberer
Thos. Frost, sarvant
Samuel Frost, sarvant
Thos. Seears, capenter
George Dickings, sarvant
Isaac Jackson, gardiner
Wm. Warring, weaver
Wm. Crandfield, capenter
Hugh Holis, vinter
John Faulkner, farrmer
Benjaman Faulkner, farmer
Peter Buttlin, sarvant
Wm. Hills, sarvant

KINGSTHORPE

A liest of the mens names in Kingsthorpe.

Peeter John Freemoux, esqr.
John Walker, buttler
Thos. Flavel, coachman
Richd. Weab, futman
Samwell Stanton, farmer
Richd. Stanton, farmer
John Lucos, farmer
Willm. Lucos, laber
Samwell Lucos, laber
⟨Thos. Butling, osler⟩ infirm
Frances Thompson, sarvint
Charles Deacon, labour
Thos. Battling, sarvint
John Barnard, sarvint
Willm. Green, farmer
Thos. Green, farmer, sener
Samwell Smith, sarvint
Willm. White, blacksmith
Willm. Cuffley, carpinder
Danell Cuffley, carpinder
Joseptch Cuffley, carpinder
Wm. Spooner, carpinder
⟨Bartlet Car, carpinder⟩ infirm
Willm. Danes, farmer
John Miller, sarvint
Samwell Hillard, sarvint
Willm. Brooks, woolstapler
⟨Roger Chumberpatch, laber⟩
   infirm
Willm. Parrot, laber
Samwell Whitsey, laber

John Johnson, farmer
Saben Luckkuck, sarvint
Thos. Parrot, labour
Thos. Dains, labour
Willm. Sibley, sivemaker
Enock Dudley, blacksmith
Willm. Steavenson, woolstapler
Richd. Dickens, labour
Richd. Capin, shumaker
Thos. Sibley, laber
Richd. Giles, laber
Thos. Wood, farmer
John Johnson, weaver
Danel Row, laber
Charles Johnson, mason
Willm. Whiting, stonecutter
James Clarke, sarvint
Willm. Buckler, britchesmaker
Edward Wells, britchesmaker
Willm. Cumberpatch, gardiner
Jeremia Boswell, labour
Henery Tibes, farmer
Robard Ammons, sarvint
Jeremiah Ellis, labour
Willm. Ellis, sarvint
James Jornes, sarvint
⟨Simmons Dains, labour⟩ infirm
Danill Parrot, labour
John Percifull, labour
Thos. Greer, farmer, juner
Richrd. Manning, baker

John Tresler, baker
Willm. Maning, miller
Abraham Abbot, miller
John Sibley, sivemaker
Charles Fitzhug, farmer
Richd. Lack, labour
John Wood, labour
John Warner, barber
Richd. Pell, mason
Thos. Percifull, shumaker
Willm. Cuffley, weaver
Thos. Lee, labour
Georg Peach, labour
Robard Kinnig, woolcomer
Willm. Healey, labour
Thos. Abbot, weaver
Frances Parbery, weaver
Robard Bassett, blacksmith
Richd. Warner, weaver
John Hollis, laber
Frances Causby, labour
Gerg. Bradshaw, shumaker
Thos. Tresler, baker
Thos. Wills, labour

Thos. White, labour
Willm. Garner, gardinner
Willm. Morris, laber
⟨John Southam, sarvint⟩ infirm
Thos. Banks, miller
Thos. Craddock, miller
John Gibson, labour
Thos. Freeman, labour
John Wheatley, sarvint
Thos. Tallis, miller
Samwell Pipping, woolstapler
Thos. Peach, woolcomer
James Percifull, labour
Joseptch Dunkley, sarvint
Thos. Lilington, sarvint
Georg Arbard, sarvint
James Horn, sarvint
John Reave, sarvint
Thos. Morris, labour
Samwell at Mr. Gudgins Lodge,
    note [not] tell his name
Jeremiah Green, farmer
John Simson, buttler

⟨Hen. Higgins, constable.⟩

MOULTON

A list of those men that are in capacity to serve as militia men in the
parish of Moulton, November the 25th. 1777.

Mr. Thos. March, yeon.
John Dawson, junr., labr.
Mr. Daniel Barber, yeon.
Easton Luck, wheavr.
Richard Britten, labr.
⟨Thos. Pool, labr.⟩
Mr. Thos. Dunkley, gentn.
Edward Buswell, labr.
Willm. Garratt, labr.
John Garratt, labr.
Thomas Garratt, servt.
William Marriott, blackth.
John Dickins, labr.
William Dunkley, bakr.
Thomas Streets ⎤
Edward Streets ⎦ wheavrs.
George Cox, junr. ⎤
William Chown ⎦ cordwainrs
John Hills, victur.
William Falkner, yeon.
Samuel Johnson, yeon.
John Clark, servt.
Henry Peach, wheavr.
Samuel Tarrent, labr.

William Tarrent, labr.
John Tift, taylor
William Tipler, wheavr.
John Mackowen, butchr.
John Kining, labr.
John Law, wheavr.
Richard Murden, wheavr.
John Corbett, labr.
William York, labr.
Samuel Jones, labr.
John Padmore, labr.
Willm. Skerril, wheavr.
Edward Knight, labr.
John Barber, vicr.
Henry Ravvish, woollsorter
William Tayler, woollcomber
Robert Smith, shopkeeper
William Blunt, wheelwright
Thomas Marriott, blackth.
Mr. John Watts, yeon.
Mr. Richard Barber, baker
John Hore, baker
Thomas Warren, maltr.
William Smith, yeon.

William Wait, cordwr.
Henry Bowers, wheaver
William Dove, tayler
John Hadden, junr., servt.
Edward Hails, labr.
⟨John Bradshaw⟩ drawn ⟨servt.⟩
Mr. Wm. Hawkes, yeon.
Mr. Aspinal, yeon.
John Whiting, servt.
Mr. Clarke Barber, yeon.
William Mabbutt, labr.
William Key, labr.
John Jeycock, labr.
Saml. Tosland, wheavr.
Robt. Jeayes, mason
William Blunt ⎱ carpainers
John Blunt   ⎰
John Grose, blackth.
William Chambers, cordwainr.
John Bradshaw, junr., cordr.
William Mollard, labr.

William Bradshaw, servt.
James Tipler, labr.
Thomas Wright, wheelwright
Mr. John Marsh, sen. ⎱ yeon.
Mr. John Marsh, junr. ⎰
William Binyen, baker
Mr. John Maule, yeon.
John Laundon, victr.
Mr. Edward Watts, mallster
Edward Haycock, labr.
Charles Cooper, servt.
Thomas Howes, servt.
David Crutchley, servt.
John Hopper, servt.
Thomas Jackson, wheaver
John Wallington, servt.
John Law, labr.
William Cox, servt.
John Steevinson, labr.
Mr. Willm. Pywell, yeon.

Willm. Pell ⎱ deputy constables for the said parish.
John Barber ⎰

OVERSTONE

A list of those men that are in capacity to serve as militia men for the parish of Overstone.

Mr. John Binyan, yeon.
Wm. Brains, servt.
John Willis, labr.
⟨John Hopkins, servt.⟩
Simon Early, servt.
Thomas Tipler, labr.
James Barnett, servt.
John Marriott, servt.
Willm. Flavell, labr.
Henry Clark, labr.

Mr. John White, yeon.
Willm. Willis, servt.
Mr. Saml. Pell, junr., yeon.
Mr. Saml. Pell, senr., yeon.
Josh. Bliss, servant
⟨Peter England, blackh.⟩
Willm. Ward, labr.
Mr. Geoe. Parker, yeon.
Mr. Willm. Luck, felmonger
Benjn. Bradwell, servt.

N.B. The justices meeting will be held on Monday the 8th. day of December next ensuing the date thereof, and those persons that think themselves aggrieved may then appeal, and that no appeal will be afterwards received as witness our hands, the 25th. day of November 1777.

Willm. Parker, deputy constable for the said parish.

PITSFORD

Novr. ye 24th. 1777. A list of all the persons in the parish of Pisford capable to serve as militia men for the county of Northampton.

Willm. Bond ⎫
John Ekins ⎬ farmers
Thos. Underwood ⎭

James Kightley, baker ⎫ trades-
Joseph Richardson,   ⎬ men
    woolcomber   ⎭

Thos. Derby, weaver ⎫
Thos. Randle, do.
Benjn. Smith,
  cordwainer
John Eady, taylor ⎬ trades-
John Baul, do.   men
John Cleaver, do.
Edward Lavy, do.
Geoe. Arthur,
  cordwainer
Wm. Baker, weaver ⎭

Wm. Judd, servant ⎫
John Bond, do.
John Merrel, do.
Wm. Carvel, do.
⟨Clark Burborow, do.,
  underage⟩ ⎬ servants
Bartin Tarry, do
Thos. Underwood,
  do.
John Williamson, do. ⎭

Samuel Chamberlain, ⎫
  labourer
Peter Richardson,
  do.
Wm. Tarry, do.
⟨Richd. James, do., ⎬ labourers
  3 children⟩
Francis Chapman,
  do.
Edwd. Chapman,
  do. ⎭

⟨John Bray, labourer, 3 children⟩
John Clifton, do.
Geoe. Williamson, do.
Thos. Williamson, do.
John Thompson, do.
James More, do.
Wm. Smith, do.

N.B. The day of appeal will be at the Peacock Inn in Northampton on Munday the 8th. day of Decr. next, and no appeal will be afterwards receiv'd.

Geoe. Stafford, constable.

SPRATTON

A list of the names of the inhabitants of the parish of Spratton in the county of Northampton between the age of eighteen and fortyfive years to serve in the militia for the said county, 1777.

Willm. Priest, servt.
Thos. Smith, junr., blacksmith
Peter Martin, grazier, son of
  Thos. Martin
John Martin, dealer, the son of
  Thos. Martin
Willm. Pearson, farmer
George Pearson, junr.
Willm. Martin, junr., farmer
Willm. Satchwell, junr., weaver
John Martin, son of Peter
  Martin, grazier
Peter Martin, son of Peter
  Martin, grazier
Willm. Chapman, weaver
Benjamin Pendered, flax
  dresser
Willm. Lantsbury, gent.
John Martin, son of Peter
  Martin, farmer
Willm. Torland, servt.
Willm. Wykes, weaver

Christopher Austin, cordwainer
Martin Pearson, farmer
Willm. Brown, grocer
John Wright, farmer
Thos. Hobson, junr., farmer
⟨John Cox, labourer⟩
Abraham Cox, labourer
Moses Cox, labourer
Richd. Balderson, weaver
Thos. Stanton, comber
Thos. Knight, carpenter
Joseph Freeman, cordwainer
John Eason, junr., wheel-wright
Saml. Hide, comber
John Collins, servt.
John Mallard, servt.
John Hanson, servt.
Charls Wills, farmer
Thos. Chapman, junr., gent.
Willm. Jones, junr., farmer
James Martin, victuler
John York, whitawer

Thos. Horn, tayler
John Wright, baker
James Pearson, baker
Willm. Alderman, labourer
Willm. Herbert, butcher
George Hobson, farmer
Willm. Palmer, blacksmith
John Deacon, carpenter
Francis Moore, junr., weaver
Willm. York, junr., weaver
Abraham Lee, junr., weaver
Aaron Norton, weaver
John Corby, servt.
John Lee, weaver
Gammage Lee, weaver

Thos. Wright, weaver
John Wright, labourer
John White, junr., weaver
John Mayne, butcher
Thos. Pearson, labourer
Robt. Mills, barber
Francis Goddard, comber
John Killburn, comber
William White, flax dresser
Thos. Smart, flaxdresser
Thos. Banbury, comber
James Redding, comber
Robt. Barker, comber
John Willcox, joiner

WESTON FAVELL

Northampton Shire. 8 Decr. 1777. Weston ffavell in the sd. county and hundred of Spelhoe. A list of all the inhabitants in the parish of Weston ffavell that are of the age of eighteen years and upwards and under the age of forty five years.

Thos. Preston, yeoman
Willm. Preston, farmer
Edwd. Nichols, ditto
John Barron, miller
Robt. White, grazier
Thos. Lansbury, ditto
Thos. Smith, mason
John Clarke, labourer
Willm. Spencer, ditto
Joseph Sutton, ditto
Jeffrey Goode, ditto
Willm. Brigs, ditto

Joseph Simon, servant
Joseph Manning, ditto
Thos. Welch, ditto
Daniell Benn, ditto
John Luck, ditto
John Woodams, ditto
Willm. Avell, ditto
Willm. Winnington, servant
James Wright, ditto
Willm. Brice, ditto
Thos. Neal ⎫
Thos. Powel ⎬ woadmen

Men that have been drawn and served by substitute.

⟨Willm. Wooding, wheelwright⟩
⟨Willm. Smith, ditto⟩
⟨Palmer Sabey, labourer⟩
⟨Samll. Dines, ditto⟩

⟨Willm. Groves, servant⟩
⟨Joseph Attewell, taylor⟩
⟨John Clarke, innholder⟩

NORTHAMPTON (CHEQUER WARD)

Chequer Ward in the town of Northampton.

John Adams, junior, ironmonger
William Davies, surgeon
John Frost, servant
John Newcome, draper
Thomas Ellis, do.
Thomas Billings, peruke maker
William Pointer, hostler
James Holton, glazier

Richard Osborne, attorney
William Linnell, whitesmith
John Fowkes, shoemaker
Thomas Hall, shoemaker
Charles Morgan, attorney
John Cox, servant
James Downing, do.
John Scofield, gaoler

Thomas Ball, turnkey
John Ward, apothecary
William Drinkwater, porter
Joseph Hall, shoemaker
Thomas Harris, chief compositor
Clark Hillyard, innholder
Jeremiah Briggs, wine drawer
William Higgins, tapster
John Hill, hostler
William Stevens, do.
Charles Matthews, postillion
Thomas Glover, do.
Rowland Pick, do.
Henry Jeffcutt, grocer
John Copplestone, tallow
  chandler
Bernard Levi, ironmonger
William Tompson, grocer
Stephen Dexter, tinman
Robert Abbey, attorney
⟨John Miller, articled clerk⟩
Thomas Fitch, grocer
Thomas Herd, do.
⟨William Mobbs, 4 children⟩
  hogman
Joshua Lucas, draper
John Drake, grocer
⟨Robert Rowell, apprentice⟩
John Holiland, chandler
John Morton, draper
William Mumford, do.
William Prowett, haberdasher
Thomas Barrick, servant
Thomas Ives, flaxdresser
John Bailey, draper
John Segary, cutler
Robert Fox, do.
⟨Samuel Cornish, apprentice⟩
John Percival, haberdasher
William Marshall, druggist
Joshua Watson, do.
William Attiwell, servant
James Dimmock, peruke maker
⟨William Cornish, apprentice⟩
Benjamin Hill, gentleman
John Coleman, servant
Robert Britten, surgeon
Thomas Mallard, servant
Thomas Campion, do.
John Wye, wine merchant
Richard Ward, servant
John Duke, wine merchant
James Whitmy, glazier
⟨James Arnold,⟩ do., lame hand

Thomas Pierce, joiner
Samuel Dongworth, printer
John Secars, servant
Henry Duke, joiner
Joseph Harding, surgeon
John Dunkley, butcher
⟨Richard Cooper⟩ do.
Thomas Trinder, schoolmaster
Christopher Smyth, attorney
⟨John Clarke, articled clerk⟩
⟨Thomas Ewesdin, do.⟩
Richard Buswell, writer
Joseph Hall, servant
⟨William Mays, 3 children⟩
  hostler
John Cornish, tapster
Westfield Lilley, postillion
Thomas Penitent, horsekeeper
Yorkshire John, under hostler
William Roddis, basket maker
Robert Roddis, do.
John Roddis, upholdsterer
Thomas Wykes, shoemaker
Robert Crabb, grocer
Michael Smith, lace dealer
John Geldard, shopman
William Trasler, victualler
William Woolston, grocer
Francis Cox, chandler
George Fish, watchmaker
William Hadden, servant
John Hutt, ironmonger
John Hall, do.
Thomas Parbery, victualler
Henry Collis, shoemaker
Robert Tompson, breeches
  maker
Henry Cook, taylor
William Tanner, shoemaker
John Wade, watchmaker
William Easton, painter
Richd. Easton, hillier
William Crutchley, victualler
William Reeder, do.
Jonathan Trippett, servant
⟨Philip Hunt, 5 children⟩ painter
⟨Francis Powell, 4 children⟩
  turner
Richard Allwood, breeches
  maker
Richard Collins, tailor
James Wyat, comber
Joseph Haddon, victualler
Benjamin Goodman, brazier

William Ager, breeches maker
John Hedge, pin maker
William Hedge, shoemaker
Samuel Hedge, clogmaker
⟨Benjamin Collins, 6 children⟩
    grocer

John Clarke, servant
⟨Paul Agutter, apprentice⟩
James Linnell, whitesmith
Joshua Steevenson, victualler
Charles Lacy, woolstapler
Joseph Mawby, shoemaker

N.B. If any person thinks himself aggrieved the day of appeal will be at the Peacock Inn on Monday the 8th. of December 1777.

NORTHAMPTON (EAST WARD)

A list of all the men at this time dwelling withing the East Ward liable to serve as militia for this county the ensuing four year's.

John Flecher, gentleman
Joseph Lomly, servant
Wm. Payne, victualler
John Perkins, gardener
James Wright, cordwainer
Wm. Hefford, mason
Wm. Dunkley, butcher
Wm. Cope, servant
John Darlow, carpenter
⟨Wm. Green, sawyer⟩
Wm. Jonson, weaver
Wm. Newet, victualler
Wm. Cole, yeoman
Wm. Cole, cordwainer
Benj. Parbery, labourer
John Cole, gentleman
John Mitchell, hillier
Henery Evans, labourer
George Briggs, cordwainer
Wm. Clever, labourer
John Martin,
    coachwheelwright
Michael Willby, cordwainer
Wm. Tompson, victualler
Richd. Tompson, victualler
Edw. Kerby, plumber
Richd. Latimer, do.
John Sanders, cordwainer
John Evans, servant
John Foxly, do.
Wm. Archer, do.
Conyors Smith, do.
John Priestley, weaver
Wm. Gleeds, do.
Wm. Aman, carpenter
John Sherwood, smith
Wm. Harris, sackweaver
John Travel, labourer
John Baker, weaver

John Richardson, carrier
Wm. Bursel, printer
Antoney French, weaver
John Boneum, do.
James Cliff, carpenter
Wm. Gates, gentleman
Fox Walker, butcher
Wm. Robinson, weaver
James Ward, do.
Thos. Baker, cordwainer
Thos. Ball, taylor
Wm. Roads, carpenter
Wm. Claridge, servant
Wm. Harris, baker
George Baston, waggoner
Wm. Willby, clark
John Markham, gentleman
Joseph Gutteridge, cordwainer
Wm. Gutteridge, do.
Robert Pointers, servant
Joel Jonson, carpenter
Wm. Jinkenson, labourer
Thos. Morris, do.
Thos. Dekin, taylor
James Hall, breeches maker
John Abbot, butcher
Richd. Boaley, labourer
Benjm. Ashby, do.
Robert Peach, cordwainer
Thos. Ward, do.
Thos. Frost, do.
Thos. Adkins, past age, do.
John Jones, slaymaker
Thos. Hogkisson, horse dealer
Robert Roberts, pipe maker
Thos. Wesly, taylor
Wm. Burges, cordwainer
Wm. Hull, do.
Dr. Fothergill, gentleman

John Tott, servant
Wm. Cook, baker
Richd. Harding, servant
John Carr, do.
Joseph Maning, labourer
Abram Roberts, taylor
Steeven Hill, cordwainer
Wm. Hall, sener, do.
Wm. Hall, juner, do.
James Whoolley, do.
John Thirkill, plumber
Wm. Gutteridge, carpenter
Robert Simms, parchmentmaker
Wm. Seabin, do.
Wm. Billingham, carpenter
⟨James Jonson, labourer⟩
Michael Gamble, mason
Benjm. Ceckley, hillier
Camp Jones, cordwainer
Edmon Joice, servant
⟨Edward Bottrill, 4 children,
    weaver⟩
George Cliff, carpenter
Charles Bason, staymaker
Wm. Cleton, gardener
Joseph Robbeness, labourer
John Cornish, weaver
Robert Trasler, baker
John Harris, do.
George Cooch, clark

Thos. Breach, cordwainer
James Maning, do.
James Hewitt, cordwainer
John Ager, do.
Edward Coulson, hillier
Robert Cox, sawyer
John Fillpot, breeches maker
Joseph Cross, innhoulder
Francis Fox, whitesmith
Abram Tite, servant
Benjm. Pewtress, gentleman
⟨Wm. Battes, lame, labourer⟩
⟨Wm. Procter, lame, do.⟩
⟨Wm. Wighthead, disabled,
    hillier⟩
⟨David Middleton, disabled,
    cordwainer⟩
⟨George Fisher, disabled, do.⟩
⟨John Ellit, 3 children,
    collermaker⟩
⟨Thos. Wootten, 3 do., post man⟩
⟨Joseph Cooper, 3 do., butcher⟩
⟨Simon Mynerds, 3 do., labourer⟩
⟨Thos. Kingson, 4 do., labourer⟩
⟨James Percival, 4 do., do.⟩
⟨Charles Morris, 5 do., do.⟩
⟨James Drew, 3 do., do.⟩
⟨James Truman, 3 do., weaver⟩
⟨Wm. Turner, 3 do., labourer⟩

Notice is here by given.

That a meeting will be held on Monday the eighth day of December next,
at the Peacock Inn in Northampton, that all person's who shall think
themselves aggrieved must then appeal, for no appeal aftterwards will be
receivd.

1777:   November th30.   J. James Boon, constable.

NORTHAMPTON (NORTH WARD)

A list of the North Ward.

Joseph Westley, baker
Francies Osborn, vitaler
James Clason, servant
Cardwell Wills, grocer
Willm. Addams, vitaler
Richd. Collison, mason
Jos. Ball, taylor
Tos. Webster, labr.
⟨Wm. Richason, brewer⟩
    3 children
Timithy Penn, sawyer
John Ives, cordwiner
Wm. Pulser, taylor

Charles Franks, chandler
Richd. Collis, woolcomber
James Brown, post boy
Wm. Watts, gardener
John Watts, gardianer
⟨Richd. Cook, cordwiner⟩
Saml. Walker, taylor
Benj. Mason, joiner
Wm. Muns, cordwainer
Henery Cooper, labr.
⟨Tos. Cross, weaver⟩ 3 children
Wm. Busby, weaver
Saml. George, yeoman

Tos. Fancot, yeoman
John Berril, weaver
Wm. Sturman, weaver
⟨Saml. Parrish, weaver⟩
⟨Tos. Halford, weaver⟩
    3 children
Edward Clarke, mason
John Salsbury, blacksmith
Richd. Wilson, sawyer
⟨Wm. Clason, cordwiner⟩
    3 children
Daniel Frost, labr.
John Price, labr.
Jos. Wright, cordwiner
Wm. Beck, cordwainer
Tos. James, cordwainer
⟨John Percifull, sawyer⟩
Wm. Penn, sawyer
Saml. Roughton, weaver
Jams. Law, taylor
Henry Law, gardianer
⟨Tos. Walker, cordwainer⟩
    3 children
⟨Zekel Warner, weaver⟩ 3 child.
Tos. Hopper, mason
Saml. March, weaver
George Yorke, brazier
Charles Penn, weaver
James Dickinson, joiner
Jos. Hall, labr.
Wm. Barnet, yeoman
Edward Morris, yeoman
Robt. Wilson, sawyer
Wm. Gester, cordwainer
Wm. Penn, weaver
Wm. Ager, weaver
John Miles, taylor
George Wod, woolsorter
Tos. Wilkison, cordwiner
John Mitimas, cordwainer
Edward Wood, glazier
Tos. Church, glazier
George Goodman, cordwainer
Tos. Causby, weaver
Wm. Swan, joiner
⟨Benj. Alliston, cork cutter⟩
    3 children
Wm. Hearbert, joiner
John Moor, turner
Tos. Cooper, butcher
Jos. Filewood, barber
⟨Wm. *illegible*, painter⟩
    3 children
Benj. Nixton, cordwainer

Robt. Green, cordwainer
John Green, weaver
Richd. Evins, labr.
Tos. Smith, butcher
Wm. Smith, gardner
Tos. Varman, butcher
Wm. Pilmore, joiner
⟨*illegible*⟩ 3 children
Wm. Bletsoe, gent.
Tos. Goode, servant
Tos. Lacy, baker
James Moore, taylor
Saml. Warrin, labr.
Wm. Dunmore, mason
Tos. Jackson, labr.
Jos. *illegible*, butcher
Isaac Keely, joiner
⟨John Woard, butcher⟩
    3 children
Wm. Hutt, servant
Tos. Dickinson, joiner
⟨John Potter, wipmaker⟩
Amas Peason, mason
Richd. Stockburn, joiner
Wm. Eayles, tinman
James Brown, baker
Wm. Hall, servant
James Barker, turner
Wm. Ferry, gent.
John Wood, woolcomber
James Huett, cordwainer
James Abson, cordwiner
Tos. Burten, cordwainer
⟨John Yeates, cordwainer⟩
    6 children
⟨Jos. Roberts, woolcomber⟩ lame
Timithy Robberts, engraver
Too Ball Cane Mellows, mason
Wm. Tear, taylor
Richd. Baker, woolstapler
John Yeatt, staymaker
Robt. Juinsley, servant
George Goldby, gardianer
Job Jermarn, taylor
Alexander Smith, book binder
James Jays, attorney
Tos. Henshaw, labr.
John Norton, labr.
Witon Edmons, vitaler
⟨Benj. Jones, cordwainer⟩
    3 children
⟨Jos. Botteril, labr.⟩ *illegible*
    children
Canity Gautharn, mason

George Allin, labr.
Wm. Still, cordwainer
Edward Pully, currier
John Roberts, labr.
Thurston Whaley, gunsmith
Richd. Alliston, cork cutter
Wm. Bennet, joiner
⟨Richd. Ward, butcher⟩ lame
Tos. Cartwright, weaver
John Paney, chimney sweep
Jos. Peason, yeoman
⟨James Warring, yeoman⟩
Saml. Camptain, yeoman
Saml. Thomas, cordwainer
Wm. Aquire, cordwiner
Wm. Stanton, yeoman
Wm. Burbury, yeoman
Richd. Stanton, vitaler
⟨Jos. Percefull, weaver⟩
   3 children
⟨John Ridington, weaver⟩
   3 child.
John Rowlett, weaver
Stephen Granborow, weaver
Wm. Reubutten, blacksmith
James Moneypeny, cordwainer
⟨Tos. Wright, weaver⟩
Wm. Parry, labr.
Tos. Tear, cordwainer
Jos. Walker, woolstapler
Jashua Walker, woolstapler
Charles King, cordwainer
⟨Jos. Wright, weaver⟩
⟨Jos. Ager, mason⟩ drawn
James James, cordwainer
Wm. Hartwell, weaver
Richd. Ager, weaver
Wm. Granborow, sawyer
Tos. Ager, weaver
⟨Wm. Ager, woolsorter⟩
   7 children
John Jackson, woolcomber
Tos. Line, servant
Tos. Smith, butcher
Robt. Gudgeon, glazier
Wm. Stephens, weaver

John Cooper, butcher
⟨Danl. Jones, servant⟩ infirm
Edward Obson, cooper
Wm. Barnett, vitaler
⟨Jos. Alliston, joiner⟩ infirm
George Eayles, vitaler
Robt. Stringer, blacksmith
Tos. Alliston, cordwainer
Wm. Knight, woolsorter
Rogger Terry, weaver
⟨Francies Yeoman, servant⟩
   drawn
Saml. Wright, blacksmith
Anthony Webb, servant
⟨John Livershidge, distiller⟩
John Addams, servant
Saml. Lucas, cooper
Jos. Bee, cooper
Richd. Obson, cordwainer
Tos. Watts, gent.
Wm. Banks, brewer
John Banks, brewer
Arter Brounsgrave, cordwainer
Wm. Lee, clockmaker
Tos. Tilley, cordwainer
Wm. Francis, confectioner
John Clason, servant
Tos. Kemp, servant
⟨Benjn. Satchel, labr.⟩
Tos. Rubberer, witesmith
⟨John Mallard, servant⟩
Jos. Gill, labr.
Robt. Collison, mason
John Bibwell, malster
Daniel Watkins, woolsorter
Tos. Robberer, weaver
Tos. Holmby, servant
Benjn. Boswort, servant
Saml. Martin, blacksmith
John Penn, weaver, senior
⟨George Henshaw, pipemaker⟩
Wm. Soans, cordwainer
John Worthington, joiner
John Cosford, servant
Tos. Page, taylor
John Penn, weaver, junior

⟨James Manning, constable.⟩

NORTHAMPTON (SOUTH WARD)

The South Ward of Northampton.

John Wilson, barber
John Knight, labourer

Henry Court, currier
John Mabbet, servant

Jonathan Lace, laceman
Thos. Adams, carpenter
Thos. Persons, collarmaker
Wm. Bateman, coachmaker
John Magure, fidler, lame
Saml. Wills, comber
Wm. Hilliry, heelmaker
Valentine Wooly, barber
John Page, felmonger
Francis Jackson, cordwinder
John Peach, woolsorter
Edward Coot, cordwinder
Willm. Hewitt, cordwr.
George Dawkins, cordwr.
Robt. Linnet, labourer
⟨George Cooper, woolcomber⟩
Wm. West, butcher
Joab Dicks, malster
Saml. Wright, millwright
Francis Hayes, papermkr.
Saml. Pool, horsebreakr.
Willm. Lyon, cordwr.
⟨Mathew Cox, 3 children,
     coach driver⟩
John Gray, woolcombr.
⟨Thos. Allen, 8 children, cordwr.⟩
James Adson, mason
James Pyner, cordw.
Peter Placett, combr.
⟨Saml. Sharwood, 3 children,
     labourer⟩
George Jones, weavr.
Thos. Cort, cordwr.
Thos. Clark, cordw.
George Rubberer, carpentr.
Francis Biggs, brickmr.
⟨John Ager, 3 children, combr.⟩
James Osbourne, locksmith
Willm. Augustus, dyer
John Law, gardener
John Johnson, turner
Willm. Brown, wheelwrite
Joseph Dilli, servant
John Baker, draper
Joseph Marret, servant
Saml. Adams, ostler
Eley Smith, collarmkr.
Benjn. Cover, shopkr.
George Charlton, cooper
Aaron Tompson, grocer
Wm. Sebeth, drawer
Wm. Coleman, ostler
James Tate, post boy
Martin Lucas, winemant.

John Voise, fishmgr.
John Fellows, cordw.
John Stanton, tayler
Joseph Dent, baker
Thos. Serjeant, baker
Thos. Law, carpenter
John Mowl, carpenter
Thos. Brown, cordw.
Joseph Brown, cordw.
Wm. Fenson, publican
⟨Edwrd. Warren, 4 child.,
     costermgr.⟩
Saml. Nichols, carriagemkr.
Wm. Etin, cordwinder
Thos. Stamford, plaisterer
⟨Wm. Miller, 3 child., cordwr.⟩
Wm. Howett, cordwr.
Joseph Camm, coachmaker
John Harris, coachmkr.
Henry Stermer, miller
James Welsh, labourer
John Yeomans, tanner
⟨John Jeffs, lame, labourer⟩
John Catan, papermkr.
John *illegible*, labourer
Joseph Webb, papermkr.
⟨Wm. Bottrell, 3 child., tanner⟩
Abram Bottrell, tanner
Thos. Turner, papermkr.
Jeffry Peacock, ditto.
Willm. Hadland, tanner
⟨Wm. *illegible*, 6 child., labourer⟩
John Galimer, cordw.
Wm. Tindale, grocer
John Puerin, wheeler
Wm. Frances, ostler
⟨Joseph Aliston, 4 child., cordw.⟩
⟨John Allen, 5 children, cordw.⟩
Joseph Hurst, woolsortr.
Edwd. Parker, combr.
Benjn. Eston, bakr.
⟨Edwd. *illegible*, infirm, fellmgr.⟩
⟨John *illegible*, fellmgr.⟩
James Sikes, fellmgr.
Wm. Serjeant, collarmkr.
Joseph Underwood, cordwr.
John Wills, combr.
Wm. Farrer, tayler
Wm. Warren, cordwr.
Richd. Maycock, painter
Edwd. Linen, cordw.
Wm. Hughes Painter, painter
Peter Peace, publican
Richd. Payne, staymkr.

Wm. Manning, woolstapler
⟨John Garret, lame, 8 child.,
    commer⟩
Wm. Harford, weaver
Thos. Otham, comber
Richd. Fox, whitesmith
Thos. Cornly, cordwr.
John Abbot, cordw.
Wm. Payne, combr.
Wm. Johnson, hilyer
Saml. Johnson, mason
Thos. Hoolet, cordw.
Charles Lethen, cordw.
Thomas Cove, sivemaker
Thos. Aorn, cordw.
Wm. Mann, cordw.
James Teaten, tayler
Thos. Luck, cordw.
John Scofield, laborer
⟨Wm. Teaten, blacksmith⟩
Lowe Howard, cord.
Robt. Tipler, ostler
Robt. Ashby, glazier
Wm. Kimdale, harnesmkr.
John Leach, cooper
Joseph Fox, weaver
⟨John Ward⟩ infirm, weaver
James Chapman, broommkr.
John Dunkley, labourer
Wm. Garret, cordw.
Geo. Munns, cordw.
Wm. Walker, weaver
John Munns, cordw.
James Clark, malster
John Dinley, servant

John Mason, currier
Wm. Howard, cord.
John Ashhtworth, carptr.⟩
Richd. Clemens, carptr.
⟨Francis Hall, 4 child., cordw.⟩
⟨John Worley, 3 child., ostler⟩
Thos. White, cordw.
⟨John Kitney, 5 chil., woolsorter⟩
⟨John Dawson, 3 child., cordw.⟩
James Cooper, leather drssr.
John Vicars, ostler
John Colton, cordwindr.
Adam Smith, cordwind.
⟨Wm. *illegible*, 3 child., labourer⟩
⟨John *illegible*, cordw.⟩
Wm. Brue, cordwr.
Saml. Bett, cordw.
Wm. Wyett, weaver
John Kelten, lace dealer
Saml. Johnson, carpentr.
James Vicars, servant
Wm. Shickle, parchmenmkr.
James Haynes, leather drssr.
⟨Christophr. Tindale⟩ lame,
    carpenter
Wm. Jones, slaymkr.
Wm. Adams, weaver
Thos. Ryely, labourer
Thos. Ribbet, labourer
Wm. Summerfield, labourr.
⟨Saml. *illegible*, 4 child., comber⟩
Thos. Clariage, cordw.
Saml. Cook, weaver
Thomas Vawn, comber

⟨Saml. Elton, constable.⟩
⟨Robrt. Kinnersley, thirdboroug.⟩
⟨Antony *illegible*, thirdboroug.⟩

NORTHAMPTON (WEST WARD)

A list of names beloning to the West Ward of Northampton liable to sarve in this county militia.

Rich. Kintt, labr.
Benj. James, shoe maker
⟨Jno. Westley⟩ uppolster
Wm. Smith, gardiner
Josh. Walker, comber
Thos. Brooks, miller
Nathl. Massey, shoemaker
Mr. Jams. Ryland, teacher
Mr. Egg, do.
Mr. Wittsey, do.

James Hewitt, vittler
James Jones, malster
Wm. Edge, shoe-maker
Jonathn. Stewart, coachman
Thos. Barns, do.
Thos. Green, labr.
Thos. Johnson, carptinter
Heny. Willson, soyor
John Cooplond, weehilwright
John Slinn, slater

Wm. Willkinson, stapler
James Cooper, labr.
Wm. Robarts, do.
⟨Thos. Thomptson⟩ 5 children,
   shoemaker
Wm. Meling, do.
⟨Josh. Johnson⟩ 6 children, do.
Thos. Holt, labr.
Wm. Penn, shoe maker
Christr. Henson, slatter
James Holmby, mason
Jams. Johnson, shoe maker
Thos. Norton, labr.
⟨Frans. Marriott⟩ 3 children
   ⟨mason⟩
Thos. Wyatt, dyor
Thos. Hewlett, shoe maker
Jonathn. Oadel, shoe maker
Richd. Brooks, do.
John Robarts, matt maker
⟨Wm. Comberpatch⟩ 3 children,
   labr.
John Spencer, carpenr.
⟨Wm. Watts,⟩ brazer
Samll. Wright, weaver
Thos. Whitney, sarvt.
John Old, do.
John Harding, labr.
Thos. Harding, do.
Richd. Erling, taylor
Edw. Gray, shoe maker
Richd. Colson, miller
Richd. Rickett, millwright
Samll. Law, weaver
John Law, shoe maker
Josh. Turne, fellmonger
Jos. Hill, labr.
Thos. Goodall, do.
John Sumpter, do.
Wm. Norton, shoe maker
John Norton, weaver
Thos. Morgan, flaxdresser
Robt. Moore, labr.
Wm. Piggott, tanner
Samll. Mellows, mason
James Neale, shoe maker
John Cox, do.
John Penn, do.
John Melows, mason
Robt. Neale, shoe-maker
John Law, gardiner
Thos. Joyner, labr.
Thos. Ringrose, do.
Thos. Welch, flaxdresser

Thos. Colman, shoe maker
Geoe. Paver, labr.
Wm. Hill, sarvt.
Edw. Pelgeram, taylor
Wm. Roughton, do
John Walker, shoe maker
Wm. Collier, labr.
Richd. Stubbins, shoe maker
John Green, do.
Robt. Bowbery, do.
Wm. Briggs, do.
John Collier, shoe maker
Wm. Bud, weaver
Josh. Hobson, shoe maker
Thos. Harris, miller
Thos. Collins, sarvt.
Richd. Bradfield, labr.
Josh. Cannon, labr.
Richd. Samwell, carptenter
John Ashworth, do.
Frans. Johnson, shoe maker
Petter Hill, do.
Thos. March, teacher
Thos. Sarjeant, do.
John Agger, do.
Wm. Timms, doctor
Richd. Farral, sarvt.
Wm. Massey, shoe maker
Nich. Battin, plumber
Thos. Tribble, weaver
Wm. Colman, labr.
Wm. Buck, whitesmith
Josh. Rubber, carptenr.
Geoe. Orsburn, shoe maker
Thos. Bayley, do.
⟨Paul Dadford⟩ 3 children, do.
Samll. Curring, gardiner
Thos. Boetterel, baker
Robt. Smith, coachman
John Willson, sarvent
Thos. Mathews, farrir
Charls. Mathews, do.
Mr. Josh. Clarke, gent.
John Marrel, sarvt.
Thos. Johnson, esqr.
John Hunt, sarvt.
Mrs. Johnsons futtman
Freemn. Taylor, curior
John York, sarvt.
Thos. Clark, sarvt.
Wm. Miles, do.
John Castel, barber
⟨Wm. Bayes, weaver, 3 child.⟩
John Collis, labr.

Geoe. Gatthwell, comber
John Fox, vittler
Wm. Foster, sarvt.
Pedega. Orsburn, white-smith
Wm. Orsburn, do.
John Willkingson, shoe maker
Wm. Cartwright, do.
Chars. Balam, sadler
⟨Frans. Dodd⟩ lame, do.
Josh. King, groser
John Haddon, shoe maker
Thos. Burnham, statchioner
Eale Boone, barber

John Spparrow, do.
James Schofield, vittler
⟨Wm. Billingham⟩ infirm ⟨labr.⟩
Edwd. Cox, cabenett maker
Thos. Old, sarvt.
John Summerfield, sarvt.
Edwd. Smith, vittler
Samll. Slater, sarvt.
Thos. Hill, do.
Samll. Treslove, gent.
⟨John Hopper, weaver⟩ infirm
Wm. Atterbury, farrer
Wm. Kent, labr.

⟨Mattw. Groocock, constable.⟩

TOWCESTER HUNDRED

Abthorpe	58	Towcester	186
Alderton	11	Wood Burcote	5
Cold Higham	25	Caldecote	9
Gayton	22		——
Pattishall	76		407
Tiffield	15		

Baker	7	Maltster	2
Baker (gingerbread)	1	Mason	2
Blacksmith	13	Miller	1
Book-keeper	1	No trade given	20
Bricklayer	6	Ostler	3
Brickmaker	2	Peruke-maker	1
Butcher	8	Plumber	1
Carpenter	11	Postboy	5
Clock-maker	1	Publican	3
Collar-maker	2	Saddler	1
Cooper	1	Schoolmaster	1
Currier	2	Servant	97
Draper	1	Shepherd	2
Drawer	2	Shoemaker	22
Farmer	17	Stay-maker	4
Farmer's son	6	Stockinger	4
Fellmonger	2	Surgeon	4
Flat-maker	2	Tailor	8
Framework-knitter	26	Tallow chandler	2
Gardener	5	Turner	2
Gentleman	1	Victualler	2
Glazier	1	Weaver	4
Glover	5	Wheelwright	1
Grocer	6	Whitesmith	1
Innholder	3	Wool-comber	2
Labourer	72	Yeoman	1
Lace-maker	2		——
Landholder	3		407
Landholder's son	2		

ABTHORPE

Northampton Shire to wit—Abthorp militia list December 16th 77.

⟨Robt. Barford, constable⟩
⟨Val. Willifer, headborough⟩
⟨Robt. Rush, victr.,
   drawn before⟩
 Richd. Hutchings, servant
 Wm. Staples, frame work knitter
⟨Jno. Floyd, drawn before⟩

Wm. Bowers, labrer
Wm. Stanley, do.
⟨Jno. Norris, victr., lame⟩
Tho. Williams, carpntr.
⟨*illegible*⟩ Meacham, labrer
Tho. Button, framework knitter
Jno. Dover, do.

⟨Tho. Snelson, do.,
  drawn before⟩
Richd. Wady, do.
Jno. Boughton, labrer
⟨Joseph Rainbow, taylor,
  4 children⟩
Wm. Sellers, framework knitter
Tho. Tims, framework knitter
Ben. Barrott, labrer
Jno. Winkles, carpntr.
Jno. Trotter, frame work knitter
Henry Allen, labrer
⟨Joseph Higham, shoe maker,
  lame⟩
Ewd. Summers, labrer
Wm. Dilly, servant
Tho. Barford, farmr
⟨Tho. Middleton, frame work
  knitter, lame⟩
Robt. Burnell, servant
⟨Richd. Burnell, servant,
  drawn before⟩
Wm. Burnell, servant
Wm. Sheppard, frame work
  knitter
Joseph Wills, do.
Ewd. Green, servant
Tho. Ward, do.

Richd. Smith, farmr
Martin Curby, butcher
Jno. Thornton, framework
  knitter
Wm. Blinco, do.
Jno. Smith, labrer
⟨Alexr. Dover, framework
  knitr, lame⟩
Emanul. Dover, labrer
Tho. Flowers, framework knitter
Tho. Knight, do.
Jno. Baker, servant
Tho. White, do.
Tho. Higham, do.
Wm. Smith, do.
Jno. Saul, labrer
⟨Chares Trotter, do., 3 childrn⟩
Wm. Paintor, servant
⟨Richd. Thornton, labrer,
  6 childn⟩
⟨Richd. Shepherd, drawn before⟩
⟨Jno. Tims, framework knitter,
  5 childn⟩
⟨Stevn Middleton, do., 5 childrn⟩
⟨Wm. Henson, do., 3 do.⟩
⟨Saml. Savige, do., 5 do.⟩
Jno. Frankling, servant

R. Barford, constable.

ALDERTON

Decr. 23rd 1777. A list of the names of the parish of Alderton lyable to serve as militia men.

Robt. Welford, shepard
Joseph Woodin, servant
John Battoms, do.
Thos. Blunt, do.
Edward Longstaff, do.
John Franklin, farmers son

John Whitlock, labourer
Wm. Rogers, do.
⟨John Travell, do., infirm⟩
⟨Joseph Travell, do., infirm⟩
Francis Elms, weaver

Wm. Slater, constable.

COLD HIGHAM

A true list of all persons between eighteen and forty five dwelling within the parish of Cold Higham with their occupations.

Land holders
John Archbold
Francis Mutton
Thos. Gibbins, juner

Land holders sons
John Wackefield
Joseph Wackefield

Robt. Archbold, inn-holder
⟨John Judkins, blacksmith⟩

Servants
Simon Meads
John Leeds
⟨Willm. Paysenall⟩
George Moor

Thos. Billing
John Webster
Thos. Goodman
Robt. Archbold
Richd. Tomkins
Robt. Tomkins
Thos. Falwell
Ambras Higham

Thos. Towshend, taylor
Thos. Hinks, blacksmith
Richd. Hands ⎱ cordwinders
Thos. Marriott ⎰

Labours

Stephen Furnis
John Huett

The day of appeal is on Wensday the 17th of this instant Decer. at the White Horse Inn in Towcester.

Thos. Gibbins, sener, constable.

GAYTON

A list of the pinhabitance of the parich of Gayton as is fit to sarve the militia.

Richd. Cue, sarvant
John Binder, sarvant
Wm. Wheatley, masener
John Wheatley, farmer
Richd. Letts, sarvant
Wm. Middleton, sarvant
Wm. Dunckley, carpinder
Thos. Branson, masener
Henry Holland, labrow
Saml. George, farmer
George Tredell, sarvant
Francis Maddock, farmer son

Charles Kingston, labrouw
Wm. Griffiths, farmer
James Harris, sarvant
John Gudgin, malstor
James Dunckley, carpinder
John Dunckley, carpinder
James Keech, sarvant
Samuel Cucknell, sarvant
John Willcox, labrouw
Thos. West, farmer
Wm. George, cunstable
Wm. Payne, thurdborouw

PATTISHALL

A list of the names of the proper persons to serve in the militia in the parish of Pattishall.

Willm. Wrighton, farmer
Rid. Pirkins, farmer
Thos. Browne, servant
George Duglas, servant
Thos. Heler, shewmaker
Samll. Heler, shewmaker
Thos. Forster, labror
Rid. Heler, servant
John Whitton, farmers son
John Johnson, servant
Rid. Croxford, labror
Frs. Duningham, servant
George Lets, labror
Samll. Waters, farmer
Willm. Wills, wool comber
Robt. Labram, jurneman ditto
Wm. Howard, colermaker
Robt. Keye, labror
John Pell, labror

Wm. Leeke, baker
Wm. Dad, servant
Thos. Steel, servant
Rid. Pell, servant
John Stamp, farmer son
Robt. Neal, servant
Wm. Pinckard, farmer
Steven Carter, servant
Benjmen Winckels, farmer son
Thos. Pell, labror
Wm. Harriss, malster
John Pinnack, servant
Thos. Cook, farmer
⟨Rid. Bodily, servant⟩
Thos. Newit, servant
Benjaman Facer, servant
Rid. Judkins, servant
Francis White, labror
Thos. Waters, labror

Rid. Phelps, farmer
John Folwell, servant
Wm. Pinckard, farmer
Lambard Waters, labror
John Pell, weaver
Thos. Abbot, labror
Haines Pratt, blacksmith
⟨Samll. Gibbs, weaver⟩
⟨Thos. Bason, labror⟩
Michel Newman, servant
Thos. Webb, shewmaker
Thos. Pirkins, farmer
Wm. West, servant
John Jones, servant
Thos. West, servant
John Horn, farmer son
⟨Wm. Winckels, labror⟩
John Ares, labror
Rid. Jesop, stokiner

Frs. Elms, baker
Samll. Cockrel, baker
Mark Folwell, butcher
Thos. Dunkley, servant
Jobe Kerton, labror
John Fountaine, weaver
Thos. Blenco, labror
Wm. Steel, shewmaker
⟨Wm. Higham, stockiner⟩
John Carter, stockiner
⟨Jos. Lucas, servant⟩
Wm. Woolfe, farmer
Wm. Warwick, butcher
Wm. Horn, stokiner
Wm. Blenco, labror
Wm. Mea, wheelright
Rid. Winckels, butcher
⟨Rid. Forster, taylor⟩
⟨Wm. Rainbow, labror, inferm⟩

John Sheppard, constable.

The day of appeal is on Wensday the 17th day of December you that think your selves aggrived must apply then no appeal will be receved afterwards at the White Horse Inn at Towcester.

TIFFIELD

A list of the mens names that are liable to serve in the militia of the parrish of Tiffield.

Willm. Faulkner
John Faulkner
Jos. Watters
Thos. Watters
Willm. Marriott
Saml. Brain
Willm. Brett
Thos. Curtis

Robt. Curtis
Thos. Pratt
Thos. als John Limon
Thos. Rattley
Thos. Hopcraft
Saml. Cole
Benj. Nibb

Cornelus Gudgins, constable.

Thos. Horn, thirdbrrow.

TOWCESTER

Towcester and Handly list.

William Waters, yeoman
William Stanton, publican
Thomas Benson, labourer
Benjamin Kibble, labourer
Richard Clark, labourer
John Yates, labourer
George Claridge, labourer
Michael Miles, bricklayer
John Capron, sheppard
George Flood, labourer

James Sharp, framework knitter
William Facer, labourer
William Sharp, labourer
William James, labourer
Jonas Collings, staymaker
Francis Hoar, sarvant
William Hoar, labourer
Joseph Emmott, frameworknitter
Samuel Moody, frameworknitter
William Ratlidge, brickmaker

George Marshall, fellmonger
⟨John Scotton, lacemaker⟩
Francis Treen, labourer
Robert Kingston,
    frameworknitter
Thomas Letts, frameworknitter
⟨William Corby, taylor⟩
Charles Lamburn, labourer
Joseph Clark, staymaker
⟨Richard Oxley, turner⟩
William Oxley, turner
John Wood, junior, butcher
Thomas Rickett, labourer
John Middleton, bricklayer
John Capron, grocer
William Hollaway, servant
Samuel Deacon, surgeon
Edward Sabin, surgeon
Joseph Kingston, servant
William Johnson, cordwainer
John Roddis, cordwainer
Simon Lovell, servant
John Flinders, servant
Robert Webb, servant
John Wood, butcher
Thomas Everett, perukemaker
Richard Brown, butcher
John Webb, servant
William Billing, ostler
⟨John Billing, labourer⟩
Thomas Ward, servant
John Blaxley, carpenter
Robert Cadwell, cordwainer
John Betts, grocer
William Carter, cordwainer
William Pinckard, cooper
William Davis, blacksmith
William Tilley, journeyman
    blacksmith
⟨Richard Tilley, postboy⟩
⟨Richard Cross, cordwainer⟩
⟨Thomas Gulliver, blacksmith⟩
Joseph Pursell, whitesmith
⟨Samuel Allington, journeyman
    tallowchandler⟩
Henry Harris, gardiner
John Ratlidge, brickmaker
Robert Johnson, labourer
Thomas Blencow, labourer
John Fretter, blacksmith
William Clark, labourer
William Antill Brown, glover
Benjamin Miles, taylor
William Waples, labourer

Daniel Basford, cordwainer
Thomas Newman, taylor
Flecher Blaxley, carpenter
Henry Wright, collarmaker
Nathaniel How, grocer
Henry Simco, baker
William Parish, baker
John Wooden, grocer
Thomas Dove, carpenter
⟨William Mickley, bricklayer⟩
James Crofts, grocer
⟨Thomas Kingstone, staymaker⟩
John Bangham, drawer
William Holland, servant
William Harris, glover
Robert Cockerill, flat maker
Ferdinando New, flat maker
⟨Willaim Eales, labourer⟩
⟨John Powel, cordwainer⟩
William Jeffery, blacksmith
William Bagley, carpenter
William Elkington, grocer
William Marshall, cordwainer
John Jarvis, blacksmith
William Smith, schoolmaster
Benjamin Haselop, fellmonger
Richard White, innholder
⟨Edward Willson, ostler⟩
George Jennings, servant
Charles White, servant
Francis Gibbs, plumber
Jonathan Todd, taylor
John Smith, publican
⟨Joseph Littler, postboy⟩
Edward Kerby, labourer
Richard Davis, innholder
Henry Harris, postboy
John Budd, servant
John Smith, ostler
Thomas Waddams, drawer
William Handthistle, servant
Thomas Palmer, postboy
⟨John Brett, labourer⟩
Richard Ashbowl, servant
Thomas Grant, surgeon
George Nurse, sadler
William Hodges, surgeon
Joseph Hium, servant
⟨Richard Capron, glazier⟩
John Davis, blacksmith
William Bland, glover
Mark Aburn, cordwainer
Walter Prestidge, clockmaker
⟨John Ross, postboy⟩

John Clark, draper
Jacob Russh, servant
John Goodman, currier
Benjamin Shackleton, servant
⟨Thomas Shackleton, carpenter⟩
⟨Thomas Kingston,
    tallowchandler⟩
⟨John Dean, servant⟩
George May, cordwainer
John Whitmoor, glover
⟨William May, currier⟩
John Nutter, labourer
Thomas Hartwell,
    frameworknitter
Samuel Todd, taylor
William Basford, gardiner
Eugene Basford, lacemaker
John Johnson, cordwainer
⟨William Timbs, servant⟩
John Allen, bookkeeper
William Lamburn, servant
John Jordan, servant
John Basford, cordwainer
Thomas Figg, servant
James Sheppard, blacksmith
Thomas Facer, labourer
William Davis, journeyman
    blacksmith
Richard Jeffs, baker
James Jeffs, servant
William Treen, labourer
Bennett Stokes, butcher
⟨Richard Mickley, bricklayer⟩
Francis Emerton, labourer

Thomas Gray, servant
John Webb, bricklayer
William Burditt, labourer

Handly

John Pinckard, gentleman
William Webb, servant
Thomas Jee, servant
Edward Hutchins, farmer
William Hium, servant
John Newitt, servant
Samuel Durham, servant
Thomas Howes, servant
⟨William Johnson, labourer⟩
⟨Richard Williams, labourer⟩
⟨Aathur Causebrook,
    gingerbread baker⟩
⟨John Hull, publican⟩
⟨George Thomason, bricklayer⟩
⟨John Buckley, servant⟩
⟨Richard Fretter, labourer⟩
⟨William Savage, blacksmith⟩
⟨Joseph Shackleton, glover⟩
⟨William Gardiner, gardiner⟩
⟨Joshua Aburn, cordwainer⟩
⟨John May, gardiner⟩
⟨William Powel, cordwainer⟩
⟨Thomas Padbury, miller⟩
⟨John Basford, gardiner⟩
⟨Samuel Wood, staymaker⟩
⟨Thomas Lamburn, servant⟩
⟨Mathew Clark, labourer⟩
⟨Bennett Sharp, farmer⟩

John Williams, constable.

Notice is hereby given, that all persons, who are aggrieved at their names, herein written must make their appeal, at the White Horse Inn Towcester, on Whensday the seventeenth day, of this instant December, and that no appeal will afterwards be received.

WOOD BURCOTE (parish of Towcester)

Wood Burcott list.

John Wass, baker
William Cooper, carpenter
William Lovell, labourer

Richard Jennings, labourer
William Long, servant

John Inns, constable.

CALDECOTE (parish of Towcester)

A list of the names at Caldicott in the parish of Towcester.

Thomas Day, cordwinder

Thomas Baylis, servant

William Ashbole, servant
James Eydon, servant
Edward Gray, servant
John Ratnit, servant

⟨James Griffin, servant⟩
James Webb, labourer
⟨John Pell, in fermd⟩

Richard Sheppard, constable.

WILLYBROOK HUNDRED

Apethorpe	21	Lutton	29
Collyweston	26	Nassington	39
Cotterstock	8	Southwick	19
Duddington	32	Tansor	21
Easton	63	Woodnewton	44
Fotheringhay	27	Yarwell	23
Glapthorn	36		___
King's Cliffe	79		467

Attorney	1	Miller	4
Baker	11	No trade given	43
Blacksmith	8	Plasterer	1
Butcher	3	Plumber	1
Carpenter	18	Roper	2
Collar-maker	1	Servant	93
Cooper	1	Shepherd	9
Farmer	37	Shoemaker	15
Farmer's son	3	Slater	27
Gardener	8	Tailor	6
Glazier	3	Tanner	1
Hemp-dresser	5	Turner	10
Jobber	1	Victualler	1
Joiner	1	Weaver	17
Keeper	4	Wheelwright	6
Knacker	1	Wool-comber	1
Labourer	97	Yeoman	6
Maltster	2		___
Mason	19		467

APETHORPE

A list of the names of the milesher in the parish of Apethorpe in the hundred of Willobroock in the countey of Northampton shire.

Mr. John King, farmer	James Winters, laber
James Freaney, farmer	Thos. Ball, shoomaker
John Cheesman, farmer	John Hersson, sarvent
⟨Robart Chapman, cooper⟩	Wm. Moles, laber
John Reead, sarvent	James Smith, sarvent
Mathew Coox, black smith	Thos. Digbey, sarvent
Wm. Lenton, laber	Wm. Faring, sarvent
Samewell Ashebey, laber	James Barick, sarvent
James Henson, sarvent	Steven Gorden, keeper
John Gordeain, sarvent	Josef Moles, sarvent
Thos. Sculthorp, sarvent	

Edwd. Ball, constable.

COLLYWESTON

Colleyweston, Northampton Shire, 1777. A list of the merlisher from the age eighteen to fortyfive.

George Bland, labour
John Boyr, roper
John Boyr, sarvant
Robert Pridmoure, slater
Robert Close, slater
Tho. Mishal, slater
John Rowlat, shomaker
William Joyce, slater
John Joyce, slater
Tho. Joyce, slater
Anthony Wortley, slater
John Close, slater
Bathomew Leaton, pennement
    in his speach

John Burlemur, sarvant
William Gudwin, farmar
John Scott, labour
John Watts, farmar
Tho. Close, slater
William Dixey, slater
John Gilbord, gardner
Francis Osborn, framar
Daniel Palmar, shepard
Samuel Stokes, butcher
John Stanger, shomaker
William Osborrn, carpanter
James Walbanks, showmaker

Thare is only one pale day will be received 1777 will be at the Talbort in Oundle on December the 15.

COTTERSTOCK

Cotterstock.

John Hamon
Thomas Hodges
Danel Gudin
John Barton

Henery Tod
James Imgram
Robin Cornyel
William Right

DUDDINGTON

A list of the now dwelling men in the parrish of Duddington betwen the age of eighteen and fortifive years, 1777.

Wm. Pain, labourer
Tho. Bonner, weaver
Joseph Bradshaw, butcher
Tho. Hibbins, mason
Tho. Wotton, tanner
George Wyles, taylor
Matthew Glithero, labourer
Jno. Cooper, servant man
Robt. Clarke
Tho. Pilmore, labourer
Val. Godfrey, junr.
Tho. Shir'lliffe, servant man
⟨Tho. Perkins, servant man⟩
Jno. Rowlatt, labourer
Jno. Hibbins, mason
⟨Tho. Laxton, baker, lame⟩
Jno. Beaver, servant man

Robt. Chappell, slater
Jno. Dyson, vitelelar
Tho. Law, labourer
Jno. Bulimer, labourer
Robt. Hibbins, cordwainer
Henery Sherlliffe, carpender
Jno. Brumhead, farmer
Jno. Tompson, servant man
Wm. Hand, baker
Jno. Hill, labourer
Jno. Goodman, miller
Benjamin Goodman, servant
    man
⟨Tho. Sapcot, farmer, lame⟩
⟨Tho. Shertliffe, labourer⟩
Wm. Moisey, cordwainer

Val. Godfrey, constable.

EASTON ON THE HILL

1777. A list of all persons between the age of eighteen and fortyfive to serve as militia men for the parrish of Easton in the county of Northampton.

James Woodward, senr., slater
Thomas Woodward, slater
Richard Woodward, plasterer
Willm. Woodward, slater
Philip Longfoot, mason
William Longfoot, mason
David Taylor, labourer
Stephen Black, yeoman
Thos. Porter, junr., yeoman
Thos. Porter (Bell), yeoman
Willm. Porter (Bell), yeoman
⟨John Porter, slater⟩
Thos. Porter, slater
William Woodward, cordwainer
James Woodward, slater
William Bacon, yeoman
John Medwell, labourer
Robert Medwell, labourer
William Duncomb, gardiner
James Kendall, gardiner
John Kendall, blacksmith
George Lemons, labourer
James Woodward (Wald), slater
John Tavernor, carpenter
William Woodward, senr.,
    slater
John Benner, labourer
John Shefield, labourer
Chas. Cotton, slater
Robert Harrison, labourer
Thos. Woodward, labourer
Thos. Cotton, slater

Jeremiah Quanbrough, weaver
John Jeffs, cordwainer
William Earl, butcher
Samuel Pridmore, taylor
William Johnson, carpenter
William Richmond, gardiner
Robert Hill, weaver
William Newboon, labourer
George Benner, junr., slater
William Hill, weaver
George Longfoot, mason
James Blake, wheelright
Anthony Waterfall, slater
William Conington, slater
Robert Goodwin, cordwainer
William Benner, yeoman
Henry Lewin, labourer
Thomas Newman, labourer
William Plumbe, servant
Charles Beebee, servant
Daniel Charity, servant
George Clemons, servant
Josiah Wood, servant
John Hudson, servant
Francis Mason, servant
Gamble Cotterall, servant
James Parker, servant
Richard Redmile, servant
William Barrer, servant
Umphry Conington, labourer
Thos. Walker, labourer
John Porter, slatar

FOTHERINGHAY

A list of ye names of those persons in ye parish of Fotheringhay between ye ages of eighteen and forty five qualified to serve in ye militia for ye county of Northampton.

Mr. Jno. Maydwell, junr.,
    farmer
Mr. Richd. Maydwell, farmer
Mr. Isaac Maydwell, farmer
Mr. Jno. Hicks, farmer
Mr. Jno. Southw, farmer
Thos. Gray, farmer
Richd. Berridge, wheelright
Charles Berridge, wheelright
Jno. Hill, baker

Cornelius Paine, baker
Daniel Wyatt, carpenter
Thos. Moulds, labourer
Jno. Smith, labourer
Robt. Bellamy, servant
Wm. Hendson, servnt &
    shepherd
Wm. Rudkin, servant
Wm. Prudey, servant
Jno. Kisby, servt. & shepherd

Wm. Freeror, servant
Thos. Jackson, servant
George Limer, servant
Robt. Ladds, cord wainer
Thos. Marshall, lobourer
Thos. Curtis, servant

Samuel Adams, servt. &
   shepherd
Edwd. Barratt, labourer
Abraham Curzens, servt. &
   shepd.

GLAPTHORN

Decembr. ye 6th 1777. A parfect list of all parsons that are liable to serve for the militia for the parish of Glapthorn and for the ensuing years.

James Cannum, mason
Henrey Charrity, laborow
Joseph Wells, laborow
Jno. Holley, laborow
Thos. Phillips, laborow
⟨Edwd. Wrightcraft, bent need,
   laborow⟩
Robt. Hillam, laborow
Thos. Hillam, laborow
Thos. Meadows, farmer &
   game keeper
Willm. Ingram, labrow
Mattw. Pridmore, labrow
Jno. Bradshaw, weaver
⟨Willm. Bradshaw, weaver⟩
Henry Flemans, shepard
⟨Robt. Coles, laborow⟩
Robt. Palmer, cartpinder
Jno. Palmer, farmer

Robt. Pinder, laborow
Robt. Jinn, laborow
⟨Gorge Manning, laborow⟩
⟨James Ingram, laborow⟩
Amus Mace, laborow
Jno. Southwell, plumer & glazer
⟨Willm. Horstead, weaver⟩
Thos. Horstead, weaver
⟨Thos. Oliver, laborow⟩
Willm. Brown, labrow
Mr. Mattw. Southwell, maltster
Thos. Palmer, cartpinder
Jno. Palmer, cartpinder
Thos. Braughton, labrow
Charles Birridge, cartpinder
Willm. Browning, servant man
Thos. Crooks, servt. man
Jno. Suter, servt. man
Thos. Edey, labrow, single man

KING'S CLIFFE

Decbr. 11 1777. This is a true list of all the persons as are now dwelling in the parish of Kings Cliffe in the county of Northampton between the ages of 18 and 45 years.

John Vines, turner
Thos. Ball, farmer
Edward Scotney, servant
Thos. Cooper, servant
Francis Cook, turner
John Town, servant
John Palmer, servant
Mr. Thos. Boughton, attoy.
Richard Fording, mason
John Cunington, junr., carpenter
John Waples, labourer
Thos. Pain, labourer
James Spire, junr., slater
John Blake, blacksmith
Samel. Blake, blacksmith
John Ventros, servant

John Harker, labourer
Wm. King, turner
Robert Godfrey, farmer
Richard Whright, servant
⟨Thos. Newbon, baker, 3 chi.⟩
John Scotney, servant
Benjamin Howes
⟨Thos. Whyte, taylor⟩
Wm. Tomlin, labourer
Wm. Carrington, carpenter
John Lightfoot, hempdreser
Wm. Lightfoot, hempdreser
Frank Rate, labourer
Wm. Williamson, joiner
Mr. Wm. Howard
Thos. Carrington, carpenter

Charles Whyman, roper
Joseph Sheffeild, taylor
Mathew Hayr, mason
John Hayr, cordwinder
Wm. Whyles, baker
Robert Smart, baker
Wm. Whyte, miller
Thos. Waterfeild, servant
Thos. Gamble, junr., miler
Hennery England, jober
John Glitherow, mason
Richard Glitherow, jun., mason
Francis Peper, labourer
James Carrington, carpenter
Charles King, wever
Joseph Harvey, wever
Samel. Harvey, comer
Leonard Dixon, junr., turner
Benjamin Dixon, turner
Wm. Sheild, labourer
George Stansby, nacker
Wm. Cole, labourer
⟨Wm. Hayr, junr., baker⟩
Richard Wadsworth, servant

⟨John Birch, turner⟩
Thos. Jackson, jun., wever
John Jackson, wever
Nathel. Dixon, junr., turner
Francis Jackson, wever
Edmund Cunington, blacksmith
James Dixon, jun., turner
Richard Blake
Benjamin Jackson, wever
Robert Baley, turner
John Leopard, labourer
George Rutcheson, farmer
Hennery Harris, jun., wever
John Wadwell, labourer
James Rayson, keeper
Wm. Hamon, servant
John Dixon, jun., turner
Benjamin Taylor, servant
Wm. Deacon
Robert Worrow, carpenter
James Chapel, jun., slater
John Baley
John Scotney, mason

The above list is taken acording to the best of our judgments by us

John Howes
Matthew Henson
constables.

LUTTON

Willy Brook hundred, 1777. Lutton. A true list of all persons between the age of eighteen and forty five loyable to serve as militia men for ye parish of Washingley come Lutton in ye county of Northampton viz:—

John Sanderson, farmer
John Boulton, farmer
John Watts, servant
John Collyer, laborour
Peter Bodger, blacksmith
Willm. Yarram, labourer
Willm. Sprigmaur, labourer
Jin Crackson, labourer
⟨John Jinks, shepard, apeald⟩
Willm. Jonson, labourer
James Rodgers, servant
James Drue, singleman, lame
  knee
James Bucknell, farmer
Willm. Baker, servant
Willm. Mitchell, servant
Thomas Chandler, labourer

John Todhissan, gardiner
Francis Earl, farmer
John Coales, shepard
Willm. Clark, servant
Geo. Ruff, servant
Willm. Phillips, servant
Willm. Leading, farmer
⟨John Nash, drawn apeald⟩
⟨Thos. Rands, poor & three
  children⟩
⟨Hugh Boar, poor, three
  children⟩
⟨Laurance Ingman, drawn man⟩
⟨Willm. Brooks, lame hand⟩
⟨John Hinch, poor, three
  children⟩

Notice is given that ye day and place of appeal is on Monday the fifteenth day of December 1777 at ye Talbot Inn in Oundle and that those yt thinks themselves agreived may then appeal & yt no appeals will afterwards be received.

By Charles Bodger, constable, Lutton hamlet.

NASSINGTON

A list of the militia men in the parish of Nassington in Northampton shire.

William Warpole, sheomaker
William Huddlestone, lab.
Josiah Johnson, glazier
William Hill, labr.
⟨Joshua the glazer⟩ unknown
John Stimpson, weaver
James Scot, taylor
Thomas Rippon, glazier
Robt. Huddlestone, lab.
⟨James Yeats, shephard⟩
Thomas Scotney, sart.
Samuell Southwell, sart.
John Handson, farmer
Edward Hart, hemp dresser
John Males, farmer
William Brauton, sart.
John Baker, sart.
William Walter, wheal right
Abraham Walter, do.
Richard Barr, labr.

Robert Emerton, weaver
Robert Jones, shoomaker
Matthew Winterton, do.
⟨John Ireland, farmer⟩
Edmund Negus, farmer
Samuell Wadwell, labr.
Thomas Ward, labr.
Robert Harrinson, labr.
William Bunning, whealrigt
John Morris, labr.
Edward Shaw, labr.
John Beasley, shumaker
William Jeffs, sart.
Daniel Taylor, sart.
John Reynards, sart.
Joseph Robberts, sart.
Robert Stainsby, hemp dreser
John Bradshaw, keeper
John Cismer, keeper sart.

They who shall think themselves aggreeved are to appeal at the Talbot Inn in Oundle on the fifteenth day of December and that no appeal will be afterwards received.

SOUTHWICK

A true list of the names of all such persons within the parish of Southwick, and at Crosswith Hand Lodge in the Forest of Rockingham as are liable to serve in the militia. December the 6th 1777.

Henry Goodyer
Henry Dalby
Josh. Clements
Henry Weekly
⟨James Lee⟩
⟨Richd. Dutton⟩
Oliver Barnes
Thos. Groocock
James Busby
James Craps

⟨Thos. Halfoot⟩
Thos. Abbot
Thos. Parker
Adam York
Wm. Kennell
Geo. Todd
Thos. Tyers
Robt. York
Wm. York

N.B. A meeting of the Deputy Lieutenants will be held on Monday the fifteenth of this month at the Talbot in Oundle, when & where all such persons as shall think themselves aggrieved may appeal, no appeal being afterwards to be received. D. Elkins.

TANSOR

1777. A list of persons to serve in the militia of the parish of Tansor in county of Northampton.

Samuel Edde, labower
Samuel Coals, labower
⟨Robert Noble, carpenter⟩
Joseph Vann, carpenter
William Killingworth, mason
John Rowell, farmer
John Tayler, servant
Richard Knighton, servant
⟨William Long, servant⟩
Henry Bellamy, servant
Francis Sutton, servant

George Rowell, servant
Richard Leach, servant
John Southwell, servant
Thomas Sawfoot, servant
Richard Grooby, labower
William Gea, labower
Matthew Woollaston, labower
John Underwood, servant
John Todd, servant
William Feelding, sarvent

That the day of appeal is the fifteen day of December next at the Talbot Inn in Oundle. If aney think themselves aggrieved may then appeal or no appeal will be received afterwards.

WOODNEWTON

A list of the persons names in ye parrish of Woodnewton for the millita in Willer Brook hundread in ye county of Northampton Shire.

Thomas Hardy, farmer
John Desbrow, taylor
John Smith, labourer
Edward Smith, labourer
Willm. Smith, labourer
Robert Desbrow, farmer
Mattw. Desbrow, gardner
Henry Moulds, labourer
Willm. Mayson, servant
John Moulds, servant
Guy Warrick, servant
George Desbrow, servant
John Dolby, farmer
Willm. England, labourer
Willm. Fitzjohn, labourer
Thomas Bell, servant
Thomas Franey, gardner
John Wright, labourer
⟨Thomas Franey, maysoner⟩
Thomas Beeby, labourer
Henry Goodyer, farmer
Mattw. Goodyer, farmer

John Thrift, servant
Robert Bullimore, carpentor
Willm. Goodyer, farmer
Robert Harker, carpentor
Thomas Sanders, labourer
Willm. Hosley, labourer
Thomas Cox, blacksmith
Robert Hale, blacksmith
Edmund King, baker
⟨James King, baker⟩
John Strickson, collar maker
John Rippon, labourer
⟨Robert Wilks, gardner⟩
John Flemming, labourer
Prusia Farren, servant
Robert Reedman, servant
Edward Redhead, servant
Mr. Hales Gryender
Thomas Andrew, servant
⟨Mattw. Hale, baker⟩
⟨Thos. Henson, farmer⟩
⟨Willm. Hale, farmer⟩

To meet at the Talbot In Oundle on the 15th Day of December next.

John Dolby, constable.

YARWELL

December the 7 1777. Yarwell. List of those persions who are qualified for to sarve on the militia.

John Truss, farmer son

Henry Foard, sarvent

John Osptial, labrour
William Irson, mason
Edward Peak, farmer son
Rogger Turner, sarvent
George Lewis, sarvent
⟨Thomas Jackson, sarvent⟩
Thomas Eat, sarvent
Thomas Irson, mason
John Irson, mason
James Thompson, mason
William Julyan, millor

William Norman, labrour
Francis Thompson, mason
John Barcker, labrour
William Green, sarvent
Charles Tood, labrour
Abraham Taylor, labrour
John Brown, molster
⟨John Alderman, hempdresor⟩
John Irson, mason, juner
Richard Harrison, farmer son

If aney of you thinks your selvs aggrived you may appeal at the Talbut
in Oundle on the fifteenth day of December after that no appeal will be
received.

WYMERSLEY HUNDRED

Blisworth	29	Little Houghton	41
Brafield	21	Milton	40
Castle Ashby	12	Piddington	25
Cogenhoe	20	Preston Deanery	14
Collingtree	16	Quinton	9
Courteenhall	12	Rothersthorpe	31
Denton	34	Whiston	8
Grendon	55	Wootton	44
Hackleton	17	Yardley Hastings	65
Hardingstone	76		
Horton	10		602
Great Houghton	23		

Ale-keeper	1	Lace-man	1
Baker	5	Maltster	3
Blacksmith	12	Mason	5
Breeches-maker	2	Miller	4
Butcher	5	Miller's servant	1
Butler	1	Miller's son	1
Carpenter	18	Newsman	2
Chandler	1	No trade given	86
Coachman	1	Painter	1
Dealer	1	Postilion	1
Esquire	2	Public house	1
Excise-man	1	Servant	123
Farmer	46	Shepherd	14
Farmer (gentleman)	1	Shoemaker	23
Farmer's servant	11	Shopkeeper	3
Farmer's son	24	Soap-boiler	1
Footman	1	Stay-maker	3
Gardener	6	Steward	1
Gentleman	4	Tailor	11
Gentleman's servant	1	Victualler	4
Grazier	3	Weaver	10
Grazier's son	2	Wheelwright	4
Groom	2	Wheelwright's son	1
Groom (under)	1	Wool-comber	1
Illegible	1	Wool-stapler	1
Labourer	136		
Lace-maker	7		602

BLISWORTH

County of Northampton. Wymersley Hundred, November ye 26th 1777.
Blisworth list then made by Joseph Hedge constable for the parish of

Blisworth of all men dwelling within the parish of Blisworth between the ages of eighteen and forty five years.

First, Edwd. Brafield, a
    gentleman farmer
William Hedge, a farmer
Thos. Langford, a gentlemans
    servant

Farmers servants

Wm. Pettifer
John Tebbey
John Bolton
John Neale
Thos. Clarke
Wm. Clarke
Thos. Hedge
James Stokes
Thos. Baldwin

Tradesmen

Francis Plowman
Charles Adkins
Richd. Goodridge

George Goode
Benjamin Goode
Wm. Faulkner
Thos. Pacey
Peter Fretter
George Marriott
John Cowley
Thos. Peach

Labourers

Wm. Willcox
John Limon
⟨Josph. Whitlock, drawn⟩

Incapacitated

⟨Edwd. Nutter, lost one end of
    a finger⟩
⟨Thos. Willcox, low of stature &
    a stammering speech⟩
⟨Wm. Collins, lame an ancle out
    of joint⟩

⟨Joseph Edge, constable.⟩

N.B. Notice is given that if any person be aggrieved ye day of appeal will be at the Peacock Inn, in Northampton on the eighth day of December next coming and—furthor notice is given that no appeal will be afterwards received.

BRAFIELD

Brafield militta list 1777.

William Cook, farmer
Richard Whiting, wheelwright
John White, servant
James Chapman, servant
Benjamin Jones, servant
⟨Thomas Smith, servant⟩ lame
⟨Langly Smith, labourer, lame⟩
Edward Robinson, servant
John Robinson, labourer
Uriah Geyton, wheelwright
Francis Robinson, servant

James Clayson, mason
William Clayson, servant
Daniel Clayson, servant
Nashon Brown, servant
William Drage, servant
John Fitczhugh, carpenter, senor
Thomas Fitczhugh, carpenter
John Fitczhugh, carpenter,
    junier
William Tompston, taylor
John Geyton, weaver

George Battison, constable.
Francis Whiting, headborough.

CASTLE ASHBY

Castle Ashby list of militia men.

Mr. John Adams
Mr. James Wooley
Mr. Samuel Green

Mr. John Buckby
William Hichcock
John Tebut

John Emmit
Edward Edins
Nickles White

George Waring
William Chapman
James Gibson

⟨John Rogers, constable.⟩

The day of a peal will be the eight day of December next at the Peearcock Inn, Northampton.

COGENHOE

A list of those betwin the age of eighteen and forty five able to sarve in ye militia in the parish of Cogenhoe in the year 1777.

Joseph Dunn, sarvant
Willm. Molton, sarvant
Thomas Valintine, labour
Joseph Moris, labrour
George James, sarvant
Thomas Devenshire, whever
Steven Spencer, sarvant
Thomas Ashby, sarvant
Danil Higgins, butcher
Hugh Higgins, farmer

Willm. Higgins, butcher
Henery Attewell, labrour
Willm. Moris, sarvant
Richard Cox, sarvant
⟨James Bedford, cordwinder⟩
John Faulkner, famer
Samuel Flindel, sarvant
Thomas Palmer, sarvant
Willm. Garner, labrour
Will. Gayton, labrour

All those that think themselfs agrved are to a pear at the Peacock Inn in Northampton on Mondey the eighth day of December at the day of apeal.

John Paine, constable.

COLLINGTREE

A list of the men between the ages of eighteen and forty five years that are able to sarve as militia men for the parrish of Collintree—1777.

Robard Brittens ⎫ sarvents
Thomas Brittens ⎭
Daniel Evans ⎫ larbras
Thomas Wingrave ⎭
Thomas Church, sarvent
William Pain, farmer
Richard Wingrive, farmer
Tobey Dibbiy, shepard
Thomas Jones, sarvent
William Sammons, labras

Thomas Cockeril ⎫ sarvent
Richard Cockeril ⎭
William Cockeril, sarvent
Thomas Labrams, farmer
Thomas Debett, labra
⟨John Abby, jorneman shoe-
    maker, three childerens⟩
⟨Richard Church, jorneman shoe-
    maker, three childrens⟩
⟨Thomas Clark, in firmd, larbra⟩

Francis Evans, constable.

COURTEENHALL

A true list of all men dwelling in the parish of Courtenhall between the ages of eighteen and forty five years of age.

Mr. John Loxly, steward
Thos. Dunkley, farmer
Ricd. Labrum, servant
Thos. Cockerill, miller
Thos. Sheppard, servant

Geo. Dunkley, servant
Wm. Dunkley, servant
John Dunkley, servant
James York, servant
Mathew Chapman, gardiner

John Phillips, labr.

Thos. Harris, labr.

Thos. Labrum, constable.

DENTON

A list of the men in the parish of Denton liabel to serve in the militta.

Thomas Roberson
Tomas Crook
James Horsborn
John Marriot
Thos. Pain
John Bailey
Edward Smith
Thos. Atterbery
Thos. Wooding
William Chapman
William Brumptam
Philip White
John Barker
William Barker
Charles White
Joseph White
George Lack
William Rainboo
Thos. Hornsby
Mark Roberson
Richard Calley
William Roberson
John Campen
John White
James White
Smith White
Vealintine Gibson
Richard Lansbre
Thomas Lansbre
William Sparrow
Thomas White
George Bearel
Thomas Morris
William Horsborn

The day of appeal will be on Monday the eight day of December at the Peacock Inn Northampton.

GRENDON

A list of the names and occupations of the parish of Grendon in the county of Northampton to serve as milita men.

John Munton, farmer
George Bletso, farmers son
Thos. Bletso, farmers son
Willm. Bletso, farmers son
Thos. Radburne, farmer
⟨Nathaniel Bates, servant, infirm⟩
Ben. Pendred, labo.
John Frost, labo.
Thos. Brealey, lacemaker
Willm. Revitt, carpenter
⟨John Hart, victular⟩ drawn
Willm. Gibs, baker
James Rattley, servant
John Underwood, servant
⟨John Wright, servant⟩
Thos. Wright, malster
Richard Bailey, victular
Willm. Mundy, excisman
Joseph Tayler, cordwinder
Willm. Cliff, victlar
John Smart, labo.
Willm. Laughton, farmers son
George Abraham, lacemaker
George Cherry, labo.
Robert Brawn, farmers son
Abraham Brawn, farmers son
Joseph Cliftun, labo.
John Thornton, lace maker
Edward Warden, gardner
  ⟨infirm⟩
John Coe, farmers son
Thos. Coe, farmers son
Camp. Cornish, shepard
Willm. Revitt, mason
Abaham Sharwood, tayler
John Staford, lacemaker
John James, labo.
⟨George Shipley, servant⟩
  apprentice
Willm. Roberson, servant
Joseph Pack, labo.
Thos. Revitt, mason

Willm. Hawkings, lace maker
Willm. Brux, lace maker
Issac Watford, lace maker
⟨John Bland, labo.⟩
Thos. Cherry, carpenter
Thos. Sanderson, sheepard
Willm Riton, servant
Willm. Sumerfield, labo.

John Spencer, blacksmith
Joseph Groome, blacksmith
Joseph Watford, blacksmith
Thos. Roberson, labo.
Willm. Hoten, labo.
Willm. Simson, butcher
Bartholomew Cherry, labo.

⟨John Cherry, constable.⟩

HACKLETON

Novembr. 26th 1777.
Hackelton, in the parish of Piddington in the county of Northampton.

Persons names—

Thos. Mercer, esqr.
Geoe. Righton, servant
John Whiting, do.
John Denton, do.
Wilm. Howes, do.
Richd. Morby, labourer
Joseph Cook, weaver
Samull Howes, labour
Wilm. York, servant

John Smith, do.
Joseph Green, cordwinder
John Johnson, wheelwright
Richd. Johnson, do.
Daniel Howes, farmors son
Thos. Old, cordwinder
Clark Nickals, do.
Thos. Goodman, labourer

John Jonne, cunstable.

HARDINGSTONE

A list of names to searve the millita in the parish of Hardingstone.

Jno. Avery, wooll stapler
⟨Richd. *illegible*, labr.⟩
Jno. Avell, cord wainer
Robrt. Basset, black smith
Thos. Bullimore, black smith
Calib Bird, carpenter
Saml. Brooks, foot man
Jno. Barriot, buttler
Thos. Bugworth, under groon
Thos. Bamford, labr.
Timmy Brice, sarvt.
Willm. Callcut, gent.
Willm. Clark, stay maker
Edw. Chapman, breeches maker
Thos. Digby, labr.
Jno. Donsher, stay maker
Richd. Edmonds, labr.
Willm. Freeman, servt.
Willm. Fisher, labr.
Thos. Furnice, taylor
Jno. Fox, black smith
Rowland Fox, black smith
Saml. Freeman, groom
Thos. Farmer, labr.

Saml. Gadsdon, labr.
Jno. Hiller, labr.
Gorge Harris, labr.
Jno. Hobson, taylor
Thos. Humphres, labr.
Willm. Jinkins, labr.
Willm. Kinning, sarvt.
Willm. Langford, sarvt.
Willm. Luck, cord wainer
Gorge Maul, gent.
Jacob More, gardener
⟨Gorge Maine, labr.⟩
Willm. Merrell, labr.
Jno. Manning, taylor
James Nickelson, coathman
Thos. Norton, weaver
Richd. Penn, carpenter
Wm. Penn, carpentor
Frans. Penn, carpentor
Wilm. Peaisland, labr.
Jno. Shargant, gardener
⟨Willm. South⟩ sarvt., lame
Jos. Shaw, farmer
Robt. Shipp, sarvt.

Thos. Shearman, staymakr
Jno. Shearman, taylor
Antoy. Tite, sarvt.
Abrm. Tite, breeches maker
Richd. Timms, labr.
Thos. Timms, farmer
Jos. Peach, cord wainer
Ralph Pulley, cord wainer
Willm. Tebbutt, postilon
Willm. Townsland, labr.
Willm. Tebbutt, cord wainer
Henry Wooding, servt.
⟨James Wickings, servt.⟩ lame
Thos. Warwick, labr.

Danil Wellford, labr.
Danil Wapoles, sarvt.
Willm. Wapoles, sarvt.
Willm. Ward, miller
Thos. Ward, sarvt.
⟨Thos. Cross, weaver⟩
Jams Brice, sarvt.
Jams Whats, lab.
Wm. Hakes, labr.
Jams. Simmons, painter
John Brice, non conpesments
Richd. Harthorp, cord wainer
John Sturges, sarvt.
⟨Richd. *illegible*, shew maker⟩

HORTON

A list of all the men now dwelling in the parish of Horton both names and occupations that are able to sarve in the militia.

Jerimiah Broocks, farmer
Valentine Tite, farmer
Thomas Caves, farmer
John Caves, farmer
William White, farmer

Fowler Ridtcherson, groome
James Person, sarvent
Henery Rogers, sarvent
John Travell, sarvent
William Smith, sarvent

John Brice, cunstable.
Novr. 30 1777.

GREAT HOUGHTON

A list of all such persons as usually and now dwelling within the parrish of Great Houghton in the county of Northampton between the ages of eighteen and fortyfive years, distinguishing their respective ranks and occupations and all such infirmities as any of them labour under incapacitating them from serving as militia men, Novr. ye 29th 1777.

Mr. Thomas Beet, gent.
Joseph Johnson, senr., grazier
Joseph Johnson, junr., grazier
Thos. Roe, junr., malster
James Pike, farmer
George Alderidge, servant
John Hunt, servant
Thomas Chaplin, carpenter
John Chapman, carpenter
William Pearson, servant
John Webb, labourer
Richard Cave, labourer
Benj. Cave, labourer
John Gibson, weaver

Saml. Robertsson, labourer
John Waterfall, weaver
John Hemery, weaver
Benj. Whitmey, mason
John Bassitt, weaver
Richard Bassitt, weaver
John George, labourer
Nathanael Gayton, woolcomber
⟨George Brice, junr., infirm,
    bad legs⟩
Hugh Higgins, publican,
    thirdborough
Thos. Roe, senr., grazier,
    constable.

LITTLE HOUGHTON

The militia list of Little Houghton, 1777.

George Manning, gent.   Francis Freear, dealer

William Manning, farmer
John Collier, farmer
Simon Collier
John Pacey
William Roe, farmer s
Thomas Coller, farmer
William Blunt, farmer s
James Marriott, farme b
Thomas Harris, farmer s
Thomas Pike, baker
William Law, gard.
William Wareing, malster
Samuel Monk, miller s
Thomas Dillow, ale keep
John Gayton, shoomaker
Joseph Hensman, shooma
William Laurance, labourer
William Walker, servant
Thomas George, servant
Richard Walker, servant

Richard Dodd, labourer
John Buckler, labourer
John Feary, servant
Thomas Spensor, servant
Charles Adkins, servant
Joseph Law, labourer
John Ashby, labourer
Edward Perkins, labourer
Thomas Kay, seepherd
William Gibbs, labourer
Robert Deacon, labourer
Thomas Clark, labourer
John Yorke, servant
Thomas Walker
William Knight
⟨Thomas Battisson⟩ ⎫
⟨John Edmonds⟩   ⎬ drawn
⟨Daniel Perkins⟩   ⎪ afore
⟨Richard Robinson⟩ ⎭

Robet Harris, constable.

MILTON

A list of the militry men of the parish of Milton.

Dennis Panter, servant
John Addinton, laborow
John Burton, laborow
Thomas Kinning, laborow
John Wellins, servant
John Ratnit, servant
Simon Twisilton, laborow
Mathew Abbey, servant
John Crass, laborow
Joseph Allin, farmer
Henry Britan, servant
⟨John Dunckley, one eye⟩
John Facer, taylor
John Collins, miller
Thomas Dunckley, farmer
William Willis, laborow
Joseph Stirman, cordwindr
John Gibbs, baker
Richard Gibbs, laborow
⟨Samuel Addinton, shepard⟩

Daniel Sparrow, laborow
William Gleed, laborow
Samuel Minards, laborow
John Muscot, servant
George Roberson, servant
John Creaton, farmer
Thomas Sirrige, cordwinder
Samuel Digby, sheppard
Charles Allin, puplick hose
Gaffield Gibbs, servant
John Caswell, farmer
⟨Joseph Sharp, farmar⟩
William Buckler, laborow
James Moorin, gardener
William Dunckley, servant
⟨Richard Jones, carpender⟩
William Brownsil, servant
Thomas Gibbs, baker
Joshua Waffern, farmer
Joseph Johnson, masoner

Jno. Frost, constable.

Note, the day of appeal is on Monday December the eighth day at the Peacock In, Northampton.

PIDDINGTON

A list of the mens names at Piddington in the county of Northampton that are liable to serve in the militia for the county, made November ye 29th 1777.

Edward Hilyr, labror
John Peason, sho maker
William Waine, servant man
John Wesly, taylor
Peeter James, farmer son
Thos. Whit, labror
John Chester, farmer son
Wolter Parker, farmer
John Smith, labror
⟨John Landon, labror with one eye⟩
James Colman, labror
John Morris, labror

John Parker, labror
John Brise, grazor
Thos. Clifon, labror
John James, farmer son
John Ritton, labror
George Willit, labror
Thos. Lack, labror
Richard Peason, servant man
Richard Brownsard, servant man
Robt. Peason, labror
Richard Ritchook, carpenter
Amos Peason, labror
Richard Paine, servant man

Robt. Cave, constable.

PRESTON DEANERY

A list of the men in the parish of Preston Deanary between the age of eighteen and forty five years.

Charles Newman, esqr.
Willm. Marriott ⎫
Willm. Ellet ⎬ farmers
Willm. Bull ⎫
John Bull ⎬ farmers sons
Richd. Bull ⎭
⟨James Crowleay, coardwinder, one bad eye⟩

Saml. Mabby ⎫
John Whiteing
James Geaton
Edwd. Pearson ⎬ sarvants
Jos. Hoarn
Saml. Green
Thos. Ellet ⎭

Thos. Roe, constable.

QUINTON

A list of the persons names qualified to sarve as militia men betwen the ages of eighteen and forty five in the parish of Quinton.

Charles Marriot, farmer
Josh. Clark, do.
Wm. Marriot, sarvent
Charles Crawley, labourer
Thos. Mallord, labourer

John Mallord, sarvent
John Bates, do.
Joseph Timms, do.
⟨Joseph Church, carpentor⟩

John Cave, constable.

ROTHERSTHORPE

November the 29th 1777. A list of the names of the people of the parish of Rothersthorpe betwixt the age of eighteen and forty five.

⟨Robert Eliott, blacksmith⟩
    lame on one arm
William Torland, servant
George Judgens, servant
William All, servant
Hennery Morriss, farmor

John Ward, farmor
Robert Coals, servant
⟨Samuel Fretter, sheperd⟩
John Howes, farmorson
William Chater, servant
Nathaniel Feniel, servant

Richard Forster, labourer
Thos. Billingham, carpenter
Thos. Wright, weelrightson
John James, sheperd
Richard Gleed, farmor
Robert Watts, servant
William Bartlet, servant
William Hipwell, farmor
Thos. Hipwell, farmorson
James Hipwell, farmorson

John Wilcox, servant
Joseph Pebordy, labourer
William Paine, farmor
Robert Frone, servant
John Watts, labourer
Stanford Farrin, taylor
⟨Samuel Trotter, consumtive⟩
⟨Francis James, badsight⟩
⟨Wm. Henman, lame on one leg⟩
⟨John Muscott, badsight⟩

John Howes, constable.

If any of you think your ⟨self⟩ you are agreevid, you must apeal at ye Peacock in Northampton on Monday ye 8th day of December next, and that no appeal will be afterwards received.

WHISTON

A list of the parrishoners of the parrish of Whishton that are able to serve as militia men.

Thos. Coles, miller
William Vallentine, miller
    servant
Benjamin Coles, farmer
Joseph Vallentine, farmer
    servant

John Roberson, shepherd
William Rattly, farmer servant
Thomas Ankinson, shepherd
⟨Thos. Barker, farmer sert.,
    inferm⟩

Thos. Coles, constable.

WOOTTON

A list of the names of all persons dwelling in the parish of Wootton who are liable to serve in the militia.

Henry Labrum, labourer
John Old, labourer
Thos. Clarke, farmer
Wm. Clarke, farmer
Plowman Jones, shepherd
John Peach, carpenter
John Harris, farmer
Wm. Harris, farmer
John Harris, servant
John Douglas, servant
Jos. Chapman, servant
Richd. Mallord, servant
Wm. Wickins, servant
Thos. Langford, farmer
Eusebius Holmes, farmer
Richd. Millar, servant
Edwd. Minards, labourer
Jno. Jeys, labourer
Jno. Stimson, shepherd
Jno. Draper, labourer

Edwd. Martin, blaksmith
Saml. Westly, labourer
Rd. Lester, chandler
John Lester, soapmaker
Richd. Cooper, servant
Bartholomew Mallord, newsman
Wm. Billingham, shepherd
Nath. Hicks, labourer
Fran. Evans, farmer
John Labrum, servant
Thos. Trusler, butcher
Thos. Robinson, shoemaker
John Old, shoemaker
Charles Jones, servant
John Cotton, newsman
John Morris, shoemaker
Thos. Peach, shoemaker
Saml. Grant, servant
Thos. Williams, victualler
John Ship, labourer

Moses Ager, shepherd
Edwd. Freeman, labourer

Richd. Couch, servant
John Ramsey, labourer

⟨John Clarke, constable.⟩

The day of appeal is on Monday the 8th day of December next at the Peacock Inn in Northampton, and all persons who think themselves aggrieved may then and there aply for relief, and no appeal to be made afeterwards.

YARDLEY HASTINGS

A list of persons liable to serve in the militia in Yardley Hastings Northamptonshire.

James Minney, labourer
Wm. Page, do.
Thos. Wooden, do.
James Whitney, do.
John Whitney, do.
John Wooden, shopkeeper
Wm. Blower, do.
James Wait, labourer
Edwd. Downing, singleman
Henry Minney, labourer
Thos. Tarry, do.
⟨Wm. Carter, taylor⟩
Wm. Allen, labourer
John Whitney, servt.
Thos. Whitney, labour
James Wooden, carpentr
James Bedford, labourer
Edwd. Johnson, do.
Thos. Berrill, do.
John Tarry, do.
Henry Wikes, do.
John Smith, servt.
Farrow Whitney, do.
Daniel Robinson, farmers son
Wm. Robinson, do.
Geo. Downing, labourer
Edw. Whitney, shopkeeper
Robt. Whitney, taylor
Wm. Walker, farmer
Wm. Brawn, labourer
John Lucas, do.
Robt. Laurance, farmer
Mattw. Wooden, labourer

John Custer, singleman
Willm. Bedford, labourer
John White, do.
Richd. Lack, singleman
John King, do.
John Carter, labourer
John Underwood, do.
Saml. Birch, carpenter
John Bent, lace man
John Longland, single man
Henry Mills, labourer
Wm. Hawkins, butcher
Thos. Archer, labourer
Charles Blunsom, blacksmith
Wm. Archer, labourer
Humphy. Hull, singleman
John Watts, labourer
Wm. Wooden, servt.
Wm. Cook, graziers son
Thos. Cook, do.
Edw. Smith, singleman
Willm. Rose, do.
Willm. Minney, labourer
James Carter, labourer
Saml. Jeffery, do.
illegible Woodwell, baker
Thos. Denton, singleman
John Underwood, single man
John Amos, labourer
Willm. Naman, servt.
James Longland, single man
Owen Wait, labourer

INDEXES

Pickering, Pickiring, Pickrin, Pickurin Jas, 140; Jn, 16, 24, 137; Wm, 155.
Picket Chris, 130.
Piddington Jn, 41; Rob, 41; Sam, 119.
Piggott Wm, 190.
Pike Jas, 212; Thos, 213; Wm, 65.
Pilgrim Jn, 137.
Pillam Edw, 54; Ric, 54.
Pillott Hen, 25.
Pilmore Thos, 200; Wm, 186.
Pinacle Fra, 86.
Pinark Ric, 100.
Pinckard, Pincard Jn, 197; Thos, 143; Wm, 194, 195, 196.
Pinder Rob, 202.
Pine, Piner, Pyner Hen, 79; Jas, 188; Jos, 28; Ric, 79; Wm, 90.
Pinfold Ric, 123; Thos, 123.
Pink Jn, 159.
Pinnack Jn, 194.
Pinny Thos, 80; Wm, 81.
Pipkin Edm, 13.
Pipping Sam, 179.
Pittam, Pittom Edw, 54; Hen, 56; Jn, 8; Sam, 51; Thos, 9, 34, 35; Wm, 35*, 126.
Pitts Jos, 90; Ric, 79; Thos, 89.
Placket, Placett, Plackett, Plackit Pet, 188; Sam, 145; Thos, 79, 143.
Plant Thos, 94; Wm, 164.
Platt, Plat, Plats Edw, 30*, 31; Geo, 30; Jn, 20, 162; Jos, 30; Needham, 24; Ric, 85; Thos, 30.
Plester Dan, 6.
Plover Wm, 23.
Plowman Fra, 208; Geo, 157; Wm, 87, 137.
Plowright Chas, 129.
Plumb, Plumbe Ben, 19; Mark, 19; Wm, 20, 201.
Plummer Jas, 49.
Pochin Jn, 165.
Pointer, Pointers, Poynter Ben, 2, 11; Edw, 10; Humphrey, 11; Jn, 11; Rob, 184; Thos, 10; Wm, 182.
Polhead Rob, 131.
Poll, Poles Jn, 166; Moses, 85; Thos, 159.
Pollard Jn, 2, 115; Jos, 117; Lawr, 125; Thos, 115; Wm, 86, 116.
Ponsford Fra, 74.
Ponton Jn, 153; Sam, 152; Wm, 152.
Pool, Poole Dan, 60; Edw, 60; Jn, 51, 66, 81, 139, 152; Jos, 168; Sam, 69, 136, 188; Thos, 73, 140, 179; Wm, 35, 41, 96.
Poriz Fra, 135.
Porter Jn, 60, 201*; Rob, 26; Thos, 26, 85, 132, 201*; Wm, 61, 132, 201.
Potherow Sam, 39.
Pottenger Thos, 124.
Potter Jn, 186; Jos, 28; Wm, 28, 56.
Potterton Sam, 23; Thos, 31; Wm, 21.
Powell, Powel Abr, 145; Fra, 183; Geo, 80, 120; Isaac, 80; Jn, 72, 153, 196; Jos, 79; Rog, 144; Sam, 66; Thos, 67, 144, 182; Wm, 81, 107, 120, 144, 197.
Powers Ben, 142; Sam, 23; Ste, 63.

Powys Thos, 110.
Pratt, Prat Ben, 152; Chas, 82; Haines, 195; Jas, 82; Jn, 28, 55*, 82; Mic, 118, 127; Palmer, 82; Rob, 28, 82; Sam, 82, 106; Thos, 62, 82*, 195; Wm, 82*, 120.
Preedy Jas, 134.
Prentice, Prentes Dan, 100; Mark, 29; Ste, 81; Thos, 158, 159.
Pressland, Presland Dan, 91, 97; Jas, 97; Jn, 97; Thos, 96, 97.
Presson, Pressen Dav, 18; Jn, 17; Jos, 100; Thos, 18.
Prestidge, Prestig Jn, 177; Thos, 55; Wal, 196; Wm, 55.
Preston Edw, 18; Jn, 130, 131; Thos, 132, 182; Wm, 140, 182.
Price, Prise Geo, 41; Jn, 186; Rob, 69; Thos, 144; Wm, 6, 82.
Pridmore, Pridmor, Pridmoure Jn, 26; Mat, 202; Rob, 22, 200; Sam, 201; Thos, 24; Tim, 157; Wm, 22, 23, 97.
Priest Wm, 181.
Priestley Jn, 184.
Pring Dan, 69.
Proctor, Procter Wm, 86, 185.
Prowett Dav, 38; Wm, 183.
Pruden Wm, 22.
Prudey Wm, 201.
Prufe Thos, 123.
Puerin Jn, 188.
Pulley, Pooley, Poolley, Pully Edw, 29, 187; Elias, 131; Jn, 171; Ral, 212; Thos, 134.
Pulser Wm, 185.
Pulver Jas, 148.
Punn Wm, 14.
Punshon Ral, 150.
Pursell, Pusel Jn, 119; Jos, 196; Thos, 126.
Puser Jos, 64.
Putt Jonah, 169.
Putter Jn, 170.
Pywell Edw, 169; Hen, 28; Jas, 156; Jn, 28, 29*, 129; Marmaduke, 101; Thos, 129; Wm, 157, 159, 180,.

Q

Quanbrough Jeremiah, 201.
Quay Wm, 40.
Quelch Thos, 45.
Quemby Hen, 94; Jn, 92; Sam, 92.
Quince Jos, 101.
Quiney Jn, 50; Wm, 50.

R

Raby Jn, 25.
Radband Wm, 141.
Radbourne, Radborn, Radburne Jn, 49; Ric, 35; Thos, 210; Wm, 90.
Radford Wm, 64.
Ragsdell Thos, 159.
Rainbow, Rainbo, Rainboo Edw, 35; Jn, 6, 11, 50; Jos, 58, 193; Ric, 5; Thos,

Sam, 92, 153; Silvester, 153; Ste, 149; Thos, 58, 81, 93, 96, 107, 215; Wm, 13, 14, 65, 81, 96, 138, 149, 158, 184, 216.

Robson Chris, 166; Jn, 48.

Rockingham Dav, 14.

Roddis, Roddiss, Rodiss, Rodhouse Ben, 51; Edw, 139; Jn, 35, 51, 142, 183, 196; Jos, 51; Rob, 183; Sam, 139; Wm, 139, 142*, 183.

Rodick Archibald, 85; Jn, 122.

Roe Jn, 140, 171; Jos, 139; Thos, 212*, 214; Wm, 137, 140, 213.

Roff Ric, 141; Thos, 141.

Rogers, Rodgers, Roggers Fra, 143; Geo, 122; Hen, 212; Jas, 203; Jn, 48, 62, 86, 139, 143, 209; Jos, 80; Mat, 172; Ric, 80, 143; Thos, 39, 46, 69, 118; Wm, 43, 55, 69, 139, 143*, 193.

Rokeby, Roocksby Jas, 105; Langham, 162.

Rollins Wm, 21.

Rooker Wm, 142.

Rose Jn, 64, 97; Ric, 5; Thos, 58; Wm, 97, 127, 216.

Rosimond, Rosomond Fra, 45; Jas, 45; Thos, 145.

Ross Jn, 57, 196; Wm, 11, 159.

Roughton Ben, 106; Fra, 103; Jn, 103; Jos, 104; Sam, 105, 106, 108, 186; Thos, 108; Wm, 106, 172, 190.

Routhorn, Routhon Thos, 113; Wm, 166.

Row Adam, 167; Dan, 178; Jas, 10, 19; Rob, 102, 174; Wm, 26, 82.

Rowell Geo, 129, 205; Jn, 17, 205; Rob, 157, 183; Thos, 44.

Rowkins Jn, 79; Thos, 85.

Rowlat, Rowlatt, Rowlet, Rowlett Ben, 109; Jas, 22; Jn, 19, 26, 29, 107, 172, 187, 200*; Sam, 29, 159; Thos, 17, 168; Wm, 17, 19.

Rowledge, Rowlidge Jn, 42; Sam, 19; Thos, 85.

Rowley Thos, 45.

Rubber, Rubberer Geo, 188; Josh, 190; Thos, 187.

Rudden Wm, 28.

Rudkin Jn, 24, 166; Wm, 201.

Ruff, Ruffe Geo, 203; Hen, 112; Jn, 132; Thos, 111.

Rush Fra, 57; Jacob, 197; Jeremiah, 35; Jn, 57; Rob, 192; Thos, 35, 57*.

Rushall, Rushel, Rushell, Dan, 48; Jn, 35, 48, 61; Jos, 36, 47; Rob, 45, 61; Thos, 47, 49, 60; Wm, 45.

Ruskin Rog, 63.

Russell, Rucill, Rusall, Russel Hen, 69; Jn, 6, 21, 34, 85, 134, 135; Josh, 34; Mic, 117; Ric, 35; Rob, 178; Sam, 2, 34; Thos, 33, 134; Wm, 45, 118, 138.

Rutcheson Geo, 203.

Rutlidge, Ruttlidge Fra, 85; Jn, 46.

Rycrass Jas, 106.

Rye Thos, 105.

Ryland Jas, 189.

S

Sabey, Saby Palmer, 182; Thos, 95, 171; Wm, 95.

Sabin, Sabins Edw, 60, 196; Jn, 60; Jos, 39, 60; Thos, 65; Wm, 24, 60.

Sachet Jn, 91.

Saddington, Sadington Jos, 129; Mat, 94; Rob, 94.

Sage Thos, 169.

Sale Jas, 66; Ric, 66.

Salmon, Sammons, Samons Jn, 55, 119; Wm, 131, 209.

Salsbury Jn, 186; Ric, 35; Sam, 35.

Samwell Ric, 190; Thos, 145.

Sanchfeild Jn, 130.

Sanders, Sandors, Saunders Bampr, 12; Hen, 86, 140; Jas, 85; Jn, 34, 41, 172, 184; Jos, 11*, 94; Kilsby, 91; Thos, 34, 85*, 205; Wm, 47, 91*, 97, 131, 159, 160.

Sanderson Jn, 63, 130, 203; Rob, 21; Sparke, 91; Thos, 211; Mrs, 130.

Sansom Wm, 104.

Sapcot Thos, 200.

Sargent, Sargin, Sargon, Sarjeant, Sergant, Serjant, Serjeant, Shargant Chas, 12; Edw, 173; Jas, 95; Jn, 86; 106, 172, 174, 211; Mm, 26; Packstone, 172; Ric, 44, 95; Thos, 172, 188, 190; Wm, 81, 188.

Satchel, Sachwell, Satchell, Satchwell, Setchel Ben, 187; Jobe, 118; Jn, 23, 25, 65, 108, 110*, 121; Jonh, 99; Ric, 23; Ruben, 30; Thos, 23, 108; Tim, 47; Wm, 22, 46, 47, 152, 181.

Saul, Saull Jn, 3, 193; Wm, 3.

Saunt Adam, 159; Edw, 151; Lewis, 157; Thos, 157.

Savage, Savige Geo, 55; Humphrey, 58; Sam, 193; Wm, 197.

Savin Wm, 117.

Sawbridge Jn, 37.

Sawer Jn, 127.

Sawford, Sawfoot Thos, 106, 205; Wm, 100.

Sayer, Sayar Sim, 85; Thos, 125.

Scarborough Jn, 131.

Scarr Wm, 10.

Schofield, Scofield Jas, 191; Jn, 182, 189.

Scotney Edw, 202; Geo, 161; Jn, 202, 203; Thos, 204.

Scott, Scot Benet, 57; Dan, 167; Geo, 10; Jas, 204; Jn, 10, 16, 29, 109, 144, 159, 200; Jos, 29; Rob, 30; Sam, 167, 171; Thos, 16, 27, 29, 30; Wm, 27, 29, 95, 167.

Scotton Jn, 196.

Scriven Edw, 141; Hen, 6; Jn, 112; Wm, 6.

Scrivner Ric, 8.

Scroxton Rob, 105; Wm, 105.

Sculthorpe, Scultharp, Sculthorp, Sculthrope, Scultrop, see Stultup Fra, 18; Humphrey, 24; Jn, 17, 19, 23*; Rob, 17; Sam, 110; Thos, 18. 19, 110, 199; Wm, 17, 24.

Seabin Wm, 185.

Jn, 3, 4, 5*, 13, 14*, 21, 23*, 27, 30, 33*,
37, 42, 43, 47, 48, 49, 51, 60, 61*, 62, 64,
65, 66, 67, 68*, 69, 70, 80, 85*, 90, 93, 95,
96, 100, 103, 104, 105, 112, 119, 121, 123,
126, 131, 138, 139, 140, 143, 144, 149,
152, 154, 164*, 167, 171*, 172, 193, 196*,
201, 205, 211, 214, 216; Jonh, 164; Jos,
29, 35, 55, 64, 91, 109, 115, 138, 144, 151,
177; Josh, 69; Langly, 208; Mic, 183;
Nat, 121; Pet, 104, 115, 151; Ric, 6, 26,
65, 80, 110*, 119, 138, 139*, 144, 193;
Rob, 7, 26, 27, 48, 108, 171, 179, 190;
Sam, 12, 36, 49, 53, 102, 104, 107*, 123,
137, 141, 154, 178; Ste, 60; Thos, 2, 9,
10, 13, 14, 21, 22, 29, 30, 37, 41, 45, 47,
48, 51, 58, 63, 64*, 65, 90, 95, 96, 110,
112, 117, 128, 129*, 138*, 151, 161, 163.
170, 178, 181, 182, 186, 187, 208; Tim,
155; Wm, 4, 6, 11*, 12, 19, 22, 23*, 27*,
33, 34, 35, 36, 42, 43, 46, 51, 61, 62*, 64*,
65, 69, 70, 80, 85*, 87, 103, 104, 107, 119,
129, 131*, 132, 138*, 144, 152, 164, 167,
179, 181, 182, 186, 189, 193, 196, 205,
212.
Snelson, Snellson Jas, 115; Thos, 193.
Snow Hen, 161.
Soans, see **Somes,** Wm, 187.
Soden, Sodin, Sodon Jn, 124, 138; Jos,
121, 122; Ric, 139; Thos, 18; Wm, 121.
Sofard Joab, 113.
Solsberry Jn, 82.
Somerly Wm, 85*, 87.
Somes Dan, 39; Jas, 85; Jn, 144.
Sorril Jas, 50; Jn, 50; Thos, 50.
Souel Rob, 4.
South Jn, 118; Wm, 211.
Southam, Southan Geo, 2; Jn, 179;
Ric, 89; Sam, 125; Wm, 8, 127.
Southwell, Southw Jn, 161, 201, 202,
205; Mat, 202; Sam, 204; Wm, 161.
Southwick Mark, 177.
Sparrow, Spparrow Dan, 213; Edw,
109; Jn, 124, 191; Jos, 109; Wm, 124,
210.
Spence Geo, 148; Thos, 164; Wm, 169.
Spencer, Spenser, Spensor Ambrose,
109; Ben, 128; Edw, 58*; Geo, 91; Jn,
16, 22, 74, 85, 136, 190, 211; Pet, 74;
Rob, 138; Sim, 46; Ste, 209; Thos, 22,
111, 213; Wm, 22, 23*, 60, 90, 101, 136,
182; The Earl, 135.
Spendlove, Spendelow Jn, 18; Jos, 23.
Spicer Jn, 3.
Spink Jas, 137.
Spiply Jn, 17.
Spires, Spire Edw, 115; Jas, 202; Sim,
122; Thos, 57.
Spokes Geo, 81; Thos, 81.
Spong Wal, 91.
Spooner Wm, 178.
Spragett Ric, 126.
Spriggs, Spriges, Sprigg Jas, 20; Jonh,
112; Rob, 19, 24*; Thos, 169; Wm, 9,
19, 74.
Sprigmaur Wm, 203.
Sprittle Wm, 8.
Squire, Squires Jn, 21; Thos, 106.

Stafford, Staford Fra, 26; Geo, 181;
Jn, 62, 107, 144, 210; Ric, 173; Rob, 77;
Thos, 16, 27, 173; Wm, 77; Zach, 16.
Staines, Stains Jn, 93; Thos, 94.
Stainsby, Stansby Geo, 203; Rob, 204.
Stamford Thos, 188.
Stamp Jn, 194.
Stanger, Stangour Jn, 18, 200; Mat,
61; Thos, 19; Wm, 58.
Stanion, Stanyan, Stanyon Chas, 157;
Edw, 30; Hen, 30; Jn, 24, 30; Jos, 30;
Rob, 24, 128; Wm, 24, 106*, 157.
Stanley, Standley And, 108; Fra, 139;
Humpy, 171; Jn, 25, 118; Rob, 28; Thos,
172; Wm, 36, 117, 192.
Stanson Rob, 17.
Stanton, Stonton Jn, 2, 37, 122*, 188;
Jos, 11; Matthias, 69; Ric, 43, 178, 187;
Sam, 178; Thos, 6, 142, 181; Wm, 104,
121, 187, 195.
Staple, Staples Ben, 158; Jn, 30, 115;
Rob, 159; Wm, 192.
Stapleton Jn, 23.
Starke, Starkey Geo, 125; Hen, 64;
Jn, 127.
**Starmer, Starmore, Starsmer, Starsmire,
Stermer** Edm, 21; Edw, 21; Hen, 188;
Jas, 21; Ral, 109; Rob, 141; Thos, 109,
142; Wm, 141.
Staunt Thos, 2.
Stead Wm, 57.
Steedon Wm, 116.
Steel, Steele Jn, 173; Thos, 115, 194;
Wm, 44, 195.
Sterman, Stirman, Sturman Jn, 177;
Jos, 213; Wm, 76, 186.
Sters Jn, 90.
Stevens, Steevens, Stephens, Stevns Abr,
39; Chas, 150; Edw, 33; Fra, 113; Hen,
44; Isacc, 100; Jn, 39, 85*, 95; Jos, 120;
Rob, 96; Sam, 85, 87; Sim, 112; Thos,
25, 33, 34, 112, 120; Wm, 25, 39, 85, 183,
187.
**Stevenson, Steavenson, Steevenson, Ste-
evinson** Jn, 155, 180; Jos, 20; Josh,
184; Wm, 178.
Stewart Jonh, 189.
Stiles Jas, 16; Jn, 172.
Still Wm, 187.
Stimson, Stimeson, Stimpson Geo, 9;
Jn, 9, 204, 215; Ric, 100; Rob, 12; Sam,
18.
Stockburn, Stockbourn Jos, 110; Ric,
186.
Stockley Geo, 123; Jn, 3; Thos, 126;
Wm, 45, 56, 124.
Stockton Thos, 42.
Stokes Bennett, 197; Jas, 208; Jn, 100;
Sam, 200.
Stonebanks Lovell, 81.
Stones Jn, 58.
Storey Thos, 11.
Stow Sam, 172.
Stratford Ben, 50; Ric, 50.
Streader Wm, 19.
Streets Edw, 179; Thos, 179.
Stretton, Straton, Streaton, Streeton

Thrift Jn, 205.
Tibbs, Tibes Hen, 178; Jn, 49, 129; Thos, 136; Wm, 136.
Tidman Jn, 42; Thos, 43; Wm, 43.
Tift Jn, 179.
Tilley, Tilly Jn, 83, 86; Pet, 14; Ric, 196; Thos, 35, 40, 85, 163, 187; Wm, 25, 196.
Timms, Timbs, Tims Jn, 116, 193; Jos, 107, 214; Ric, 212; Thos, 193, 212; Wm, 190, 197.
Timson Ant, 153, 171; Dan, 107; Edw, 23, 30; Hen, 94; Jas, 16; Jn, 5, 102; Sam, 171; Thos, 16, 99, 153; Wm, 16, 24, 29, 163.
Tindale Chris, 189; Wm, 188.
Tingle Phil, 110; Thos, 110.
Tipets Thos, 56.
Tipler Jas, 180; Jn, 108; Jos, 63; Rob, 189; Thos, 63, 180; Wm, 179.
Tipping Wm, 24.
Tirral, Tirrel, Tirril, Tyrel, Tyrrell, see **Turral** Adam, 31; Chas, 150, 172; Jn, 172; Jos, 13; Josh, 150; Thos, 25.
Tite, Titte Abr, 185, 212; Ant, 212; Ben, 13; Jn, 9, 54; Valentine, 212.
Titman Edw, 132; Jn, 132, 160.
Toach Ric, 46.
Toasland Jn, 163; Wm, 163.
Toay Wm, 123.
Tobb Ben, 36.
Tobet Dan, 154.
Toby Dan, 87; Sam, 87.
Todd, Tod, Tood Chas, 206; Geo, 204; Hen, 103, 200; Jas, 158; Jn, 205; Jonh, 196; Rob, 157; Sam, 197; Thos, 105, 128, 159; Tim, 105; Wm, 91, 131.
Todhissan Jn, 203.
Tolton, Tolten, Toulton Fra, 102; Jn, 149, 164; Rob, 164; Thos, 126, 165; Wm, 164.
Tomalin, Tomblin, Tomlin Ben, 60; Dan, 110; Jas, 111, 128; Jn, 60, 66, 173; Jos, 60; Rob, 6; Sam, 64; Thos, 62, 173; Wm, 202.
Tomb, Tombs, Toombs Jn, 8, 153; Thos, 11; Wm, 11, 153.
Tomkins, Thomkins, Tombkins, Tomkings, Tompkens, Tompkins Chas, 18; Edw, 90; Jn, 1, 47, 63, 143*; Martin, 143; Ric, 194; Rob, 194; Thos, 90, 143*; Wm, 123, 125.
Tomlinson Coles, 85; Sam, 86; Thos, 152; Wm, 107.
Tomons Wm, 64.
Tongue Edw, 171*; Jn, 86; Thos, 171; Wm, 172.
Tooby Jn, 42*; Thos, 40.
Tookey, Tooky Sam, 158; Wm, 79.
Topper Wm, 18.
Tosland, Toseland Jn, 155; Ric, 129; Sam, 180; Thos, 74.
Tott Jn, 185.
Towers Jn, 65; Ric, 40.
Town Jn, 202.
Townley, Townly Ant, 79; Art, 146; Jn, 74, 79, 169, 170; Sam, 109; Sim, 109;

Thos, 49, 79, 161; Wm, 169.
Townsend, Townensend, Townshend Jn, 49, 76; Sam, 68; Thos, 60, 108, 194; Valentine, 45; Wm, 61, 118.
Townsland Wm, 212.
Townsley Thos, 101.
Toy Thos, 117; Wm, 127.
Trainey Rob, 158.
Trantom Mat, 106.
Trusler, Trasler, Treslar, Tresler, Trestler, Trusler Jn, 47, 71, 179; Ric, 9; Rob, 141, 185; Thos, 138, 140, 141, 179, 215; Wm, 137, 183.
Travil, Travel, Travell Dan, 8; Jn, 184, 193, 212; Jos, 193; Rob, 12*; Shem, 9; Wm, 12.
Trayfoot Isaca, 132.
Treadle Sam, 5.
Treadgold, Tredgold Edw, 50; Geo, 134; Jas, 135; Jn, 169; Jos, 134; Thos, 134; Wm, 134.
Treadwell, Treadell Geo, 194; Jn, 56, 58; Phil, 115; Thos, 115.
Treen Fra, 196; Jn, 11; Wm, 197.
Trench Jn, 85.
Trenton, Trentom Geo, 125; Jas, 123; Jn, 127.
Treppass Ric, 49.
Treslove Sam, 191; Wm, 81.
Tribble Thos, 190.
Trifin Jn, 9.
Trinder Thos, 183.
Trippett Jonh, 183.
Trolley Jn, 85; Sam, 85.
Trossel Jn, 93.
Trotter Chas, 193; Jn, 193; Johnson, 56; Sam, 215.
True Jos, 109.
Truman Jas, 185.
Truss Jn, 205; Jos, 120.
Tucker Hen, 54; Rob, 119; Wm, 56*, 117.
Tuckey, Tucky Edw, 116; Geo, 122; Thos, 2, 116; Wm, 117.
Tue Edw, 4; Jos, 126.
Tugwood Jn, 38.
Tunnell Nat, 109.
Turland, Torland Edw, 135; Fra, 85; Jn, 136; Nat, 85; Ric, 36, 149; Thos, 82, 136; Wm, 81, 97, 181, 214.
Turnall Jn, 177.
Turnbull Jas, 87.
Turncliff Jn, 106.
Turner, Turne Burrows, 170; Edw, 55, 68, 108; Jn, 3, 34, 110; Jos, 119, 151; Josh, 190; Nat, 62; Pet, 46; Phil, 56; Ric, 69, 107; Rog, 206; Sam, 33, 166; Thos, 4, 35, 95, 188; Wm, 3, 33, 46, 56, 115, 185.
Turnsley Jn, 171.
Turpin Wm, 13.
Turral, Turrell, see **Tirral** Jas, 38; Jn, 18; Wm, 119.
Turvey Jn, 115, 127; Ric, 13, 46.
Tutchinor Jn, 137.
Tweltree Rob, 92.
Twigg Wm, 169.

18; Thos, 210, 216; Wm, 86, 135, 182, 216.

Woodruff, Woodrof Chas, 86; Jn, 93.

Woodward Jas, 201*; Ric, 201; Thos, 10, 201*; Wm, 201*.

Woodwell, Woodell Mic, 125; —, 216.

Wooley, Whoolley, Wooly Jas, 185, 208; Valentine, 188.

Woolfe Wm, 195.

Woollard Jn, 110; Thos, 107.

Woollman Edw, 165.

Woolston, Wollston, Wollstone, Woollaston, Woollston, Woolstone Hen, 160; Jn, 25, 82, 86, 87; Jeffery, 105; Mat, 205; Sam, 25; Ste, 109; Thos, 86, 103, 105; Wm, 22, 25, 86, 105, 183; —, 86.

Woolward Jn, 22.

Wootton, Wooton, Wootten, Wotton Geo, 9; Jn, 116, 121; Ric, 117; Thos, 24, 125, 185, 200.

Worley, Worly Geo, 82; Jn, 140, 189; Rob, 134; Wm, 136.

Worlidge Wm, 130.

Wormleton, Wormleighton Ebenezer, 62; Sam, 47, 68.

Worpool Sam, 30; Wm, 30.

Worrel Wm, 35.

Worrow Rob, 203.

Worster Jacob, 69; Ric, 69.

Worth Wm, 154.

Worthington Jn, 112, 187; Jarves, 112.

Wortley Ant, 200.

Wright, Write Brookes, 142; Currer, 73; Edw, 130, 134, 157; Hen, 196; Jas, 90, 160, 182, 184; Jeremiah, 74; Jn, 26, 56, 61, 66, 71, 82, 91, 94, 96, 130, 131, 142*, 181, 182*, 205, 210; Jos, 49*, 61, 113, 186, 187; Josh, 81; Mason, 144; Moses, 71; Nat, 135; Ric, 63, 81, 167, 177, 202; Sam, 86, 102, 113, 187, 188, 190; Ste, 39; Thos, 21, 49, 73, 90, 91*, 104, 105, 107, 108*, 132, 134, 139, 142, 157, 158, 177, 180, 182, 187, 210, 215; Wm, 29, 47, 49, 54, 55, 72, 81*, 86*, 90*, 142*, 144, 150, 154.

Wrightcraft Edw, 202.

Wrighton Thos, 48; Wm, 125, 194.

Wyatt, Whiot, Whyat, Wyat, Wyett Dan, 201; Edw, 121; Geo, 60; Jas, 183; Jn, 3, 121; Neley, 124; Rob, 6, 121; Thos, 57, 124, 190; Wm, 4, 189.

Wye Jn, 183.

Wykes, Wikes Hen, 216; Jn, 62*, 64; Thos, 62, 64, 69, 90, 183; Wm, 64, 90, 181.

Wyles, Whyles, Wiles Geo, 200; Jn, 17, 99; Wm, 203.

Wyman, Whyman, Wiman Chas, 203; Dan, 91; Jn, 23, 91, 97, 145; Jos, 16; Rob, 23; Thos, 18.

Wymont Jos, 83.

Y

Yakesley Ric, 151; Thos, 151.

Yard Thos, 151.

Yardley Thos, 158.

Yarn Aaron, 66.

Yarram Wm, 203.

Yarrow Jn, 109.

Yarwell Wm, 157.

Yates, Yeates, Yeat, Yeatt Geo, 125; Jas, 204; Jn, 41, 116, 186*, 195; Jos, 41; Ric, 124.

Yearl, Yerl, see **Earl** Nat, 8; Phil, 56; Sam, 56.

Yeoman, Yeomans, Yeoumans, Yomans Edw, 166; Fra, 187; Jn, 188; Jonh, 166; Jos, 166; Ric, 166; Thos, 172; Wm, 33.

York, Yorke Adam, 204; Dan, 18; Edw, 95; Geo, 64, 173, 186; Jas, 77, 209; Jn, 18, 40, 64, 68, 86, 105, 145, 155, 181, 190, 213; Pet, 91; Ric, 151; Rob, 18, 204; Sam, 69, 77, 155; Thos, 64, 65, 91, 141; Watson, 18; Wm, 129, 154, 173, 179, 182, 204, 211.

Youls, Yooul Jn, 80; Thos, 157.

Young, Yong Edw, 27; Jn, 105; Nic, 123; Rob, 105; Wm, 27, 93, 95.

INDEX OF PLACES